GREATEST GAMES
QUEEN'S PARK RANGERS

GREATEST GAMES
QUEEN'S PARK RANGERS

MIKE DONOVAN

Reprinted 2025

First published by Pitch Publishing, 2013
Pitch Publishing
A2 Yeoman Gate
Yeoman Way
Durrington
BN13 3QZ
www.pitchpublishing.co.uk

© Mike Donovan, 2013

All rights reserved. No part of this book may be reproduced, sold or utilised in any form or transmitted in any form or by any means, electronic or mechanical, including photocopying, recording or by any information storage and retrieval system, without prior permission in writing from the Publisher. A CIP catalogue record is available for this book from the British Library.

ISBN 978-1-90917-879-3
Typesetting and origination by Pitch Publishing
Printed and bound in India by Replika Press Pvt. Ltd.

Contents

1 Fulham 1893 11
2 Brighton United 1899 15
3 Wolverhampton Wanderers 1900 19
4 Plymouth Argyle 1906 23
5 Manchester United 1908 27
6 Brentford 1911 32
7 Watford 1920 36
8 Arsenal 1921 40
9 Swindon Town 1930 44
10 Bristol Rovers 1937 48
11 Swansea Town 1948 52
12 Grimsby Town 1950 56
13 Watford 1957 60
14 Tranmere Rovers 1960 64
15 Southend United 1961 68
16 Hull City 1962 72
17 Mansfield Town 1966 76
18 Birmingham City 1967 81
19 West Bromwich Albion 1967 85
20 Oxford United 1967 91
21 Aston Villa 1968 95
22 Leicester City 1968 101
23 Derby County 1970 106
24 Nottingham Forest 1972 110
25 Cardiff City 1973 114
26 Liverpool 1975 119
27 Leeds United 1976 123
28 SK Brann 1976 129
29 AEK Athens 1977 133
30 Coventry City 1979 139
31 Luton Town 1981 143
32 Tottenham Hotspur 1982 147
33 Fulham 1983 152
34 Newcastle United 1984 157
35 Partizan Belgrade 1984 161
36 Liverpool 1986 165
37 Chelsea 1986 170
38 Arsenal 1990 174
39 Liverpool 1991 178
40 Manchester United 1992 182
41 Everton 1993 186
42 Port Vale 1997 190
43 Barnsley 1997 194
44 Crystal Palace 1999 197
45 Oldham Athletic 2003 201
46 Sheffield Wednesday 2004 205
47 Watford 2011 209
48 Liverpool 2012 213
49 Fulham 2012 217
50 Chelsea 2013 221

Acknowledgements

FIRST AND foremost I would like to thank Gordon Macey, the Queens Park Rangers official club historian, for his support. His personal advice when we met up at that charming public house in Woking was invaluable. I appreciate him taking time out, even providing verbal instructions over the phone to direct me to the venue off the motorway!

The information in his books on the club – *The Official History of Queens Park Rangers Football Club* (QPR) and *Queens Park Rangers The Complete Record* (Breedon) – provided crucial resources on which I was able to build the stories of many of the matches, especially those dated before the Second World War.

I would also like to thank Gordon for the pictures he has supplied for the publication. Again, an invaluable contribution.

I would like to thank Les Ferdinand for doing the foreword. 'Sir Les' is a proper legend of the club, a great role model and all round top bloke. I appreciate the efforts of Melissa Chappell and John Fennelly, head of publications at Tottenham Hotspur Football Club, in helping to get it all together.

I felt and feel honoured to have met up again with Ian Gillard, the loyal Rangers left-back during the club's halcyon days of the 1970s, and for him to share his memories along with those of another Rangers legend, Mark Lazarus.

Other former Rangers stars such as Glenn Roeder, Clive Allen, Warren Neill, John Byrne, Chris Kiwomya, and Les Ferdinand have also gone down Memory Lane with me.

I would like to thank Paul Morrissey, QPR's media manager, for taking time out to meet me, organising a match day visit to Loftus Road for me to continue my research, putting me in touch with players and helping to enable the book to be recognised as an official publication, and his colleague Ian Taylor. Plus my gratitude is extended to all at Pitch Publishing, especially Paul and Jane Camillin.

I appreciate the fantastic input of Queens Park Rangers fans such as Nick and Jan Saloman, Debbie Wileman, Rosemary Donovan, Paul Harris and others.

Thanks to Paul Barber and Peter Hannon at the Football Association, Andy Dodd and Tony Brown at the Football League, the enfa.co.uk website, and the Premier League.

I appreciate the assistance of the British Newspaper Library – and its helpful staff – in Colindale, north London. I enjoyed my visits and being able to read the actual newspapers which reported on Queens Park Rangers right back to the club's beginnings in the 19th century.

Shooting To The Top by Rodney Marsh (Stanley Paul), *Stan Bowles The Autobiography* (Orion), *Ollie The Autobiography of Ian Holloway* and *Made in Sheffield My Story* by Neil Warnock provided prime sources.

Newspapers such as *The Sun*, *The Guardian*, *The Observer*, *The Daily Telegraph*, *Daily Mail*, *Daily Star*, *Kilburn Times*, *Ealing Gazette* (which published interviews your author had with QPR managers such as Alec Stock, Steve Burtenshaw, Tommy Docherty, Terry Venables, Alan Mullery and players like Gerry Francis, Stan Bowles, Gary Waddock, John Gregory, Tony Currie, Arthur Jefferson and Mike Keen) have been more than useful, and magazines such as *Backpass* too (keep up the good work, Mike!).

I would like to thank the official QPR website, BBC Sport, QPRnet.com, Indyrs.co.uk and other recommended sites such as 11v11.com – and its posters.

The inspiration provided by my mum, wife Rosemary, brother and sister, son Matthew, brother-in-law Charlie and the rest of my family has been helpful.

Also Kevin and Pauline Rogers, Mark Friedlander, Dave Harley, Tony Harris, Mike McNamara, Graham Cumming, Mims, Kate and Keith, Tilly and Ronnie, Marc and Louise Whitmore, the Loughton Five-a-Siders, the Bexhill Mob, 6 Music Radio and all I have crossed positive paths with during the writing of the book … And tea.

Mike Donovan

Dedications

To my mum.
To Nick, who has supported Rangers through thick and thin.
To the memory of Louis Haar.
To the memory of Ray Jones, a Ranger cut down as he was blooming (28 August 1988–25 August 2007).
To all Rangers fans.

Foreword

I HAVE a real soft spot for Queens Park Rangers as Rangers is where it all started for me. I was born in Paddington and lived in the Ladbroke Grove area and I used to walk past Loftus Road every day on my way to secondary school.

When I first joined the club there wasn't one local lad playing for them. All our youth team players either came from Wales, Scotland or Ireland. No one from the local community was playing in the youth team and I never thought I was going to be a professional footballer.

I loved playing football, so I went to Viking Sports in Ealing while I was still at school. I stayed there a couple of years and moved on to Southall. I went from the youth team into the reserves and made my way up into the first team. Playing for Southall I had my first taste of Wembley in the FA Vase Final.

Unfortunately we lost! I always remember the manager standing in the middle of the room before we went out saying, 'Perhaps one of you may have the opportunity to play at Wembley again in your careers.' Everyone looked around the room and wondered who it could be. We had some good players but no one ever thought it might be me. Years later I managed to play there with England.

From Southall I went to Hayes. A guy called Bobby Ross, a QPR scout, saw me play there and told Frank Sibley, a loyal servant to the club as a player, manager and coach for 34 years, came to watch. Eventually manager Jim Smith came down and signed me on the same day.

I'd been working as a painter-decorator, doing driving jobs, all sorts, anything that would enable me to get away to train on Tuesday and Thursday evenings and play on a Saturday. Now I was a professional footballer. It was amazing.

I had a year in the reserves and a brief spell on loan at Brentford. I wasn't really breaking into the team and I remember Jim Smith saying he thought I had what it took but I wasn't going to get an opportunity in the team at that time. So he felt it was a great opportunity for me to go out and play in Turkey and play under an English manager at Besiktas with Gordon Milne, the former England and Liverpool player, who was in charge there. I didn't know anything about Turkey. All I I knew was that I needed to go and play football.

I felt playing abroad would be helpful to get away from the distractions of London. Going out to Turkey gave me that education on what it was like to be a professional footballer.

I came back and, thankfully it started to happen for me and Queens Park Rangers gave me some unforgettable years.

My favourite QPR team-mate? Clive Wilson. There were so many players that made my time with the club enjoyable but Clive is godfather to my daughter and I am the same to him and he's a great friend.

Favourite Rangers manager? I worked with a few like Jim Smith, Trevor Francis and Don Howe but probably the one I got on with most and the one that got the best out of me was Gerry Francis. He came in, put his arm around me and said, 'Look, you are my centre forward.' He told me, 'I think you've got everything it takes to play for England.' I laughed at him at the time. But he was proved right.

One of the great things about Queens Park Rangers at the time – and I think most of the boys would tell you – was the atmosphere in the dressing room. We had a mix of

Foreword

very good players and we had a great group of sociable lads. I still say that the chat we had at Queens Park Rangers was the best I have had at any football club I've been to and I have been fortunate enough to be at some good clubs as a player like Newcastle United, Tottenham Hotspur, West Ham United, Leicester City, Bolton Wanderers, Reading and Watford.

There were a lot of characters. Alan McDonald, sadly no longer with us, was a top man. Ray Wilkins was a character, Ollie (Ian Holloway) was definitely one. Gary Penrice was a big personality. Everyone got on with everyone, no cliques. I've been involved in a lot of dressing rooms and sometimes you can get little cliques. But there wasn't anything like that at Queens Park Rangers. Everyone seemed to get on with everyone. That's the way it should be.

There were some great on-the-field moments for me personally too, like when I scored a hat-trick against Everton to complete a second successive treble when QPR finished fifth in the first season of the Premier League. And when I was part of the first Rangers team to beat Liverpool at Anfield.

Mike Donovan has featured them in this enjoyable and fascinating book which covers 48 other great games from across the club's long history from their first bit of silverware in 1893 to Harry Redknapp's side going to beat west London rivals and reigning European Cup holders Chelsea at Stamford Bridge in an otherwise tough 2012/13 season for the club.

Rangers and their brilliant fans – who gave me my Sir Les nickname (although I still don't know how it came about) – will enjoy the read too, along with many other football supporters. Many have a genuine affection for the club.

A lot of people used to say to me they weren't Queens Park Rangers supporters – they might have followed Tottenham, Arsenal or whoever – but if their team was away from home they would go down to Loftus Road and watch Rangers because they were always guaranteed to see a good game of football. QPR have always had that reputation of being a good footballing team.

Also Loftus Road is a nice little stadium, it is close to the pitch. And when you get a few people in there it has a great atmosphere.

It has a lot of history with some great players down the years like Stan Bowles and Rodney Marsh.

I'm flattered if I am well thought of at Queens Park Rangers. One of the things I remember when I went to Newcastle was that on my return to Loftus Road I got the biggest standing ovation you could hope to get as a player going back to his old club.

It made me feel that I did it the right way when I left QPR. There was no turmoil. It was just the fact I felt I needed to try and improve and develop as a player. I'd gone as far as I could go. I think the supporters appreciated that and showed that by the ovation they gave me at the end of the game.

I honestly feel I've been so lucky to be able to do something I love doing and still love doing with my coaching at Spurs. I've had a good life through football and I can't complain.

And it all kicked off for me because of the faith Queens Park Rangers and their supporters showed in me. I will be forever grateful. Now read on and enjoy the book.

Les Ferdinand MBE
London July 2013

Introduction

THE 'GREATEST' is an adjective used to underline either something or someone who has a superior quality so I set about which Queens Park Rangers games were deserving of such a prefix over the club's long history which had expanded to 131 years on publication of this book.

I began the process of whittling down the thousands of matches to 50 by asking all Rangers fans what they would include, via the club's match programme during the 2012/13 Premier League season.

I also wanted to touch on my own emotions and memories of a club that has been a big part of my professional and personal life. A visit to Loftus Road to plug in the phones for reporters and then read over their copy to copy-takers was my first assignment as a budding sports journalist. And then I covered the club as sports editor of the *Ealing Gazette* during the 1970s and 1980s. I also had a wife and another best friend who supported them. And they were the nearest league club to where I grew up in London.

But the head had to have a say in the final choices and it insisted on ground rules.

The choices had to include matches which represented a 'first' for the club. It is like life, we all remember the first time.

So it was crucial to include the first trophy, promotion, title, big FA Cup win, Charity Shield appearance, League Cup Final, FA Cup Final, top-flight showing and European tie.

It was necessary to go back to the club's beginnings to ensure perspective, from when a group of Paddington schoolboys from Droop Street got things started. To the nomadic nature of the early years with ground-changing a regular occurrence before Loftus Road was settled upon. It was important to include the ups and downs of promotion and relegation fights (supporters have suffered a rollercoaster of emotions down the years), and to look at the return to the Premier League under Neil Warnock then the subsequent Harry Redknapp era. It was essential other high points such as victories over big names such as Manchester United (at Old Trafford), Liverpool and Arsenal were included. There was the west London derby factor, of course. Victories over Brentford, Fulham and Chelsea (one when the Blues were European Cup holders) had to be in there. The big comeback games had to be featured such as epics against Newcastle United and Port Vale.

Matches which represented great individual achievement such as Alan Wilks's five goals against Oxford United, Dennis Bailey's hat-trick at Old Trafford and Clive Allen's debut treble as a teenager all feature, as do games which highlighted the impact of icons who heightened the club's profile as one capable of producing entertaining football.

Managers from James Cowan to Dave Mangnall to Alec Stock to Gordon Jago to Dave Sexton to Terry Venables to Gerry Francis to Ian Holloway to Neil Warnock to Harry Redknapp are all in.

Mavericks who wore the fabled number 10 shirt from Rodney Marsh to Stan Bowles to Simon Stainrod to Tony Currie to John Byrne to Adel Taarabt all feature, along with other legendary players such as Mark Lazarus, Evelyn Lintott, Tommy Cheetham, Cyril Hatton, Reg Allen, Brian Bedford, Gerry Francis, Dave Thomas, Don Givens, Phil Parkes and Ian Gillard, plus loyal players such as the indomitable Alan McDonald, who tragically died in 2012, and Tony Ingham. A host of characters who supplied a wealth of memories are all covered in this book. Sit back, put your feet up and read all about them.

Mike Donovan

v Fulham 3-2

West London Observer Challenge Cup. Kensal Rise Athletic Ground
22 April 1893. Attendance: Not known

QUEENS PARK RANGERS:	FULHAM:
Creber	May
Rushbrook	T. Shrimpton
Teagle	Curry
McKenzie	Cardross
Harvey	Newport
Maund	King
Wallington	Pearce
Ward	Fearon
Davies	Withington
Morris	King
Collins	Sermon

Referee: Mr Gregory (Uxbridge)

IT ONLY took a decade for Queens Park Rangers to win their first trophy. They did so by lifting the West London Observer Cup with a 3-2 win over near-neighbours Fulham after extra time at Kensal Rise Athletic Ground on Saturday 22 April 1893.

But let me tell you first about a cat's tale which led to it and beyond to the present day ...

Jude the cat sat on the lap of Queens Park Rangers fan Jan Brown in the season ticket holders' section of the South Africa Road stand at Loftus Road in the late 1990s.

Many supporters were warmed by the black feline curled up on them during cold afternoons and evenings. The friendly, comfort-seeking stray given free rein of the Loftus Road ground during the 1990s and 2000s. Such was its association with Rangers the club adopted the animal. And the moggy even inspired the R's mascot, which was named after him, although Jude the Stadium Cat depicts the real Jude as seven feet tall and capable of walking on two feet.

But when the club was taken over by Italian owners in 2007, the cat and mascot were history, the feline reportedly rehoused with a member of the Rangers staff and the human version retired.

Jan and her family, who have supported the R's for more than 40 years, believe the owners took the decisions for superstitious reasons, believing black cats to be unlucky (although the new owners restored the mascot). The name of the cat and its mascot equivalent, though, will forever be in QPR's DNA. It dates back to its origins.

Pupils of Droop Street Board School in Paddington, west London, formed a youth football club called St Jude's Institute in 1882.

It was done with the help of Jack McDonald, Fred Weller and Reverend Gordon Young and acted as a youth club team on a new west London housing estate, with the facts detailed in club historian Gordon Macey's excellent *The Official History Of Queens Park Rangers Football Club.*

Queens Park Rangers' Greatest Games

Rangers' home pitch was a piece of waste ground near Kensal Rise Athletic Ground and the Institute itself was used as headquarters. They were known as St Jude's.

Queens Park Rangers was adopted as a name four years later when the club combined with an equivalent outfit on the same estate, Christchurch Rangers, which had also been founded in 1882, by George Wodehouse (whose family had a 60-year association with the club as players and directors).

The get-together came about when a friend of Wodehouse – whose name could have been either Jeeves or Wooster for all that has been left to posterity – suggested it while watching his pal play for Christchurch against St Jude's.

Queens Park Rangers was suggested as the name of the new amalgam by an E.D. Robertson with most of the players living in Queens Park.

And the moral and financial backing of Walter Cross, who became a director, guided them through their small beginnings.

Their only assets were four posts and two lengths of tape for crossbars at their first proper home, Welford's Field, rented for £8 a year from a dairy on ground at the back of the Case is Altered public house south of Kensal Rise station. They even had a shortage of shorts, scrounging 11 sets of jodhpurs from a fan who owned a riding stables for their first unrecorded game. The first season was made up of friendlies against the likes of Tottenham Hotspur, Brentford and Fulham also, of course, in their early incarnations.

Growth was swift and they began a nomadic existence by moving to an enclosed London Scottish ground at Brondesbury the following season (1888/89) at £20 per annum. But the pitch was prone to waterlogging and they found another, albeit temporary, home at Barn Elms for the second half of the 1890/91 season which saw them take part in competitions for the first time.

Their first competitive game saw them draw 1-1 with Spurs in the London Senior Cup in November 1890, although they were pipped 2-1 in the replay.

Rangers had a bash at the West London Challenge Cup, an eight-team tournament which turned into a farce that term.

First-round opponents St John's Hammersmith pulled out before the tie against QPR was played, claiming they had a 'weakened team' (and were later crushed 8-0 by Rangers in a hastily-arranged friendly). Semi-final opponents Hanwell simply did not show for the showdown at Barn Elms.

Rangers felt they should have been given a walkover into the final but were refused, although they managed to make it through 4-2 after Hanwell made an appearance for the re-arranged date.

Yet, after all that, the final was never played for reasons which have never been divulged.

The haphazard nature of Rangers' early competitions was prevalent again in their first taste of their third competition, the West London Observer Challenge Cup, during that campaign.

After a bye, their first tie – against Kensington Rangers – took almost a MONTH to be decided. First off, QPR insisted they were not informed of the venue arranged for the match. Then they protested about the state of their hosts' pitch before reaching the semi-final with a 5-1 win over Kensington at Barn Elms. The journey ended in the last four with Rangers going down 4-1 at the Half Moon, Putney, to Stanley, a team rated the kings of west London football.

The next season – 1891/92 – proved a damp squib for Rangers as far as competition was concerned after moving to Home Farm (their fourth home if you are still counting),

v Fulham 1893

walloped 7-1 in the opening round of the London Senior Cup at Old St Stephen's and knocked out of the West London Observer Cup in their second game by Vulcan at their new base.

But fortune changed the following term (1892/93) which proved an historic one for the club – it brought that first trophy.

And back then it was a change of shirt colour and design rather than a black cat which proved lucky.

They had settled on Oxbridge dark and light blue halves for the early years of existence. But it was decided that season to wear hooped shirts for the first time. The kit was so similar to the one worn by Glasgow Celtic as to make no difference. That meant green and white hoops, white shorts and black and green socks.

They had also changed home once more, sharing the Kilburn Cricket Club ground with the bat-and-ball brigade at Harvest Road in Queens Park.

It marked their first season of league competition. The West London League was made up of ten clubs and among them was Paddington.

A rivalry had built up between QPR and Paddington, formed by the Christchurch players who did not become part of the amalgamation.

And it was a home fixture against Paddington which witnessed the Rangers 'Bhoys' displaying the green and white for the first time.

It was a controversial affair from which Paddington emerged 2-0 victors. The ill feeling, in fact, was part of the reason QPR refused to play the return fixture. That, and an under-strength team. You wonder how football authorities of today would have reacted to Rangers' stance. QPR were resplendent in their hooped kit as they lifted the West London Observer Cup.

They received a bye in the opening round but faced Stanley, who, with Fulham, had previously lifted the trophy named after the local newspaper, in the semi-final.

But the R's roared in the last-four showdown and blew Stanley away, winning 4-0 thanks to goals from Bert Morris, Bill Ward, James McKenzie and Ted Wallington.

The final test seemed even harder. They faced Fulham, also previous winners of the trophy, at Kensal Rise Athletic Ground. The Cottagers were fresh from being crowned West London League champions and, of course, determined to complete a double. And they had a fervent following who cheered their favourites to a deafening decibel level when they trotted on to the pitch.

The setting and name of the venue might have lacked the romance of either Wembley Stadium, the Camp Nou or the Maracana, nay Celtic Park, but Rangers weren't about to suffer any heartbreak.

The athletics venue was rather exposed and Rangers were soon blowing in the wind following the 4pm kick-off. Or rather, trying to playing into strong gusts. Fulham tried to take advantage of the weather conditions by banging away at the QPR rearguard. But unlike many performances in the 2012/13 Premier League season, the R's defence remained resolute, stonewalling Fulham for the entire first half.

QPR duo Herbert Teagle and Bob Rushbrook protected goalkeeper Harry Creber. They were aided, though, by wayward shooting from their opponents with Withington and Fearon missing opportunities for the Cottagers.

The R's even managed a breakaway after Tom Harvey broke up a Fulham attack to put Wallington away and the front-runner forced a save from Cottagers stopper May as the pace and excitement grew.

Queens Park Rangers' Greatest Games

The Super Hoops in green and white soon put the wind up the Cottagers in the second half. And they bombarded the Fulham goal with May in impressive form.

Two smash-and-grab raids by Ward and Wallington, goal heroes in the semi-final, of course, put QPR 2-0 up.

The first goal from Ward owed more than a little to the wind with May unable to judge its flight. It left Rangers supporters 'nearly frantic with delight'.

QPR maintained the pressure and May was forced to block efforts from Morris, Ward and Wallington.

But the Fulham stopper was beaten by a drive from Wallington inside the penalty box. QPR had one hand on the trophy.

Unfortunately, Rangers were unable to hold on to their advantage and Fulham pulled one back 20 minutes from the end of normal time when Withington skipped by the QPR defence to flash an unstoppable shot beyond Creber.

The thrills and tension mounted as every player on the field stepped it up with the crowd increasingly involved and ten minutes later the scores were level.

Rangers conceded a free kick close to their goal, not dissimilar to the one conceded by Stephane Mbia against Wigan Athletic during the relegation scrap at Loftus Road in April 2013 and, like Mbia's slip-up, of course, it resulted in a late equaliser.

One report insisted the referee blew for time SEVEN minutes early 'according to numerous watches held by the spectators', before ordering an extra half an hour to be played to decide the outcome.

Play became 'fast and furious'. Morris had a shot saved by May before Ward beat the stopper with a high shot as the goalkeeper slipped to make it 3-2 in the first period of the 30 added minutes. Surely, QPR would hang on this time?

Indeed they did with their defence reverting to its earlier mode of resolution. And, it seems, a spot of time-wasting. One account states, 'There was not much play in the final quarter-of-an-hour owing to the leisurely manner in which Rangers brought the ball back from out of play.'

Victory was secured. It was a proud Rangers team which gathered for the presentation ceremony. The cup was made of sterling silver and stood 16 inches in height and weighed in at 38 ounces, but the first experience of collecting silverware was a little tarnished as the organisers had no medals to hand out to the winners. The association pleaded poverty. And, besides, it was argued, previous cup holders had forked out for their own.

This led to a stand-off between QPR and the powers-that-be. The following year Rangers reached the final again. But their unknown opponents declined to play the match for unspecified reasons and the association demanded the R's returned the trophy.

The club declined, arguing no one had beaten them for it. They also insisted they would hang on to the trophy until receiving the medals to mark their triumph the previous season.

Brighton United 6-0

Southern League. Kensal Rise
2 September 1899. Attendance: 6,000

QUEENS PARK RANGERS:
Clutterbuck
Knowles
McConnell
Crawford
Tennant
Keech
Smith
Hayward
Beddingfield
Turnbull
Cowie

BRIGHTON UNITED:
Howes
Ashby
Crawford
Mills
Francis McAvoy
Willocks
Mercer
Oakden
Maurice Parry
Malloch
Hill

Referee: Mr Stark

THERE WAS good news for the female supporters of Queens Park Rangers when their club switched from amateur to professional status. Rangers would let them in for half price (3d) with the promise of their own tea room. How the fairer sex must have squealed with delight at being able to sip their drinks and scoff their cakes without pesky, boorish men around and have bonus spending money left in their purses. After all, I'm sure the gestures were no doubt well-meaning rather than patronising.

Even better, though, would have been the sight of the players they had come to support getting it together to batter Brighton United 6-0 in their first appearance as members of football's paid ranks at Kensal Rise in front of 6,000 paying customers which included season ticket holders ensconced in the pavilion, having paid either 12s 6d or 6s 6d for the entire campaign depending on your gender.

The men must have had a high old time discussing the afternoon action while their partners also had the bonus of deciding on whether to have it white with or without.

They had plenty to converse about as, with just 90 minutes' experience as professionals under their belts, Rangers had put themselves on top of the Southern League table.

The favourite topic must have been about the effectiveness of their strike force, in particular Andy Cowie, who had bagged FOUR goals, two in each half, or their favourites' chances of lifting the title at the first attempt after such a promising start. Expectation levels were forever thus.

Fred Beddingfield put the R's in front and Peter Turnbull also chipped in with a goal.

Rangers' decision to go professional was forced on them partly by one of their players seeing red and a subsequent £4 fine.

Sammy Brooks received his marching orders in an FA Cup tie against hosts Richmond Association, who went on to defeat their reduced opponents 3-0, in September 1898.

The London Football Association took exception to Brooks falling foul of officialdom and closed Rangers' ground for 14 days besides issuing the fine.

Queens Park Rangers' Greatest Games

QPR's noses were put out of joint and they sniffily pulled out of every competition they were involved in under the auspices of the capital's FA.

Their action punched a massive hole in their fixtures, as all their main ones had disappeared at a stroke. Their players were not best pleased and seemed open to the temptations put before them by rival clubs.

It was clear the inducement of money would provoke an outbreak of loyalty to sweep through the unsettled playing staff.

There was also the increased demand for top football in the capital to replicate northerly areas of the country making up most of the membership of the developing Football League.

Rangers had seen the growing interest first-hand with the friendly they had organised with the Throstles of West Bromwich Albion.

The powers-that-be at the club sat down for an extended pow-wow at St Jude's Institute to form a professional set-up. A committee came into being and Queens Park Rangers Football and Athletic Club came into existence in December 1898 with G.H. Moussell appointed secretary and a board of directors including Taylor, Cleverly, Lythaby, Cross, Hiscox, Saxby, Devenish, Wood, Teagle and Hawkes.

QPR were accepted into the Southern League for 1899/1900 while finishing off friendlies as the reserves signed off the club's time as amateurs by lifting the West London League First Division title, going unbeaten and conceding only two goals in 12 fixtures.

Moussell gave an interview with a west London newspaper in the build-up to the visit of Brighton United.

It took place, the paper reports, at the club headquarters, 89 Lancefield Street in Queens Park.

Moussell spoke of the challenge Rangers faced in the Southern League and the Southern Counties League for midweek jousts against the likes of Reading, Woolwich Arsenal, Tottenham Hotspur and Portsmouth, plus a smattering of more friendlies against top Football League opposition. When quizzed as to whether Rangers would again be in the FA Cup, Moussell replied in an expression reminiscent of late British comedian Terry-Thomas, 'Rather!'

Of the players, he said, 'Well, I think that we have a good lot, and if they play up to their reputations I shall be much disappointed if we are not among the first three.'

He picked out centre-forward Fred Beddingfield as the QPR player to watch and heaped praise on Jock Campbell, insisting he was 'the best-known football trainer in the world'.

No pressure on Jock to produce, then?

Well, Campbell and Beddingfield certainly lived up to expectations against Brighton United. Beddingfield, a capture from Aston Villa, put Rangers ahead after just 16 minutes. And Peter Turnbull was on target after 35 minutes.

But it was Cowie who stole the show when he hit the ground running with his four goals. He doubled Rangers' advantage two minutes after Beddingfield's strike. Cowie made it 4-0 three minutes before the interval.

And the ace Cowie secured a hat-trick 20 minutes after the re-start before completing his haul eight minutes from time.

Brighton withdrew from the league before the end of the season and the result was expunged so Rangers ended up below Moussell's estimate in eighth. They also took a big financial hit and it was only due to the generosity of the directors who ploughed in cash that the club were saved from going bust.

v Brighton United 1899

It was no wonder Moussell said of the board, 'If success comes to QPR, no one knows better than I that it is solely the work of our directors, most of whom are sound businessmen, and men who have served Rangers well for years. I only hope the public will appreciate their labours.'

But at least the R's will forever be able to boast that when they blinked into the professional sunlight they shone brightly.

QPR had ticked over in the wake of winning the first bit of silverware for the trophy cabinet in the shape of the West London Observer Challenge Cup.

There was little time to reflect on the glory. Yet another ground move had to be organised – from Harvest Road to the Gun Club in Wood Lane by Wormwood Scrubs prison – for 1893/94.

They also had to withdraw from the West London League after just a season in it (finishing a respectable sixth with 16 points) and go back to largely playing friendlies, with Brentford and Fulham on their fixture list.

But they found a small get-out-of-jail card the following term. QPR managed a run in the London Senior Cup for the first time – reaching the fourth round – after four exits following their introduction to the competition, with The Casuals ending their participation. The same season, though, saw them fall at the second hurdle in their Middlesex Cup debut.

And the following season saw them enter the FA Cup, the most famous domestic knockout competition of them all.

The magic of the cup was already very much a part of English football's psyche. Rangers' opening-round tie against near-neighbouring foes Old St Stephen's – who became Fulham – attracted the biggest crowd in Rangers' history, an estimated 3,000, at Harvest Road on 12 October 1895.

It witnessed Ward hitting the target for the R's but the game ended 1-1 and Rangers lost the replay at Wormholt Farm by a lone goal in front of half the number which had created a memorable atmosphere for an historic occasion in the first attempt to separate the sides.

Ward clearly had his shooting boots on in national cup competitions for QPR that season.

He netted both Rangers goals as they overcame Surbiton Hill 2-1 in their first ever game in the FA Amateur Cup.

The Casuals, rated among the best amateur sides in and around London, did for them again as they did in the county knockout competition.

Smith scored their only goal in a 5-1 tonking. All the more galling for Rangers as it was in front of their own supporters.

Rangers packed their bags at the Gun Club for Kensal Rise Athletic Ground in 1896 on a ten-year lease with rent starting at £100 and increasing to £150.

And after three years of friendlies-dominated football they joined a league, the London League, playing in its Second Division. Expectations were high with Rangers managing to get a top trainer on board. Jock Campbell – a long time before Terry Neill attempted a similar trick – had looked after Arsenal (then with the prefix of Woolwich) and Tottenham Hotspur.

Crowds were on the increase with matches against long-standing rivals Fulham and Brentford. The Bees pulled a record crowd into Kensal Rise for the final game of the season. Some spectators were so keen to get to see the action they climbed the fences surrounding the ground.

Queens Park Rangers' Greatest Games

Campbell's boys, though, were unable to pull up many trees that season. They fell at the first hurdle in the FA Cup to Marlow, who had taken part in the first year of the competition won by Wanderers in 1872. A guess who scored Rangers' only goal in the 3-1 loss? Correct, it was Ward.

Rangers made it through two rounds of the FA Amateur Cup and London Cup. R's were unguarded against 1st Scots Guards and put out of their misery in their opening tie in the Middlesex Cup.

Organisers put Rangers in the First Division of the London League for the following campaign but the team pulled out after just four fixtures for unexplained reasons.

Yet they managed to break their FA Cup duck when goals from Evans (two) and A. Wallington earned them a 3-0 win over Windsor and Eton at Kensal Rise. And then they attracted 6,000 for a 4-0 crushing of Chesham Generals before Clapton pricked the bubble.

They made the semi-finals of the Middlesex Senior Cup and London Charity Cup and got through one round of the London Senior Cup.

Despite failing to rise to the high hopes at the start of Campbell's reign, QPR had created enough of a name for themselves to attract West Bromwich Albion for a money-spinning friendly. More than £140 was made at the gate and shared 50-50 between the clubs.

Money was becoming increasingly significant and the move into professionalism was made the following season, triggered by THAT sending off.

v Wolverhampton W 1-0
FA Cup. Molineux
31 January 1900. Attendance: 7,000

QUEENS PARK RANGERS:	WOLVERHAMPTON WANDERERS:
Clutterbuck	Baddeley
Knowles	Davies
McConnell	Blackett
Crawford	Griffiths
Hitch	Pheasant
Keech	Fleming
Turnbull	Bryan
Haywood	Harper
Bedingfield	Bowen
White	Owen
Hannah	Miller

Referee: Arthur Kingscott (Derbyshire)

*A*BIDE WITH Me is a hymn traditionally sung before the FA Cup Final. It would have been appropriate with 7,000 present at Molineux on Wednesday 31 January 1900 for a first-round replay in the greatest domestic knockout club competition of them all.

You see there is a line in it which opines 'fast falls the eventide'. In other words the sun has lowered in the sky sufficiently that twilight, the short prelude to darkness, to offer limited vision. And when you are playing football that certainly can be a hindrance.

Back in the day when Queen Victoria was still on the throne, Thomas Edison invented electricity and football floodlights followed. But their use was limited in England to exhibition matches with the governing body banning them.

So every football match – bar non-competitive games – had to be completed prior to the fall of darkness.

But twilight was, so to speak, a grey area. Certainly referee Arthur Kingscott thought it light enough when he ordered Queens Park Rangers and Wolverhampton Wanderers to play extra time after a second lot of 90 minutes had failed to separate them.

The players of both sides took the opposite view. The light they felt was too bad to continue and pleaded with the Derbyshire official to call it a day, or rather, in their eyes, night. Now, rather like Margaret Thatcher, Kingscott was not for turning. It was a trait which brought the late British Prime Minister face to face with controversy.

And Kingscott was to underline he was of the same persuasion by allowing a hotly disputed equaliser for Sheffield United which took the FA Cup Final of the following season against Tottenham Hotspur, played in front of 114,815 witnesses at Crystal Palace, to a replay.

Spurs won the reconvened encounter at Bolton Wanderers' Burden Park with Kingscott in charge to thus become the first – and so far only – non-league club to lift the famous trophy.

Queens Park Rangers' Greatest Games

But travelling back a season Rangers, who played alongside the north London club in the Southern League First Division, had no such pretensions. And that was even though they were only pipped 1-0 while being the opponents for Spurs' first league game at White Hart Lane and managing a goalless draw in the reverse fixture against the eventual champions.

Yet that, of course, was not allowing for Kingscott taking charge of their tie against a strong Wolves outfit.

They had enough on their plate as it was with Wolves being the obstacle into the second round.

The team in old gold from the Black Country were founder members of the Football League in 1888 and were headed for fourth spot in the First Division during the campaign.

More pertinently Wolves had already won the FA Cup, defeating Everton 1-0 in the final just seven years earlier (in the only one held at Fallowfield, Manchester, with captain Harry Allen scoring the match-winner). It was already their third final in the competition.

A mere four years previous to taking on QPR in the competition, Wolves were pipped 2-1 by The Wednesday (now Sheffield Wednesday). And in 1889 they lost 3-0 to Preston North End on an historic occasion which saw the Deepdale 'Invincibles' complete the first Football League and FA Cup Double.

The Midlands outfit were also to march to glory for a second time in the competition by overcoming Newcastle United 3-1 in 1908.

Get it? The draw had cast Rangers very much in the role of underdogs. But the magic of the Cup has always been about the Davids taking on the Goliaths and slaying them. Thus provoking the epithet 'giant-killers' whenever this is achieved.

And this was the label that was eventually stuck onto Rangers when their marathon tie against Wolves was concluded thanks in part to the intransigence of referee Kingscott.

So were we to expect the unexpected when Wolves arrived at Kensal Rise for the first attempt to separate the sides? Not really. A mid-table Southern League outfit against illustrious opponents used to dining at the top table of English football. What were the odds?

Rangers anticipated a big crowd and opened the gates three hours before kick-off. Ground conditions were heavy, which was in Rangers' favour as they attempted to combat the advantages a Football League side possessed over a non-league one.

Adam Haywood ensured the hosts held Wolves to a 1-1 draw. Surely that was as good as it was going to get?

But Rangers refused to concede their best opportunity had deserted them as they faced Wolves the following Wednesday on Molineux's superb playing surface, which, pre-match, was thought to offer another advantage to hosts who had plenty to be going along with as it was.

The same XI which had performed so valiantly in the first match were present and correct. And how. Rangers had to defend early doors with defender Alf Hitch clearing a dangerous Wolves attack.

On the counter, QPR almost drew first blood through Frank Bedingfield. His effort, following a sweeping move involving him, Bill White and Haywood, was saved by Tom Baddeley.

Hitch and Bedingfield went close as Rangers clicked into gear while Miller forced QPR stopper Harry Clutterbuck to save as the game developed into an entertaining end-to-end showdown.

v Wolverhampton Wanderers 1900

Rangers had a penalty appeal turned down by Kingscott after Adam Haywood 'went down like a log' after 'two heavy backs charged very viciously'. Clutterbuck cleared balls by George Bowen and, with his head, from Jack Miller. James Hannah thought he had put Rangers in front from a Peter Turnbull cross but his effort was ruled offside. From the free kick, George Harper scored for Wolves before Kingscott ruled he had blown for a foul on him by Rangers' Alex McConnell.

Wolves began to turn the screw shortly before the interval and after it but the Rangers defence stood firm, with Clutterbuck, McConnell and Joe Knowles outstanding. As Wolves tired, Rangers pressed but both sides had chances. Clutterbuck saved from Davis and White shot wide.

Ted Pheasant hit the post from the penalty spot after McConnell was adjudged by Kingscott to have handled, no doubt distracted by Clutterbuck moving to the six-yard line before the rule about goalkeepers having to stay on their line was brought in five years later.

The official heightened his role centre stage by ordering extra time in the growing gloom, rather like Clive Thomas, the Welsh referee who disallowed what would have been a winning goal by Brazil's Zico against Sweden in the 1978 World Cup as he argued he had blown the final whistle with the ball in mid-flight.

Or, more recently, the likes of Uruguayan referee Jorge Larrionda who disallowed Frank Lampard's goal for England in the second round of the 2010 World Cup against Germany with the ball yards over the line.

Or Mark Clattenburg, caught up in a racism row with Chelsea out of which he was exonerated.

Kingscott, Derbyshire's finest, blew his whistle and had to wait patiently after ignoring desperate overtures to reconsider his decision to play on with the daylight beginning its descent to dusk.

It is reported that the teams had left the ground and only returned to the field of play reluctantly, no doubt persuaded to do so by connections of both sides fearful of repercussions from the governing body of English football and the spectators as well as the immediate wrath of the immovable Kingscott.

Thankfully the spotlight fell away from the Man in Black and onto a player. Giant-killings need a hero, or even a super hero. Frank Bedingfield had no blue tight figure-hugging onesie and red cape to wear. Nor did he have a telephone box to twirl round and magic himself out of his civvies into such an outfit. The striker merely settled for Rangers' hooped kit to perform the role of match-winner.

And the irony was that Bedingfield had had experience of scoring in a match effected by fading light. He had netted an equaliser for eventual Football League champions Aston Villa against Sheffield Wednesday the previous season before referee Arthur Scragg abandoned the game on 79 minutes, with his side's Yorkshire opponents leading 3-1, due to 'failing light'.

In fact, controversy was also connected to that fixture with the Football League ordering the two sides to play out the remaining 11 minutes FOUR months later with Wednesday winning and Bedingfield replaced by Billy Garraty.

Rangers won the toss for choice of ends. And it proved a lucky pick thanks to Bedingfield.

The striker with the eye for goal had been forced to leave his side with ten players to take on the might of Wolves in the second half of normal time due to a leg injury.

Queens Park Rangers' Greatest Games

But it was decided the striker would battle through the pain barrier and/or any other inconvenience caused by his physical ailment for extra time.

And what a difference his presence made. A contemporary report had it that Rangers immediately went at their opponents 'hammer and tongs'.

Like the wolf in the scary children's tale of the Three Pigs, Rangers huffed and puffed and finally blew down the house of their opponents thanks to Bedingfield.

The Wolves resistance was razed to the ground three minutes into the second period of the added time.

Bedingfield latched on to the ball and went on a solo run which left his opponents dazed and confused before rifling the ball into the corner of Tom Baddeley's goal.

Rangers continued to go for the throat to make sure rather than sit back on their crucial breakthrough goal.

In fact, the report stated that Bedingfield's strike 'seemed to rouse Rangers to even greater energy and dash'.

And Turnbull, taking a ball from White in his stride, fizzed an effort just wide.

But there was a nerve-jangling moment for the Southern Leaguers in the final seconds as Wolves picked themselves off the floor to launch a final attack. But Kingscott returned to his position in the limelight by giving a free kick to QPR, adjudging that the hosts had drifted offside. Then he blew his whistle. Those wearing Rangers' favours celebrated at the ground and on the return journey to west London.

It proved a case of 'after the Lord Mayor's show comes the dust cart', or, in clearer language, an anti-climax in the second round when Southern League rivals Millwall Athletic came to Kensal Rise and went away with a 2-0 win. It was the same QPR side which had stunned Wolves, bar Tom Smith for Turnbull at outside-right.

But an epic afternoon and 'eventide' at Molineux had provided a shining light for QPR to try and follow.

They had had to overcome London Welsh, Fulham, West Hampstead, Wandsworth and Civil Service in the preliminary rounds to earn the right to be in the hat for a plum draw in the first round proper. They got one in Wolves. And the fruits of their labour paid off. Big time.

Bedingfield went on to top score for Rangers with 21 goals to help them finish mid-table in the league in his only season with the club before joining Portsmouth.

Tragically the north-easterner – born in Sunderland – died aged just 27 four years later after emigrating to South Africa. But he will always be remembered by die-hard Rangers fans for his contribution in Rangers' first big impact on the FA Cup.

v Plymouth Argyle 1-0
Western League First Division
Agricultural Showground, Park Royal
17 April 1906. Attendance: 6,000

QUEENS PARK RANGERS:
Howes
White
Newlands
Gardner
Hitch
McGargill
Sugden
Fletcher
Yenson
Ryder
Roberts

PLYMOUTH ARGYLE:
Not known

Referee: Not known

IAN HOLLOWAY, a Queens Park Rangers player in the 1990s and promotion-winning manager in the 2000s, is now, first and foremost, known for being a successful boss having guided Blackpool and Crystal Palace into the Premier League in the space of three years.

Secondly, his reputation has also been forged by his ability to coin memorable phrases like, 'We need to tweak the nose of fear and stick an ice cube down the vest of terror' during Palace's successful play-off bid in 2012/13.

Some of which, like 'I couldn't be more chuffed if I were a badger in mating season' when recalling a promotion with Rangers, no doubt, have their origins in his upbringing in his home city of Bristol, where he played for Cadbury Heath as a youngster.

There is a family picture of a freeze-frame of a young, fair-haired Holloway off the TV in his autobiography *Ollie* playing for the club formed in 1894.

Perhaps his descendants may have been kicking a ball around on the playing fields of Heathens' Springfield home.

Back in those Victorian times there seems to be no record of the club playing competitive football, but these days they are in the Premier Division of the Western Football League.

And that league provided QPR with their first title as a professional club, having joined the paid ranks in 1898, sealed when a Bill Yenson goal was enough to give Rangers a 1-0 victory over reigning champions Plymouth Argyle at the Agricultural Showground, Park Royal, the day after Easter Monday in 1906.

Edward VII was just four years into his reign but when the 1905/06 season kicked off at the Agricultural Showground in Park Royal (their NINTH ground following Welford's Field, London Scottish, Barn Elms, Home Farm, Kilburn Cricket Club, Gun Club by Wormwood Scrubs, Kensal Athletic Ground and Latimer Road) Rangers' crown jewels consisted of just two trophies.

Queens Park Rangers' Greatest Games

There was the West London Observer Challenge Cup, which your author wrote about in the opening chapter. And the second was achieved in their final season as amateurs when Rangers' reserve team finished on top of the West London League First Division having finished the campaign against six rivals, including Shepherd's Bush, Hammersmith Athletic and Kensington Rangers, unbeaten, having conceded a mere two goals in total.

But a third was most welcome to sit alongside them in the trophy cabinet at their Park Royal headquarters. Proof that the nomadic club had found their feet in the full-time game.

To do so they had to go further afield than the capital. The Western League had formed as the Bristol and District in 1892 (adopting its current name three years later). It consisted, as the name suggests, of teams from the west. And as it was in England that meant teams from counties such as Gloucestershire, Wiltshire, Dorset, Somerset, Devon and Cornwall.

The founder members reflected just that with the likes of Eastville Rovers (who became Bristol Rovers), Bedminster (who combined with Bristol South End to become Bristol City), Clevedon (who became Clevedon Town), Clifton Association, Mangotsfield and St George (who combined to become Roman Glass St George), Trowbridge Town, Warmley and Wells.

But by the time Rangers joined it for their first season in 1900/01 membership had spread to involve clubs from London and the South Coast, with Bristol Rovers and Swindon Town the lone representative geographically situated in the West Country.

And five terms later the capital investment had increased with Tottenham Hotspur, West Ham United, Fulham, Brentford and Millwall turning it into a London League in all but name. Optimism was far from high in the Rangers camp when they kicked off their 1905/06 campaign in the Western League.

QPR had far from pulled up many trees in their brief acquaintance with the league, with two mid-table finishes and one just four spots off the bottom in their first three campaigns.

And the previous season had seen them finish rock bottom with Plymouth Argyle flying the flag for the West Country by finishing top of the pile.

A 5-1 victory against Millwall in front of 2,000 at the Agricultural Ground was some late consolation for QPR. Generally, though, defeats against Southampton (5-0 and 4-1) and the Lions (3-1) were more reflective of a disastrous campaign in the league. They only managed to collect a paltry 15 points from their efforts in it during 1904/05, while Plymouth doubled the amount.

But all that changed the following campaign of the midweek league which allowed Rangers to also play Southern League fixtures at the weekend.

Rangers had a new look. Bolton Wanderers midfielder Bill Yenson had replaced John Bowman, the player-secretary who left for Norwich City after serving QPR for four years.

Sid Sugden had arrived from Nottingham Forest and Matthew Kingsley signed from West Ham United. But the most significant signing was James Cowan, who hooked up with the west Londoners after a glittering career with Aston Villa.

Cowan had won five Football League titles and two FA Cups with Villa and was to become Rangers' first manager (more later).

The captures seemed unable to give the club's performances in the Southern League a consistent lift.

They managed a decent start – two victories out of the first three matches with a Sugden debut hat-trick helping seal a 4-0 win against New Brompton – and a spectacular finish

v Plymouth Argyle 1906

which saw them wallop Watford 6-0 and create a club scoring record in the competition as Bristol Rovers were beaten 7-0 with Fred Ryder, Jack Fletcher and Fred Bevan each scoring twice and Andy Thompson once.

But in the meantime results were not so hot and despite Ryder top-scoring with 15 goals in 34 matches Rangers finished 13th.

And interest in the FA Cup only lasted a game after they received a bye into the first round proper – only their second appearance at that stage – with Fulham pipping Rangers 1-0.

But it was a different kettle of fish for The Midweekers in the Western League.

They were in a tough league which included Southampton, Plymouth Argyle, Tottenham Hotspur, West Ham United, Millwall, Brentford, Fulham, Portsmouth and Reading.

They might have been Southampton's whipping boys the season before, but new-look Rangers turned the tables on the Saints by completing the double over the South Coast outfit from Hampshire in the space of a month. A 5-1 home victory on 30 October was followed by a 3-2 success in Southampton's back yard.

Rangers also delighted the home support in a 3,000 crowd at the 40,000-capacity Agricultural Showground – with one large grandstand and a smaller structure inside a horse-ring enclosure on a 100-acre site – by taming the Lions 2-1 and holding Millwall to a goalless draw in the reverse fixture.

But the race for the title came down to the wire with the decider against the reigning champions in the final game.

Rangers went into their showdown with Plymouth Argyle knowing defeat would see them end up third behind Southampton and their Devonian opponents.

The money folk at Rangers took advantage of the occasion. The club had, as we have discovered, a roller-coaster existence as far as their finances were concerned, so those who held the purse strings upped the admission price to 3d per person for the clash on the Tuesday after Easter Monday.

Plymouth were not going to give up their title without a fight and made the near 500-mile round trip in determined mood.

But Rangers had clearly adopted a sensible approach over the holidays – no doubt avoiding Easter eggs and too much alcohol and food consumption – and managed to squeeze a 1-0 win thanks to a Bill Yenson winner to ensure the West London Observer Cup and West London League trophy had company.

It was clear from the kick-off it would be a keenly contested encounter. And it turned into a thriller of two missed penalties.

Plymouth were unwilling to roll over and give up their fight to retain the title. And Bill White felt the force of their effort when he was clattered by Argyle inside-right Wright, who was booked for the challenge.

Sid Sugden had two golden opportunities to put Rangers ahead but squandered both. Fred Ryder was presented with the ball by Yenson in front of goal but allowed the Plymouth defence to clear.

Rangers forced a series of corner kicks and from one of them Yenson got a firm contact to bullet the ball past Plymouth goalkeeper John Sutcliffe and give QPR the lead, the match and the title.

But Plymouth remained a threat. Rangers goalkeeper Arthur Howes fisted a shot from Harry Wilcox away after the Plymouth player had got by White.

Queens Park Rangers' Greatest Games

Rangers threatened to double their lead, though. Bill Roberts made a fine run before being fouled by Argyle defender Clarke. Then Yenson had another effort kept out by England international stopper Sutcliffe.

QPR had their backs against the wall following the interval with Plymouth securing three corners in as many minutes. From one Dave Buchanan shot wide.

Rangers had their best chance yet to increase their lead when Yenson won a penalty as he was fouled by Clarke but Sutcliffe saved the spot-kick from Gardner.

Both sides threw the kitchen sink at each other and Plymouth were awarded a penalty for a challenge by White on Wilcox. Again it was the goalkeeper who emerged the hero, saving the eight-yard effort from Plymouth captain Clarke to enable Rangers to hang on.

QPR had pipped Saints by a point, bagging 26 in all, with Plymouth third on 24.

The club might have ended the term £400 in debt, according to contemporary reports, but at least there was something to show despite the loss.

It proved the only season in which the sun shone for Rangers in the league. They made a fist of their defence but ended runners-up to Fulham while the club suffered their worst ever Southern League season. Their final two seasons in it saw QPR finish three off the bottom and runners-up.

These days the Western League is entirely made up of teams from the south-west with the likes of Bristol Manor Farm, Melksham Town and Ilfracombe Town joining Cadbury Heath in the top flight, while a second division includes Barnstable Town, Chippenham Park and Shepton Mallet.

The divisions of what is now known as the Toolstation League are the ninth and tenth tiers on the pyramid system into the Football League, known as Steps 5 and 6.

West Country football has produced modern-day striker Bobby Zamora, ex-players Gary Penrice and, of course, Holloway for Rangers, while QPR legend Gerry Francis has managed in it (all having been at Bristol Rovers).

The capital's love affair with the Western League, though, has long been confined to dust-covered history books. Largely, so it was believed, down to the competition being considered merely one in which its reserve teams participated. Just an opportunity to mix developing talent with coming-back-from-injury players and the odd triallist.

The conclusion was reached, with many of the London clubs also playing in the prestigious Southern League, rated the finest outside the Football League.

But it has been recently uncovered that it was very much for its frontline sides.

So anyone interested in Queens Park Rangers specifically is advised to wipe those books down and pore over their pages of yellowing paper. They will discover details of a little gem of a year in the history of the Super Hoops.

v Manchester United 1-1
FA Charity Shield. Stamford Bridge
27 April 1908. Attendance: 12,000

QUEENS PARK RANGERS:
Shaw
McDonald
Fidler
Lintott
McLean
Downing
Pentland
Cannon
Skilton
Gittens
Barnes

MANCHESTER UNITED:
Moger
Stacey
Duckworth
Bell
Roberts
Downie
Wall
J. Turnbull
S. Turnbull
Bannister
Meredith

Referee: J.T. Howcroft

THEN AS now Manchester United were considered a scalp no matter what level the opposition were: high or low; Bayern Munich to Barnstable Town; Barcelona to Belford Red Row Welfare.

It was David v Goliath when Queens Park Rangers took on the Red Devils in the first FA Charity Shield match at the end of one of the most momentous seasons in the west London club's history.

Non-league Rangers had won the Southern League as United were crowned Football League champions.

And one bright spark came up with the idea that to pit each of the title holders against each other would provide the perfect match at the end of the season to raise funds for good causes; an idea which evolved from the Sheriff of London Charity Shield which saw a professional and amateur team lock horns to win it.

It provided Rangers with the biggest occasion in their history and the country's leading scribes were there to record it; the nearest the sport came to blanket media coverage BS (Before Sky).

Fortunately for Rangers they had an individual in their camp who had more than an idea of how to cope and the standard his club had to attain to get any sort of result against the Mancunians from Old Trafford, who had celebrated their first of now 20 top-flight titles with a 2-1 win over Preston North End two days earlier.

James Cowan had been become Rangers' first manager in May 1907. Up until then QPR relied on player-secretaries like G.H. Moussell and John Bowman to combine administrative and team duties to see them through.

Cowan had arrived at the club's Agricultural Showground in Park Royal, west London, two years before as a player with massive experience. And a glittering career which would have stood comparison with any player of his time, whether they wore United's red shirt or not.

Queens Park Rangers' Greatest Games

The dominating centre-half had won FIVE league titles with Aston Villa during his 14 years at Villa Park in which the club bestrode English football like a Colossus. He also had two FA Cup winners' medals in his display cabinet at home. He helped them to defeat West Bromwich Albion in 1895 and Everton two years later.

Cowan was the rock on which Villa's back line – and their success – was built. And he was considered, according to contemporary observers, to be one of the best players of his era. His forte was pace, a quality still rare in today's game in many quarters. His sprinting abilities enabled him to win the renowned New Year Sprint at Powderhall, although the achievement cost him a club fine as he skipped a Villa match to take part.

After 354 Villa appearances, Cowan moved into the backroom in 1902 and became a coach to the club juniors before moving out of football to become the boss at the Grand Turk public house in Aston, the district of England's second city where Villa was based.

But he re-laced his boots when an opportunity to move to west London and link up with QPR came about.

His playing comeback, though, swiftly came to a halt aged 37 after just one Southern League appearance for Rangers, one in which he managed a goal as QPR put the boot into the Cobblers from Northampton in a 6-1 victory in front of 8,000 fans at the Agricultural Showground Park Royal.

But it was clear his acumen off the field combined with what he had experienced on it would make him an invaluable asset if Rangers wanted to make their mark on the bigger stages. Rangers had struggled in the Southern League in Cowan's debut season and the pattern got even worse the following term after they lost leading scorer Fred Bevan who asked to be put on the transfer list and was sold for £340 to Bury.

Rangers reached the nadir of their existence in the league that term by finishing just three places off rock bottom.

And this was in spite of an influx of players including Joe Fidler from Fulham and John McLean from Millwall and, because of an effective scouting network in the north-east of England, Newcastle United's Sid Blake, Tom Green from Middlesbrough, and Sunderland's Dennis O'Donnell, plus Ted Anderson, down from Sheffield United.

Rangers had a couple of big home wins that were earned against struggling Northampton Town and Swindon Town, 5-0 and 6-2, while Tottenham Hotspur, FA Cup winners seven years earlier, were beaten 3-1 in front of an impressed 15,000 at Park Royal.

But away from HQ, victories seemed as rare as hen's teeth – with QPR managing just two – and none of their strikers hit double figures in the goalscoring charts for the season, Sid Sugden going closest with nine.

Even the FA Cup left QPR wanting, losing a home replay against Bristol Rovers to extend their search for a victory in the competition to five years.

The fact Rangers were left homeless when their landlords, the Royal Agricultural Society, were forced to sell their ground to dig themselves out of a financial hole must have had QPR folk believing their glass was more than just half empty.

Something had to be done and Cowan's appointment to take his place in the managerial hot-seat proved an inspired one.

A home was found in the close season. A quick reconnaissance of potential bases in the west London areas of Shepherd's Bush, Kilburn and Notting Hill was made before the club settled on one just half a mile away from the Showground in Park Royal. Its owners, the Great Western Railway, even supplied the venue with its own station besides a stadium which held 60,000.

v Manchester United 1908

With a TENTH headquarters settled upon, Cowan began the task of building a team worthy of it. And he did not let the grass grow under his feet and almost completely revamped the side which looked strong on paper and lived up to the hype.

He acquired goalkeeper Charlie Shaw, a fellow Scot, from Port Glasgow, who only missed two league games in six seasons. Right-back John McDonald joined from Grimsby Town, Nottingham Forest striker Alf Walker came, as did wingers Fred Pentland and Billy Barnes from Brentford and inside-left Alf Gittins via Luton Town.

But twin coups de grace were the captures of Archie Mitchell and Evelyn Lintott. The manager returned to Villa to pick up Mitchell.

The defender was, like Cowan, a dominant centre-back and he progressed to being a Rangers regular for 14 years after an outstanding debut season. One wonders whether the manager saw the player he was at Villa in the defender.

And half-back Lintott, who linked up with the west Londoners from West Country Plymouth Argyle, proved a class signing.

He only scored once in guiding Rangers to their first Southern League title in 25 appearances – in a 5-2 crushing of Clapton Orient – but he shone so brightly he earned a full England cap in a 3-0 away defeat of Northern Ireland in Cliftonville.

It made Lintott, who was tragically killed in action during the First World War, the first Rangers player to be given one. The size of the feat is borne out by the fact QPR did not have another full England international until the legendary Rodney Marsh 64 years later.

Cowan's side spluttered at the start of the campaign which began at the Showground, with Rangers having to beg a favour from its owners with the finishing touches being put to their new home.

But after two draws and a reverse, QPR clicked and went on a fabulous run of 15 games in which 11 were won and only one defeat, which came against Millwall on their debut at the new stadium in front of 16,000.

QPR were level on points with Plymouth Argyle – the team they pipped for the Western League crown just two years before (see earlier chapter) – on 27.

The rivals set a Southern League attendance record when 29,768 attended Rangers' new home to witness a goalless encounter on Christmas Day.

Rangers got a firmer grip on the championship race in the New Year and won five out of six – including a completing of the double over Clapton Orient – from the beginning of March. But Plymouth still held on to their coat-tails. QPR's reverse fixture against the Devonians on Good Friday was reckoned the clash to see where the crown was headed. The 1-1 draw in the West Country fell in Rangers' favour with their hosts needing both points (in the days before a victory earned three).

QPR missed their first opportunity to make sure of the title with a shock loss to Northampton Town at Park Royal.

But a Frank Cannon hat-trick and a Pentland strike against West Ham United ensured a 4-0 win and the crown at the second time of asking 48 hours later in front of 10,000 ecstatic supporters.

Two heavy losses – 5-2 and 8-3 against Southampton and Swindon Town – in the final fixtures gave an anti-climactic feel to the season in which the two Alfs, Gittins and Walker, ended up joint top scorers on 16.

But the fact remained that just seven days after lifting the Southern League title Rangers had to make the short journey across west London to Stamford Bridge for their Charity Shield encounter against United.

Queens Park Rangers' Greatest Games

It was a daunting task. Their opponents had secured their first top-flight title a mere two days earlier when Ernest Mangnall's team pipped Preston North End 2-1 at Old Trafford thanks to a strike from Harold Halse, a £350 capture from Southend, and an own goal by hapless Tommy Rodway. Their points tally of 52 was a Football League record.

The following season United were to lift the first of 11 FA Cups (at the time of publication) by defeating Bristol City 1-0 at Crystal Palace thanks to a goal from Sandy Turnbull (who only played when Mangnall had his arm twisted by his captain Charlie Roberts to include the half-fit striker because he 'might get a goal').

And just two terms after that Mangnall – setting a high benchmark for United managers to follow and which proved a comfortable one for the recently retired Sir Alex Ferguson – guided United to their second title, a 5-0 victory against Sunderland completed with strikes from Halse, two, Jimmy Turnbull and Enoch West, plus an own goal by the Mackems' Albert Milton.

And the Fergie of his day had the Turnbulls and Roberts to pick from as they warmed up to take on the R's.

Crucially, Mangnall also had Billy Meredith, a superstar, to call upon. Yet Rangers had their potential heroes too, such as Lintott, the international right-half.

It was rated the biggest, most glamorous game that Rangers had been involved in.

Poor weather put spectators off attending the prestigious occasion, with only 12,000 scattered around the terraces and seats of a ground with a capacity of around 70,000.

It meant, of course, that the charities selected would get less than anticipated. But those who did brave the inclement conditions were given a football treat.

Rangers, resplendent in their green and white hoops, might have been intimidated by the event and the reputation of their illustrious opponents, but there was no sign of twitchiness.

QPR looked determined to prove the gap between the Southern and Football League was paper-thin, if not non-existent. They oozed confidence with Pentland and Cannon looking a handful for the revered visitors to the capital.

The pair gave notice when they combined to force a back-on-their-heels United to concede a corner. Rampaging Cannon was charging towards goal when Bolton referee Howcroft accidentally blocked his path and United defender George Stacey was able to clear the danger.

Shortly afterwards Rangers took the lead. Left-winger Barnes found his inside-left Gittins, who fed Cannon. The striker stepped up a gear to speed forwards and drive home beyond helpless United stopper Harry Moger, one of the country's top goalkeepers.

Rangers refused to rest on their laurels and looked to double their advantage soon afterwards. Moger's goal again came under threat but the man in black darkened their mood when he halted play to discipline the Red Devils' Jimmy Turnbull.

All United had to show as an attacking force was an early effort from Sandy Turnbull following a George Wall cross which Charlie Shaw saved. And Rangers continued to dominate. Moger was forced to save a Gittins effort shortly before the interval.

Rangers began the second half where they left off the first and Percy Skilton and Cannon threatened the United rearguard with only a last-ditch intervention from Roberts preventing a second goal.

United began to turn the tide and Shaw made two superb saves. One was a particularly fine stop from Jimmy Turnbull who had sashayed his way by two Rangers defenders before the goalkeeper whipped the ball off his toes.

v Manchester United 1908

Both sides maintained a fast pace throughout despite the pitch getting heavier and heavier due to the unseasonable bad weather to thrill the fans who had braved the elements. Eventually, there appeared a chink in Rangers' display as Gittins suffered in the conditions. The crowd urged him, according to a contemporary account, to 'get at it Gittins'.

The next second saw United up their tempo and it paid off with the equaliser from outside-right Meredith. The Welsh Wizard had been kept quiet by Rangers' left-half Sammy Downing, who did a fine man-marking job for much of the game.

But when Meredith broke free of Downing's shackles he cracked a shot from distance against the upright and post before the ball rebounded into the opposite corner of Shaw's goal with the stopper needing more than snookers to judge the flight of the 'cannon'. It was a wonder goal. As the report pointed out it was one 'only seen once in a hundred matches and one which perhaps no player but Meredith could make'.

United's tails were up but Rangers stood firm and almost grabbed a winner. Percy Skilton and then, from a Pentland pass, Cannon went close.

And Gittins was dispossessed as he tried to beat an opponent, with Cannon and Skilton unmarked.

The match was hailed worthy of one between champions, 'fast and scientific'. Both goalkeepers earned praise, as did the defenders, such as John McLean and midfielders, like Lintott, Bill Barnes and Pentland, while forwards such as Skilton, Cannon and Gittins 'were as clever as one could desire'.

One observer said, 'One cannot speak too highly of the play of the Rangers. It was one of the finest games I have seen them play.'

Lord Kinnaird, president of the FA, was full of compliments and called upon Rangers and United to replay just before the start of the following season.

Kinnaird would be presented with the original FA Cup for 21 years of service to the governing body after playing in nine of the first 11 finals and Rangers and the Reds were happy to go along with such an esteemed football person in his desire to see an outright winner of the Shield.

It came to pass back at Stamford Bridge in August with Rangers losing it 4-0 with Jimmy Turnbull hitting a hat-trick and George Wall adding the other goal.

Each side then visited the West End to watch a 'bioscope' replay of the game at the Alhambra Theatre in Leicester Square. It consisted of a cinema screen showing of the action.

A bioscope was usually part of a fairground show put on by a travelling cinema fronted by an organ with dancing girls putting on the entertainment between showings.

If that was the case on the evening of 27 April 1908 it might have provided a break from what must have been one of the first video nasties in the eyes of QPR – unless highlights of the first game, when QPR stood tall and proud, were shown.

Rangers' share of the gate receipts, which has been reported as totalling £100, was divided between St Mary's Hospital, Willesden College Hospital, Acton College Hospital and Willesden Children's Aid.

6 v Brentford 4-0

Southern League First Division. Park Royal Stadium
7 October 1911. Attendance: 15,000

QUEENS PARK RANGERS:	BRENTFORD:
Shaw	Ling
McDonald	Rhodes
Ovens	Cleverley
Whyman	Richards
Mitchell	Hamilton
Wake	Hickleton
Smith	Brown
Revill	Sibbald
McKie	Anderson
Thornton	Rouse
Barnes	Hendren

Referee: Not known

IAIN DOWIE, who has served QPR as a player, coach and manager, coined the phrase-in-a-word 'bouncebackability'. It entered the *Oxford English Dictionary* following a campaign to include it led by Sky TV's *Soccer AM* football show.

The esteemed tome defined the expression as: (especially in sport) the capacity to recover quickly from a setback.

It is apt for describing Rangers as they completed a second Southern League title victory – with a 4-0 west London derby win over Brentford the highlight – and FA Charity Shield runners-up double two years before the outbreak of the First World War.

The R's had punched above their weight as they took on the mighty Manchester United in the first ever FA Charity Shield in 1908 (as written about previously) after lifting their first Southern championship.

But they were forced to pick themselves off the canvas to make their second Shield appearance on the back of a second Southern trophy success four years later.

QPR could have been dealt a knockout blow shortly after holding United in the charity match thought to be the brainchild of Lord Kinnaird, the FA Cup legend and president of the governing body. Buoyed by earning championship status, Rangers quit the Southern League and applied for membership of the Football League with Stoke City resigning from the Second Division.

Unfortunately their upwardly mobile ambitions were hit as their attempt to get amongst the big boys was rejected. The league's AGM voted in favour of Tottenham Hotspur, who had trailed QPR by seven spots and ten points. Rangers were angry and shocked and thrown into crisis. An achieving club with good players and a ground but no one to play having resigned from the Southern League. The only option appeared to be the South Eastern League, which was considered of a standard beneath reserve football.

It could have seen Rangers dissipate, disintegrate and disappear, just leaving the memories of a roller-coaster three decades of existence.

v Brentford 1911

It was time for a hero to enter the scene. A super hero. Mr Wood, the club secretary, might not have had a Batmobile, but he certainly saved the situation.

He picked up Rangers' begging bowl and took it to the Southern League's management committee. Negotiations were protracted and no doubt the midnight oil came into use. But Mr Wood convinced the people on the other side of the table that Rangers would be a useful late addition to the fixture list. The committee voted to re-instate Rangers by increasing the number of clubs in their top division from 20 to 21.

But there was a caveat. Rangers had to play all their games midweek as the fixtures secretary had already published his efforts which left weekend dates unavailable.

That, of course, presented another problem. Rangers had had their financial travails. Now they could be hit in the pocket again with having to play their matches during normal working days. It was the days before competitive floodlit football so the club was unable to stage it in the evening after their fans' nine-to-five labours had been completed.

The players were understandably unsettled by the club missing out on a Football League place and the club were running scared of a mass walkout.

Manager James Cowan, who had masterminded the title glory which brought about the showdown with the Red Devils, tried to re-group his wavering troops. It was no easy task. Morale had been kicked below the waist.

Star winger Fred Pentland was concerned enough about situation to move to Middlesbrough for a club record £350. He had been pushing for an England call-up and considered hopes would evaporate if he stayed in west London. Even the carrot of a £4 a week wage – a considerable sum in those days – dangled in front of Pentland could not tempt him into a u-turn.

Evelyn Lintott decided to up sticks soon after the season started. The reported £1,000 Rangers received from Bradford City for the England international half-back sweetened the pill of his loss, but Lintott's departure had left a huge hole in the QPR back line.

Yet Cowan tried to make a fist of it by bringing in Harry Duff from Manchester City, Alonzo Drake from Birmingham City and Lincoln City's J. MacDonald. He also fought off competition from Preston North End to land his biggest fish, Bill Greer, who became an Irish international when he faced England with Northern Ireland at Bradford in February 1909, adding two more caps the following month to complete his country's Home International campaign against Scotland and Wales. Cowan did his best but losing players with the influence comparable to a Gareth Bale and Dave Mackay in Pentland and Lintott looked insurmountable as a roller-coaster season unfolded.

The defence of the title, albeit one they would have preferred to swap for the bragging rights of being a Football League club, ended with Rangers in 15th.

They only managed four goals in the opening eight games, although held firm at the back by only conceding the same number.

They triumphed in five of the next six games, but then couldn't buy a win in the following five. Billy Barnes tried to keep spirits up with ten goals, but it wasn't easy with QPR also tripping at the first hurdle in the FA Cup against West Ham United.

Mr Wood was unable plug the dyke out of which cash flowed with crowds down and most results far from encouraging. Rangers lost £866 on the season but the debt was offset by the sales of Pentland and Lintott and fund-raisers by supporters answering SOSs from club HQ.

But the tide began to turn the following season. They were back playing on weekends – which helped boost crowds – and the side was more stable.

Queens Park Rangers' Greatest Games

Rangers were unbeaten in eight and had only suffered one reverse after 11. They were not defeated away until Christmas and were top going into the New Year. QPR eventually finished third after losing three of their final four games with William Steer, signed at the start of the season, bagging 27 goals.

They even managed to reach the quarter-finals of the FA Cup for the first time with Steer netting five in their three rounds against Norwich City, Southend and West Ham United before a 1-0 defeat at Football League outfit Barnsley.

It caused great excitement among supporters. As the team returned to Paddington from Yorkshire with their steam train bedecked in their green and white colours, supporters surged for the compartment with some players hopping out on the opposite side to the platform and legging it back to the previous stop at Royal Oak.

QPR's reserves made the semi-finals of the Southern Charity Cup and the bean counters reported a profit of £253 (in stark contrast to the previous term, of course).

Rangers kept most of the same players for the following season, with the likes of Dan McKie from Chorley, Oldham Athletic pair Bert Butterworth and Bob Browning and Norwich City's Horace Brindley coming in, and finished sixth, with a first-round exit in the FA Cup to Bradford City.

Proof positive of Rangers' capabilities of winning their second Southern League title back came at the start of the 1911/12 season. Cowan bolstered the squad yet again with Ted Revill from Chesterfield, Bristol Rovers' Gilbert Ovens, Harry Thornton and Arthur Smith from Brierley Athletic moving to Park Royal.

And the new boys made an instant impact, particularly in the goalscoring department. Neighbouring Brentford, who were to become strong Rangers rivals, discovered just what these hot shots were about in early October. Dan McKie bagged a double, one from the penalty spot, while Revill and Smith also hit the target in an emphatic 4-0 victory which showed how little time the recent signings had taken to bed in.

The showdown attracted one of Park Royal's biggest crowds of the season – 15,000. Rangers had made a flying start to the season and the Johnny Come Latelys had gradually boosted the attendance through it, having kicked off their home fixtures season with a third less.

There is nothing like winning – with a bit of style, of course – to pull in the punters.

The sting was taken out of the Bees to the delight of the vociferous majority in green and white favours as Rangers posted their biggest victory of the season.

A victory which not only extended an unbeaten opening run to six games, of which five were won (with the first four producing an average of ten goals scored and none conceded), but ensured Rangers would be taken seriously in their quest to secure the Southern League crown for the second time in four years. QPR had a firm grip and were not about to loosen it. At the end of the month they walloped West Ham United 4-1 at Park Royal in front of a massive 25,000 with Cowan's astute working of the transfer market still in evidence with McKie, Smith, Revill and Thornton firing home.

The dynamic duo of McKie and Revill hit the goals in a 2-0 away win against Bristol Rovers in the next game to ensure Rangers remained unbeaten for the first ten games, eight of which finished with the R's collecting maximum points

In the meantime ALL but one of their goals had been scored by Cowan's latest captures. McKie had scored in all but two, totalling ten (and was to net in the following two games as QPR tasted back-to-back defeats). Revill was just one down while Smith and Thornton each managed a pair.

v Brentford 1911

Rangers were setting a scorching pace at the top and recovered after their stumbles – which were against Swindon Town and Northampton Town – before a couple more reverses as they turned the year with 31 points with half the fixtures played, three ahead of the Cobblers.

QPR held their nerve and still led at April with Plymouth Argyle leapfrogging Northampton and hovering just three points behind.

But it shredded as the Green and Whites could only scrape two victories from their last seven games.

Rangers' West Country rivals – a team they had beaten to clinch the Western League (as written about earlier) – won all their final six matches to leave QPR needing to avoid defeat in their last fixture at Norwich City to seal the title. A Smith strike gave them a 1-1 draw and the crown by just one point.

The achievement, of course, gave them their second tilt at the FA Charity Shield. They again gave a good account of themselves against the Football League champions despite the teeming rain which limited the opportunity to provide a memorable spectacle. But were they pipped 2-1 by Blackburn Rovers at Tottenham Hotspur's White Hart Lane with Revill on target for the R's.

The proceeds of £262 from the 4 May meeting were sent to the Titanic Disaster Fund just 19 days after the British liner had sunk.

7 v Watford 7-0

Football League Third Division South. Cassio Road
4 September 1920. Attendance: 9,000

QUEENS PARK RANGERS:	WATFORD:
Hill	Williams
Blackman	Barnshaw
Grimsdell	Gregory
Grant	Bassett
Mitchell	Hoddinott
O'Brien	Ronald
Faulkner	Horsman
Birch	Waterall
Smith	Toone
Gregory	White
Middlemiss	Wilkinson

Referee: Not known

JIMMY BIRCH arguably became the first of Queens Park Rangers' icons when he scored the goals at Watford which gave the R's their first ever win in the Football League on Saturday 4 September 1920.

The number 10 shirt has become synonymous with Rangers' playing heroes in the modern day, with the likes of Rodney Marsh and Stan Bowles epitomising the goalscoring maverick associated with it.

But if Birch had worn a number it would have been a number 8.

The inside-right performed in the era before spectators could glance down at the team sheet in their programme to identify a player by the numerical figure printed on their back.

R's fans had no need of means other than their own eyes to make out the diminutive, stocky forward of 5ft 7in in his long shorts which tapered down to just above his knees and were pulled up over his waist. Even his hairstyle – smart, short and swept over with a sharp left-sided parting – caught the attention.

He grabbed even more, though, with what he was able to produce on the field with his bustle, ball control and dead-eye finishing.

Regularly he feinted this way and that to leave an opponent dizzy before slamming home a goal. The Birch swerve was most likely reminiscent of the Bowles swerve. Crowds love that sort of skill and it is clear Stan the Man did not have exclusivity on being the only QPR star with the ability to pull it off judging from contemporary reports which bigged up Birch.

And it was entirely appropriate that Birch figured in a series on momentous matches for Rangers besides his stinging of the Hornets that spanned the club ending its time in the non-league after their second Southern League title triumph written about earlier and finding its feet in the Football League.

He netted Rangers' last ever goal as a non-league club in the FA Cup in a 2-1 defeat against Football League giants Aston Villa in front of 33,000.

v Watford 1920

And he was the first QPR player to hit the target as Rangers made their Football League debut in a 2-1 reverse against Watford at Loftus Road just seven days before he starred in the historic first victory.

QPR had their first manager, James Cowan, to thank for bringing Birch to the club in the autumn of their 1912 championship success.

The boss, a former Aston Villa superstar central to the serial pot-collecting by the Birmingham club (written about earlier), had done his homework on the striker from Blackwell in Derbyshire: how he was understudying England ace Harry Hampton at his former place of employment; how Birch had hit an impressive 49 goals in two seasons for Villa's reserves and yet had been unable to dislodge either Hampton or any other Villa player for that matter while knocking so loudly on the first-team door; how, at 24, the timing was right for the fringe player to prove his worth beyond the stiffs.

Birch might not have shared Cowan's penchant for moustaches but it was clear he was a cut above, repaying the Scot's faith in him in spades. And it did not take him long, scoring both goals in a 2-1 victory over Plymouth Argyle on his QPR debut on 5 September 1912 as Rangers kicked off their Southern League title defence at the Park Royal Stadium. Birch had left a good first impression with the 10,000 present.

The forward proved he was more than a one-hit wonder, building a reputation for consistency as he finished his first season an ever-present and top scorer by some distance. Birch managed 18 goals with his nearest challenger, Billy Gaul, not having the 'Gaul' to match him, finishing ten down on the new boy who had been one of two big signings for the R's (the other being Bill Thompson from Plymouth) that season.

Birch took over as captain from Archie Mitchell and continued his goalscoring exploits by finishing top scorer for the following two seasons, bagging 20 and 17.

The Great War limited him to a smattering of London Combination appearances. But he resumed where he left off after the hostilities ended as the Southern League got going again in 1919/20, finishing on top of the Rangers scoring charts with 17.

The question was could he – and indeed his team-mates – step up to the challenge of playing in the Football League?

The short answer as far as the inside-right was concerned was a resounding 'yes' as Birch went on to complete the achievement of being leading club scorer for five seasons and netting a total of 123 goals in 328 games while completing a 14-year career with the R's. The number of strikes puts Birch firmly in the Rangers Hall of Fame as the club's third highest scorer of all time. And who is to say he would not be standing on top of that list but for the Great War?

Any doubts which existed as to Birch's abilities to adapt to the Football League were immediately wiped away, of course, when he scored in their Football League debut on 28 August 1920 with 20,000 packed inside Loftus Road.

Rangers had found the ground which became their 12th home – and one which has remained so almost all the years since – in 1917 by enforcement rather than design. Their Park Royal Stadium was turned into allotments by the government to assist the country's war effort, with the Great Conflict continuing. A base had to be found to fulfil London Combination fixtures.

Rangers scoured the neighbourhood and a new headquarters was found. It was an open field on Ellerslie Road in Shepherd's Bush bordering White City's exhibition site, a venue which boasted white marble cladding on pavilions (hence its name) and the athletics at the first London Olympic Games four years earlier.

Queens Park Rangers' Greatest Games

QPR were familiar with that part of the area as a rail strike had necessitated them playing two games at White City in Easter 1912.

The only facility the 'field' had was a pavilion along its south side which was not deemed a suitable structure, with Rangers replacing it with a revamped stand from their previous home, complete with dressing rooms and an office tucked under the spectator area. And it was soon re-christened Loftus Road after the street running along its east side.

In comparison to the grandeur of QPR's Park Royal base it left something to be desired. But the venue left empty when its tenants Shepherd's Bush Football Club broke up at least enabled them to carry on.

Rangers had it in a presentable state by the time they applied to the Football League for membership again in 1920. The process was rather easier than when they had their noses put out of joint as Tottenham Hotspur gained entry at their expense in 1908. Even though they could only manage sixth place in what proved to be their final Southern League season from 1919/20.

There was a proposal that the league should create a third division. Rangers were joined by all the other 21 clubs in the Southern League First Division to form it. With champions Portsmouth and runners-up Watford, Crystal Palace, Cardiff City, Plymouth Argyle, Reading, Southampton, Swansea Town, Exeter City, Southend United, Norwich City, Swindon Town, Millwall, Brentford, Brighton and Hove Albion, Bristol Rovers, Newport County, Northampton Town, Luton Town, Merthyr Town and Gillingham, R's became its founding members (it was regionalised the following season when teams from the north sought league status).

If Rangers were expecting to fly, borrowing the title from one of musician Neil Young's early songs, they were, Birch apart, deceiving themselves. To labour the point from another Young title, flying on the ground is wrong. High hopes are very well, and new manager Ned Liddell (successor to Jimmy Howie, the replacement for the ailing Cowan who had passed on in 1915), certainly had them based on his signings.

Left-half Mick O'Brien, who was to become an Irish international with Rangers (and manager), linked up from South Shields. Tottenham Hotspur's Bert Middlemiss, stopper Len Hill from Southend, Millwall's George Grant, Bob Faulkner from Blackburn Rovers and Ernie Grimsdell from Guildford United all came in.

The influential Hampstead player Arthur Chandler joined a third of the way through the campaign with Liddell proving a wheeler-dealer because R's only dished out a total of £25 for all the newcomers.

The loss against Watford on the opening day gave them a warning shot across the bows that adapting to life in the Football League would be no cruise.

And it seemed it had not been heeded in the second game at Loftus Road four days later. Birch did his bit against Northampton by getting on the scoresheet once more but at the end of the 90 minutes in front of 14,000 QPR had lost their second game. And by the same score as that suffered on day one.

Liddell decided it was time to ring the changes. Rangers were, as we know, to face Watford seven days after they had been defeated by them – and it proved third time lucky.

Liddell had plenty to think about as Rangers travelled across to Hertfordshire to Cassio Road, the first home of Watford and now the site for a cricket pitch at the West Herts club (it was two years before the Hornets switched to Vicarage Road).

And he decided to bring in Hill and left-back Grimsdell for their debuts in place of Ted Price and Joe Wingrove, who had both taken part in the back-to-back defeats. Experienced

v Watford 1920

Archie Mitchell was recalled at centre-half with Grant switching to right-half in place of Tom McGovern.

The alterations stiffened up the defence in front of the goalkeeper and Hill was able to keep a clean sheet.

Birch's confidence was sky-high after finding the net two games in a row. And it was no surprise when he was the go-to forward for Rangers central midfielders like O'Brien and wingers Bob Faulkner and Middlemiss. And Birch rewarded the blood, sweat and tears of his colleagues with his double strike for a 2-0 victory.

It had proved third time lucky after the frustrations of the two openers and sparked Rangers into going on an unbeaten five-match run. The defence provided a strong backbone with QPR letting in just one goal throughout it.

A roller-coaster couple of months followed with three wins, three defeats and three draws before Rangers' rearguard moved back into stonewall mode as they helped the side to four victories on the bounce.

The second half of the season was up and down. R's only managed four points from five matches before they went six games escaping a loss and conceding a miserly one goal.

They eased to the end of their first campaign with six more wins and two deadlocks in ten. The efforts earned them third place and R's finished just six points off champions Crystal Palace. A more even and less bumpy season might have seen them crowned Third Division champions in the inaugural season.

But Liddell had positives to glean from the fresh experience of being on a national stage.

Grant and Jack Smith were models of consistency and did not miss a game.

Smith added to his reputation by finishing the club's top goal scorer with 19 goals from his 44 appearances.

Inevitably, Birch got his fair share to underline his ability to step up a level, firing in 16 in just 27 games to put him second on the list.

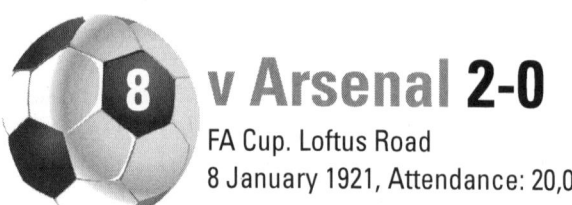

v Arsenal 2-0

FA Cup. Loftus Road
8 January 1921, Attendance: 20,000

QUEENS PARK RANGERS:	ARSENAL:
Hill	Williamson
Wingrove	Shaw
Grimsdell	Hutchins
Grant	Butler
Mitchell	McKinnon
O'Brien	Toner
Manning	Rutherford
Birch	Pagnam
Smith	White
Chandler	Voysey
Gregory	Blyth

Referee: Not known

FAME IS 'being known or talked about by many people, especially on account of notable achievements'. The chattering classes among Queens Park Rangers folk were – in 1921 – likely to be talking about Arsenal louder than any opponents to their favourites in the past.

Especially in the wake of the day QPR's Green and White Army came into face-to-face combat with the Gunners out of the military base at Woolwich in South London (and now transplanted in the north of the capital) for the first time.

And that the occasion was in the FA Cup, unquestionably the most renowned domestic knockout competition on the planet, merely added to its kudos.

Most significantly of all, the volume was turned up to a *Spinal Tap* 11 because R's stuffed them, delivering a late, second knockout blow (literally – more later).

It allowed Rangers to join Arsenal in the national Hall of Fame, with the Gunners perhaps believing they might have to one day in the not-too-distant future look over their shoulders at the club which might yet prove to be more than Third Division upstarts.

QPR deserved to be feted as famous, even if it was just for the result of their endeavours over 90 minutes.

Yes, Rangers had faced Aston Villa, the serial champions and FA Cup winners and founder members of the Football League in the competition the season before. But that meeting did not pull off the required result for the lads from west London, with, as we have read, R's returning from Birmingham licking their wounds, denied a giant-killing in their final campaign in non-league football.

Arsenal shared Villa's status of being among the clubs to kick-start league football. Not a bad boast. They also had an ambitious chairman, Henry Norris, who is said to have engineered a place in the Football League's top flight for his fifth-placed second-tier outfit through his friendship with the league president, Liverpool owner John McKenna, two years prior to their debut meeting with Rangers.

v Arsenal 1921

It was an action which took the gloves off a simmering rivalry with Tottenham Hotspur who lost their First Division spot to the Gunners and were already less than delighted Arsenal had moved in as neighbours six years earlier due to the potential of splitting the affections of football supporters in the area.

And it was Norris who appointed Herbert Chapman, the legendary manager as the Gunners completed a hat-trick of titles in the 1930s, a mere four years after the visit to Loftus Road. Arsenal also had a manager who sowed the seeds for the Chapman era with the signings of the likes the Gunners' 1930 FA Cup winner Alf Baker in the dugout in front of the stand which had been moved across from the Park Royal Stadium for the Saturday showdown with Rangers.

Leslie Knighton, who later brought in title medal winners Bob John and Jimmy Brain, and was succeeded by Chapman, had been in charge of Arsenal since the return to the top flight.

He had seemingly had a fractious understanding with Norris with the Arsenalfc.com website stating, 'The (Knighton) autobiography suggests that Norris and Knighton enjoyed a General Melchett/Captain Blackadder type relationship, in which the walrus-moustachioed chairman conjured up all sorts of imaginative ways for his manager to endanger himself for the club's cause.

'But, despite the tight transfer budget, he was able to utilise the talent he had shown at his previous club, Manchester City, for spotting and developing potential footballing talent with a respectable ninth in the First Division in 1920/21.'

Arsenal were just the sort of giant the Davids of QPR wanted to cut down whether green, jolly or otherwise. And when Knighton's team arrived at Loftus Road they faced a side determined to achieve the sort of victory denied in England's second city while finishing off the club's Southern League career.

R's had also developed a respectable record in the Cup over the years considering they had competed as a non-league side.

After winning just one game in four years, they made the second round proper after six qualifying wins and the victory over Wolverhampton Wanderers (featured in an earlier chapter).

They made it to the last eight twice in four years (1910 and 1914) and the last 16 in 1915 after three consecutive reverses against Luton Town followed by other qualifying exits against Fulham (twice) and Brentford, Bristol Rovers, Swindon and West Ham United. And Liddell believed he had the players to turn the dream into a reality. He had the outstanding Jimmy Birch to call on (on whom this tome has waxed lyrical in a previous chapter), but R's were far from a one-man band.

Mick O'Brien had settled in comfortably after his switch from South Shields, establishing himself as a regular.

The nomadic left-half, with Rangers the ninth of 16 clubs he played for, showed why he had attracted Glasgow Celtic to sign him from Blyth Spartans before the First World War, in which he served, displaying his versatility by looking equally comfortable at the back and going forward, form which eventually earned him Irish international honours.

Arthur Chandler was rated an important capture when he signed from non-league Hampstead for a nominal fee, probably only just into double figures – as discussed earlier.

He had local hero credentials as a Paddington boy, born within a stone's throw of the area where Rangers first breathed life through the St Jude's Institute, Droop Street Board School and Christchurch Rangers.

Queens Park Rangers' Greatest Games

Chandler was to make his name as Leicester City's all-time record goalscorer with 273 goals (with Gary Lineker having to eat his heart out, one figures). He also became the oldest Fox to score, aged 39 years and 34 days, and the player to net most goals in one season for the Leicestershire outfit, 34, a target he reached twice.

That's not the end of it because he still tops the City charts for the number of top-flight goals, 203, the most hat-tricks or more, 17, the longest scoring run, eight matches, and the most goals in one game, six – against Portsmouth.

Even so, Chandler did his bit for Rangers as he learned his craft over his three years with the club.

His goals ratio might not have been as prolific as it became but he notched 18 goals in 86 appearances.

And in his debut season, which began more than halfway through the 1920/21 campaign, he only managed three in 14. But, significantly, one of them arrived against Arsenal.

Expectancy was in the air as 20,000 filed into Loftus Road. Rangers faced the first test of their abilities to cope with the big boys since their arrival in the Football League just a few months earlier.

After all, whether the Gunners were in the First Division by fair means or foul – judging on where you stand on the stories surrounding their formidable chairman – they were in the top half of a division two levels above their hosts.

Rangers drew confidence from the fact they had not conceded a goal for five matches, with the ever reliable Archie Mitchell organising his defensive troops to his side's best advantage.

Another consideration which might also have helped to level the playing field was the condition of the pitch.

Rain had left it appearing no more than a quagmire. A mud-heap which might have been deemed more suitable for farmers to plough than football.

Arsenal had quality in their line-up. Joe Toner, a future Irish international who went on to make a century of appearances for the Gunners, played on the visitors' left wing.

And Baker was also included. The former miner reputedly signed after a shift at his Derbyshire pit by Knighton, was highly thought of by his manager who was to make him captain in 1924.

Knighton appreciated the versatility of the player who debuted for the Gunners in Arsenal's first ever top-flight game at Highbury (against Newcastle United) two years earlier.

Baker could operate with equal efficiency either as a right-half or right-back and he had established a regular slot in the first team in the lead-up to the meeting against Liddell's side.

But it was believed in the home camp that the heavy conditions – in the days before the development of more pristine sand-based pitches through scientific advances – just might limit the newcomers to north London out west.

And that is how it proved. Rangers displayed more stamina than their more illustrious opponents which allowed them to cope with them.

Ernie Grimsdell came in for Fred Watts at left-back for the R's, while the Gunners had midfielder Clement Voysey and defender Jack Butler for Alex Graham and Alf Baker.

Liddell's troops were slow to get stuck into the battle after skipper Mitchell won the toss for choice of ends.

v Arsenal 1921

Aggression was the name of the game Arsenal employed and the hosts were forced to adopt a rearguard action early on. They were forced to concede a series of corners with wingers Jock Rutherford and Joe Toner planting some dangerous kicks into the heart of the QPR defence but impressive goalkeeping from Len Hill and his back line kept the visitors at bay.

Rangers weathered the persistent storm to come thundering into the game. Chandler and centre forward Jack Smith gave Gunners stopper Ernie Williamson cause for concern with goalbound drives.

The game unfolded into a thrilling tit-for-tat encounter with play moving swiftly from end to end, with Arsenal having the edge thanks to their superior link-up play.

But the tie swung in the R's favour as the second half started with a bang. From Chandler's boot, to be precise. And it came from a slip-up by Williamson within five minutes of the restart.

The Arsenal goalkeeper under-hit a goal kick and Chandler seized on it out wide on the left. The flanker cut in, with the ball under close control, before letting fly and leaving Williams groping fresh air.

Liddell's troops, though, were pushed on to the back foot as Arsenal pressed for an equaliser.

Jackie Rutherford waltzed through the Rangers defence before squaring the ball in to the path of striker Fred Pagnam who just had Hill to beat from two yards, but the goalkeeper managed to block the forward's effort 'more by luck than judgement' according to a contemporary report of the encounter.

Rangers' hearts were in mouths shortly afterwards when Hill lost his footing after making a save and possession of the ball and presented it back to his opponent. Fortunately for QPR the Gunners player sent the ball just wide of the unguarded net.

It enabled the Green and Whites to set the seal on victory five minutes from time – in controversial circumstances.

Winger John Manning sent over a high, dipping cross which Williamson caught under his own bar on the goal line. Before the stopper had an opportunity to clear his lines, Smith bundled Williamson and the ball into the net with records crediting O'Brien with the final touch.

The goalkeeper was spark out and remained unconscious as he was carried off the pitch. To add insult to injury for the Gunners, arch north London rivals Spurs went on to lift the famous trophy at the end of the season.

Arsenal gained revenge in the competition the following season when they returned to Loftus Road for a replay after QPR had forced a goalless draw at Highbury.

But Rangers would forever have the memory of the day they rose to the challenge against a famous club – the only one yet to be relegated from the top flight since the Football League resumed after the Great War – soon to dominate English football for a decade. They had come a long way from the pitch owned by Welford's Dairy. And it wasn't until 1990 that they had the chance to try and repeat it.

v Swindon Town 8-3

Third Division South. Loftus Road
12 April 1930. Attendance: 7,534

QUEENS PARK RANGERS:	SWINDON TOWN:
Cunningham	Nash
Pollard	Penn
Pierce	Girvan
Foster	Dickinson
Armstrong	Humphries
Whatmore	Archer
Coward	Denyer
Burns	Dowdall
Goddard	Morris
Rounce	Roberts
Howe	Thorn

Referee: Not known

HISTORY HAS handed down a few George Goddards of significance. All rather diverse. There was the English Mormon, the United States Air Force Brigadier and the one nicknamed Sonny who was a worldwide lobbyist for the Trinidad and Tobago steel drum movement.

With religion, armed forces and music covered, surely there must be one linked with sport? Indeed there was. A busman from Redhill in Surrey who drove into the Queens Park Rangers record books, swapping his garage uniform for the freshly-adopted blue and white hoops of his new employers in 1926.

The phrase 'scoring for fun' might not have been around in the 1920s and 1930s but it most certainly applied to Goddard, who became the greatest goalscorer in Rangers' history.

It was not until Rodney Marsh happened along in the 1960s that his total goals tally for a season record was broken. But to date no QPR star – no matter how big a legend he may be to the fans and posterity, albeit Marsh, Stan Bowles et al – can match him for the amount of goals for the club.

With the ability to find the back of the onion bag the swift route to immortality in the eyes of the one-eyed R's supporters, Goddard wrote his name in the largest of letters after finding his way to Loftus Road from his bus depot and stopping for eight seasons – at his and no doubt Rangers' request – to accumulate 186 goals, 174 in the Football League and 12 in the FA Cup.

The ratio of his league strikes was phenomenal as he only had an appearance total of 243. He was a byword for consistency and the club's leading marksman for SIX campaigns on the bounce.

Goddard was certainly no flash in the pan after bagging 23 in his debut season for the R's. And he managed to hit 16 hat-tricks or more in a single game, including FIVE in a season when he broke his own club record of goals in one campaign with 39.

v Swindon Town 1930

But he outshone himself with a quartet as he helped swamp Swindon Town 8-3 one memorable April afternoon in 1930 at Loftus Road.

Boy, was Goddard needed when manager Bob Hewison persuaded the amateur striker, a prolific scorer in the Athenian League with Redhill, to turn professional with Rangers.

Rangers had struggled to establish themselves in the Football League. They seemed to have made a reasonable start to their career in it.

The FA Cup success against Arsenal (written about previously) alone had given them cause for optimism that they would adapt from non-league to Football League.

A fifth-placed finish in their second term – with the Third Division regionalised – underlined their confidence might be well founded.

The highlight was a six-goal revenge mauling of the Lions of Millwall, the team which pricked their FA Cup balloon in the next round after the win against the Gunners in their debut season.

They slipped six spots in their third campaign but there appeared no cause for alarm, especially as they were able to reach the quarter-finals of the FA Cup for a third time.

The Cup run, given added incentive with Wembley Stadium to stage the final for the first time, caught the imagination among R's followers with 18,000 and 23,454 attending as they eased by Crystal Palace and Wigan Borough before defeating South Shields.

It ended when they were pipped 1-0 by Sheffield United in front of 20,000 at Loftus Road.

Unfortunately the positivity proved deceptive as QPR were forced to re-apply for membership after finishing bottom in 1924 by only managing to collect 31 points from their 42 fixtures, reflecting the worst season for the far-from-Super Hoops since turning professional.

Money talks and, as in the case of Rangers back then, lack of it precipitated the slide to propping up the division with the club's decision to reduce ticket prices to attract paying customers for 1922/23 backfiring as gates often dipped below five figures due largely to disappointing results and performances. The building blocks cracked with QPR unable to rival more well-off clubs.

With only one club promoted to the Second Division each season it was essential squads had to be the strongest possible to capture the single spot. Then as now professional players wanted the best deal to financially benefit themselves and their family before tying their colours to the mast of clubs, even those with such pretensions.

Rangers' financial plight led to two key performers unwilling to accept the offer put on the table to them.

Left-winger John Gregory, an England junior international rather than the more modern namesake who went on to play for and manage R's, departed to Yeovil after 11 years at the club.

Experienced Harold Edgley, the former Chelsea player, gained an extra 'e' by moving to Edgeley Park and turning out for Stockport County. A third departure, no doubt to ease the cash flow, was Arthur Chandler, the Paddington-born striker, to a glittering career with Leicester City for a club-record £3,000.

Rangers used 29 players to find a winning formula the following season after being given a reprieve but Ned Liddell's outfit was only able to pull away from the re-election zone with three wins and a draw in their last four games.

The bell tolled for Liddell who was dismissed and replaced by Hewison in the summer of 1925.

Queens Park Rangers' Greatest Games

Unfortunately it got worse. Goalkeeper Len Hill and Ben Marsden quit for Southampton and Reading, each after five years' service, while leading scorer Colin Myers ended up at Exeter City.

There was an influx of newcomers who struggled to gel, illustrated by the fact only one victory was obtained in the opening seven games. It seemed clear the defence had trouble coping with the new offside rule, which meant only two rather than three of its members had to be between the attack and the goal.

The second half of the season was an unmitigated disaster as the R's managed just a solitary win in 20 matches. Rangers finished losing 27 of 32 and anchored to the bottom once more, 14 points adrift of Charlton Athletic and the average attendance from their entry into the league had been reduced to 8,000 from 14,000.

Rangers were let off once more and this time they repaid the faith shown in them by the Football League when hero Goddard entered the fray as QPR dumped their green and white Celtic lookalike hooped kit for the now familiar blue and white.

Just seven players were retained as Rangers cut the dead wood. Eight new boys were brought in during the summer, including winger James Lofthouse, before two more were added, Lincoln City midfielder Jimmy Eggleton (who was to become trainer, assistant secretary, groundsman, boiler operator and maintenance chief) and, of course, the inimitable Goddard.

Goddard hit the ground running, netting on his debut in a 4-2 derby reverse against Brentford at Griffin Park on 11 September 1926. By the time he had completed a dozen games the striker had bagged TEN goals, including doubles in victories against Aberdare Athletic (which gave the Hoops their first win of the season at the sixth attempt) and Norwich City.

Goddard was also on target in four-goal wins against Plymouth Argyle and Northampton. The Gomshall goal-getter had breathed life into a side so bereft of it in recent seasons. It sparked an increase in the average home gate which went up to close to 10,000.

The 1926/27 season ended in a flourish with R's producing wins and clean sheets in each of their final away games and a 5-1 dismantling of Merthyr Town at headquarters. A third visit to the 're-election panel' was avoided with R's comfortable in 14th largely due to Goddard, who ended top of the club's scoring charts for the campaign with 23 goals.

With the support of incoming non-league forwards George Rounce and Jack Burns, from Uxbridge and Crypto, Goddard helped QPR up to tenth the following season by banging in three more than the previous term.

Goddard clearly had the taste for it and set a club record which has lasted to this day of netting 37 league goals as the Blue and White Army marched into sixth spot in the 1928/29 term.

It was clear that the three-pronged spearhead of Burns, Goddard and Rounce – all former amateurs – had taken to the professional ranks like a duck to water with Burns and Rounce chipping in 22 goals between them. Merthyr Town can best testify to the hurt the trio could inflict on opponents when Goddard (four), Burns (three) and Rounce were on target in a record 8-0 league win for the R's.

The main man, though, was hungry for more goal records – and he achieved his aim with one more the following season with 42 from 46 appearances.

Goddard was just insatiable and unstoppable and he most clearly illustrated the points with his quartet against Swindon on 12 April 1930.

v Swindon Town 1930

The open-faced Goddard had a smile which could light up a room but when he donned his blue and white shirt, which left a floppy collar when unbuttoned, he turned into a Smiling Assassin.

The Robins had no answer to him as the third lowest attendance of the season at Loftus Road, a mere 7,534, was treated to a masterclass in goalscoring.

The transition from amateur to professional has proved too large a chasm to clear for many. The likes of Stuart Pearce and Graham Roberts, who played at the top level after a career in non-league, managed it. And Goddard obliterated any lingering doubts of the ultra-cynics as he rocked the mid-table Robins.

Goddard fired in four awesome foursomes in his Super Hoops career but his third helped his side equal their highest ever position in the league and was their best since a regionalised Third Division had been introduced.

Third place might not have secured R's promotion but was the result of a second successive promotion challenge – and a whole lot better than seeking re-election.

Inside-forward Rounce also had a share of the headlines with a hat-trick against Swindon, an achievement which also acted as gaffer tape over the mouths of those who doubted the ability of part-time footballers to establish themselves in a full-time role (underlining the point by scoring 59 goals in 171 R's appearances before securing a switch to the Second Division with Fulham, although tragically he died from tuberculosis before playing for the Cottagers).

Bill Coward, signed two seasons before and a club servant for five years, proved brave enough to help make up the eight-goal haul.

But it is Goddard, with a little help from his friends, who shone brightest while doing most to restore so much pride in the Rangers shirt as they entered a new decade. He went on to precede the likes of Pearce and Roberts and play in the top flight with Sunderland.

There has only been one Goddard to earn a full England cap and be associated with QPR. That player was Paul rather than George. But, by George, the Goddard who routed the Robins in 1930 would no doubt have done so if Rangers had been a premier outfit during his time with them after coming off the buses.

v Bristol Rovers 8-1

FA Cup. Eastville
27 November 1937. Attendance: 7,000

QUEENS PARK RANGERS:	BRISTOL ROVERS:
Gilfillan	Nicholls
Smith	Roberts
Jefferson	Preece
Lowe	McLean
James	O'Mahony
March	McArthur
Cape	Warren
Mallett	Mills
Cheetham	Hartill
Fitzgerald	Prendergast
Bott	Sullivan

Referee: Not known

BYKER GROVE was a 1980s, 1900s and 2000s children's television programme which launched the careers of presenters Ant and Dec. Anthony McPartlin and Declan Donnelly played PJ and Duncan in the drama before turning into cuddly national treasures who popped up side by side fronting up prime-time gogglebox shows such as *I'm A Celebrity Get Me Out Of Here*.

Now let's borrow Dr Who's blue telephone box and travel back in time to when the district of Newcastle Upon Tyne after which Ant and Dec's original show was named was known for producing decent footballers rather than a pair of smiley Geordie celebrities.

And one in particular who would have been more than capable of surviving in tougher jungle conditions than those experienced by the B-to-Z list celebs introduced by a couple of former child actors. His name? Tommy Cheetham, who would hit a hat-trick to ensure a record FA Cup 8-1 victory for Queens Park Rangers against Bristol Rovers two years before the outbreak of the Second World War.

Back in the time machine. We are now roaming the immediate years in the north-east of England before the first conflict to involve most countries around the globe – the Great War – when mining was the chief occupation and football the main pre-occupation on Tyneside. Cheetham is born.

Return to Dr Who's mode of time transport and we are in a period just after the First World War and the strapping Cheetham is playing for Byker FC and earning a reputation as a junior player of note. But he puts any ambitions he might have held to escape a future in the mines by opting for the Army rather than in professional football. He serves in India for the Royal Artillery while regularly swapping his soldier's uniform for a football strip on the sub-continent. Cheetham comes to Queens Park Rangers' attention and, when he returns to the Army's English base at Aldershot, new manager Billy Birrell makes his move.

Birrell had been looking for a reliable marksman after a period of instability for the club which had seen the sale of all-time star striker George Goddard.

v Bristol Rovers 1937

His predecessor Mick O'Brien – the fourth QPR manager in 18 months in succession to Archie Mitchell who followed a third former Rangers player, John Bowman, into the hot seat after Bob Hewison departed in November 1931 – had been forced to sell Goddard to Brentford to ease a cash crisis. And promotion-pushing Rangers became mid-table obscurists the following season, 1934/35.

First, given his status in the military, the arrangement was for Cheetham to turn out for the Super Hoops as an amateur, but he soon signed on as a professional, making his debut in a 1-1 away draw against Brighton and Hove Albion a month before his 25th birthday in 1935.

Cheetham had lots of time to catch up on having gone a roundabout route to pursue the career much of the male population of football-mad folk on Tyneside dreamed about.

And he didn't waste any of it. He hit the ground running. After three matches he had bagged six goals despite drawing a blank in his opener against the Seagulls. He netted a double on his home debut, a 3-2 return victory over Brighton, and six days later managed FOUR against the team representing the town he had just left for the capital, Aldershot.

Now that is the way to become a crowd favourite. And he proved he was far from a five-minute wonder. Or even an individual satisfied with the 15 minutes of fame the late artist Andy Warhol always insisted was the minimum every individual around the globe enjoys.

Supporters drooled at the way the former soldier went into battle for the Rangers' Blue and White Army on the football field.

A QPR fan called 'Martin' on the Independent R's website posted in October 2012, 'Together with George Goddard, Stan Bowles and of course Rodney, Tommy Cheetham was one of my Dad's all time favourite R's players.'

In an extraordinary first season Cheetham averaged more than a goal a game, ending up with 36 in 35 league matches to guide Rangers to fourth.

It appeared Cheetham was the key to Rangers' fate in each and every game. Rather like Gareth Bale was at the start of his Tottenham career – but in reverse, as Spurs were unable to claw a victory when the Wales international's name was on the team sheet in those days in stark contrast to the perception of his talents in the modern day with Real Madrid.

If the former soldier was called up and scored it would, more often than not, guarantee the R's would finish with maximum points. In fact there were only five matches when he scored and they failed to do just that throughout the 1935/36 campaign. The Super Hoops stormed through the opening two months of Cheetham's prolific spell, only losing twice. From the end of October he managed an astonishing 12 goals in just seven outings.

And the striker completed an historic personal run of scoring in NINE home league games on the spin which made home very sweet for the Byker who sent many an opponent on their 'bykes'.

It began a month to the day after he celebrated turning 25 on 11 October 1935.

Exeter City – who were to finish rock bottom by the end of the campaign – fell victim to Cheetham who notched two goals in a 3-1 win.

Bristol Rovers were the next in line for the Cheetham treatment as the forward converted a penalty as QPR claimed a 4-0 win – a portent of things to come for the West Country side, of course.

Bournemouth could not stop him and neither could Crystal Palace, who succumbed to a treble from the soldier firing bullets in the form of a leather ball.

Cardiff City leaked two, Southend United one and Watford another two as the former soldier marched on. Torquay United failed to halt him to set up a further double against

Queens Park Rangers' Greatest Games

Reading which ensured Cheetham had scored in nine consecutive league games. And QPR had won ALL of them.

And by the end of the year Rangers had only lost a single game on their own turf – and that came against Millwall on the first day of the season, with Cheetham yet to play for the club.

Cheetham's individual efforts earned him an England trial in a Possibles versus Probables match in March, although his hopes were dented by opposition defender Alf Young with *The Times* reporting, 'Cheetham did not receive a pass for nearly half-an-hour' before adding 'considering the brilliance of Young, the play of Cheetham could hardly be considered unsatisfactory'.

Expectations of a Cheetham-inspired Rangers elevating themselves into the Second Division for the first time, though, were undermined by disappointing away form.

They blasted into the New Year with four victories on the bounce, including a nap hand against Swindon Town, with Cheetham unhinging the West Country team in a similar manner to his predecessor as goalscorer-in-chief, George Goddard.

The bubble burst with a 6-1 crushing at Coventry City. Rangers' home form went to pot with back-to-back losses against Northampton Town and the revenging Royals of Reading. Form was up and down with Cheetham only hitting the target once in the final eight games.

But the Geordie only just scraped into double figures the following season – 1936/37 – on 11. His goals that term included one in a 7-2 demolition of Southend United.

Another flickering highlight from the campaign was a run of one defeat in nine which fleetingly took R's to fourth, but the Hoops ended just above mid-table, 13 points off champions Luton Town.

Cheetham showed his confidence in front of goal remained high for his third season – 1937/38 – at Rangers.

He netted 18 goals in 29 matches that term to pave the way to the top of the table for Rangers before they slipped to an eventual third.

Cheetham did his bit for the R's in the league. He got them off to a winning start against Brighton and by halfway his side were well poised for a promotion assault, having lost only four of 21.

His team led the pack after a decent run to lead Millwall by nine points but stuttered with one triumph in five and despite rallying with five maximums in their final five fixtures the Lions pipped them by just three points, leaving the Loftus Road outfit reflecting on an early-season home defeat against their South London rivals.

But he saved his best performance of the campaign for the sinking of the Pirates of Bristol Rovers in the FA Cup, the greatest domestic club competition in the world, on 27 November 1937 as R's totted up their biggest ever victory.

The city which founded the league that gave them their first league title triumph as a professional club, the Western, did not receive a hint of gratitude from Rangers who were rampant with Cheetham in irresistible form.

The Geordie had managed three double strikes during the league campaign but he was able to go one better against the Bristolians with his confidence sky high and flying wingers Jack Cape, formerly of Manchester United, and Wilf Bott running the hosts ragged.

Wave after wave crashed against the Rovers rearguard which merely crumbled.

Inside-left Alf 'Paddy' Fitzgerald, signed from Reading in 1936, also grabbed a treble en route to top-scoring for the club by the end of the campaign with 21 in 40.

v Bristol Rovers 1937

Winger Bott, a capture from Newcastle United, also underlined his ability to guide the ball into the net with a double in a campaign in which he ended up one ahead of Cheetham, who rated the defeat of Rovers among his QPR highlights.

He said in an article in the *Topical Times* for January 1938, 'For the first fifteen minutes the game was fairly even, but after that our boys simply overwhelmed the Rovers. We scored 8. It might just as easily have been 28!

'The Rovers made great efforts to put our scoring machine out of action, even going to the extent of a colossal switch-round of positions. I had the satisfaction of scoring a hat-trick, as did Paddy Fitzgerald, our strong, foraging inside-left. On that day's play we could have beaten almost any team in the country.'

The big centre-forward, with a penchant for turning up his collar a la Eric Cantona, might have had a tooth or two dislodged by opponents since quitting the forces for Civvy Street but he certainly did not lack bite in front of goal.

He netted 22 in 26 the following season, bringing his Rangers total up to 93 goals in 135 appearances, before moving into the top flight with Brentford in a £5,000 deal in March 1939.

And it was clear he had revelled in the challenge of being given the opportunity to prove himself as a Football League centre-forward with QPR.

He said in the contemporary article, 'Centre-forward? Yes, I like it. I enjoy these tussles with my friendly-enemies – the "stoppers" of football. He is trying to do the best for his side. So am I. May the best man win!'

11 v Swansea Town 0-0

Football League Third Division South. Loftus Road
26 April 1948. Attendance: 27,500

QUEENS PARK RANGERS:	SWANSEA TOWN:
Allen	Parry
Rose	Feeney
Jefferson	Keane
I. Powell	Paul
Ridyard	Weston
A. Smith	Burns
Adams	Payne
Stewart	James
Hatton	R. Powell
Mills	Morris
Hartburn	Scrine

Referee: Not known

ARTHUR JEFFERSON put his feelings into simple words. Short and sweet. The bullish Jefferson skippered Queens Park Rangers on the day they gained the required point in a goalless draw against Swansea Town at Loftus Road on 26 April 1948 to seal the club's first Football League promotion and championship.

The left-back, who had stood in for injured club captain George Smith against the Swans, told your author in 1983, 'The promotion year was memorable.'

When we spoke, it seemed Jefferson preferred playing golf at the Ealing Club and making sausages at his son-in-law's butcher's shop nearby to football as Rangers busied themselves celebrating a third Football League elevation.

He said, 'It's a different game these days and I don't really enjoy it.'

But there was no question the passion remained for the experience of helping a talented team pulled together by manager Dave Mangnall to create club history, a team packed with characters.

Jefferson certainly was one himself. After hooking up with the Super Hoops from non-league Peterborough, there were few thrills with the Yorkshireman.

If the ball came in his direction he would swiftly thunder it upfield. He established a fearsome reputation as a left-back who would snap away at opponents like a dog with a bone in order to gain possession.

He was rated king of the slide tackle, an ability which would be frowned upon in these days of more limited contact.

And he often suffered injury through his fearless physical approach. He endured concussion, a broken collarbone and, for three months, was sidelined with a broken leg. Jefferson might well have auditioned for a part in TV's *Casualty* as he also sustained cartilage damage, which necessitated its removal, and a fractured arm.

Alongside Jefferson against the Swans was another remarkable figure. Alf Ridyard, a 41-year-old centre-back, had been recalled for the previous game, a 1-0 home victory against Newport County, following an injury to club captain George Smith, who had been signed for a record £2,000 from Brentford at the start of the season.

Ridyard might have been the club's chief scout but it was clear Mangnall still believed he was made of stern enough stuff to aid Rangers' campaign to finish the season guaranteeing R's Second Division football for the first time.

That was not surprising as the imposing Ridyard was 6ft 3in and built like an outhouse, a rock of a defender on which many attacks crumbled into the sea.

And he always had the mental strength to deal with any challenges, being a larger than life figure.

He had been known to hold up the start of a game in order to pass his false teeth to the Rangers trainer to keep safe. And the story goes, according to *Heroes In Hoops* by John Marks, that the Yorkshireman was milking a cow on his home Handsworth Farm near Barnsley when Rangers signed him a year prior to the outbreak of the Second World War.

Jack Rose, the right-back who replaced George Powell (himself a substitute for double broken leg victim Reg Dudley) against Newport and Swansea for his only appearances of the season, presented a dapper image, but had extra motivation to ensure Rangers went up at the end of the 1947/48 season. He appreciated it was either now or never for him having endured three operations on his cartilages.

Goalkeeper Reg Allen was an all-action hero on and off the field. He served as a commando in the Second World War after signing as a professional with Rangers on being discovered playing amateur football for the team of workers at the Corona soft drinks firm.

After conceding seven goals on his Rangers debut in a reserve game he went on to become a stopper rated by eyewitnesses as the best Rangers have ever produced, which is saying something when you think of the likes of Phil Parkes and Julio Cesar.

The Baron – as Allen was known – was considered to have a solid positional sense, be a good handler of crosses and, according to Jefferson (who would have known, of course!), a good communicator.

In fact Allen got so good he was rated the best uncapped keeper in the land and attracted a £10,000 offer on the eve of the season which he agreed to before a change of heart.

Inside-forward Don Mills, yet another Yorkshireman, born into a mining village, had established himself in the first team two-thirds of the way through the season.

His slim frame caused concern – he was loaned to Torquay in the hope the sea air would build him up – but his potential was clear, particularly with his eye-of-a-needle passing. Leading scorer Cyril Hatton would have vouched for the accuracy of a ball from Mills, who was to become a traffic warden in Torquay after retiring as a player, as he netted 21 goals in the league and 25 overall.

And there was reliable Welsh international wing-half Ivor Powell, who entered the *Guinness Book of Records* as the world's oldest coach aged 93 in 2010 while at Team Bath. Powell played in all but one of Rangers' league fixtures during 1947/48.

Mastermind Mangnall deserved his reward. He was at the club when the seeds of the triumph were sown during the war.

Mangnall was a prolific goalscoring striker for R's as he helped the Ted Vizard-managed side win the 1940 League South B competition put together after the Southern League was abandoned due to the outbreak of hostilities.

He was joined by Jefferson, Ridyard, and guesting Cyril Hatton and Jack Rose as teammates with the Super Hoops netting third spot in the 1943/44 Football League South title race.

Queens Park Rangers' Greatest Games

And the club stepped up a gear when Mangnall succeeded Vizard in the hot seat as the club took the 1946 Third Division South (North Region) title in the final year of the war, with Allen, Jefferson, Ridyard and Rose performing along with future manager Alec Stock, while Powell, signed before the war when he served in India, joined them to reach the semi-final of the division's cup.

And as peace broke out and the Third Division South resumed for the 1946/47 season, Mangnall took them even further.

It was clear Rangers were big players in the division as they splashed a record £1,000 to sign Hatton full-time from Notts County and Mills joined as a professional, with Johnny Hartburn linking up from Yeovil on the advice of Stock, now managing the Glovers, to add to the nucleus of a blossoming group of players. They finished runners-up after being top shortly before Christmas. It gave out a warning to their rivals.

Rangers made a flying start to the 1947/48 campaign with five victories on the bounce, going 12 unbeaten with maximum points from TEN of those games. And Hatton was on fire, averaging almost a goal a game with Rangers ripping up the division.

It was breathtaking and the crowds were flocking to watch Mangnall's men in action with more than 20,000 regularly packing out grounds capable of holding so many.

Something had to give. And it did. R's suffered back-to-back reverses against Swindon Town at home and Swans away. Fortunately for the west Londoners it proved a blip. They stormed on, occasionally dropping to second, but generally keeping the heat turned up to gas mark nine on their rivals.

Bournemouth held on to their coat-tails and the evening showdown between the front-runners at Dean Court on 14 April 1948 was viewed as a match which could eventually prove to have decided the title.

It caught the imagination with 26,000 shoehorned into the Cherries' headquarters, including hundreds of Rangers supporters who had travelled down to the South Coast from London in a convoy of coaches.

The 10,000 who were locked outside the ground were given a running commentary as the championship pace-setters locked horns.

An early goal from Super Hoops striker Fred Durrant proved the difference between the sides. Victory gave the R's a four-point advantage over their hosts and, with a game in hand, the visitors were left needing only five points from their remaining five matches to ensure promotion.

They followed up with another away victory against Exeter City, thanks to a goal double from Hartburn.

The wheels came off with a crushing 5-2 defeat at Norwich City, with skipper Smith sustaining the injury which ruled him out of the final three matches.

But Powell scored his first goal of the season, ironically against a Welsh club, as Rangers beat Newport County 1-0 at home in a performance which deserved a more emphatic result in favour of the hosts. QPR had put themselves within one point of title glory.

Just two days later Rangers' supporters were put out of their misery. A crowd of 27,500 squeezed in at Loftus Road for the last home fixture of the season.

The Swans, another, of course, from the Principality, made it a nervy night for Mangnall's men and their followers on a Monday evening which crackled with tension for those of a Super Hoops persuasion.

Rangers were unchanged from the team which had done for Newport. The QPR rearguard was largely a mean machine, blunting any goalscoring pretensions Swansea

v Swansea Town 1948

might have had, although Allen was forced to save from Ray Powell and, in the second half, Frank Scrine.

Generally, Rangers held the initiative with the midfield promptings carving out a series of opportunities but found Swans stopper Jack Parry in impressive form.

Rangers' front line lacked the edge they had displayed against Newport largely due to the propensity of high balls which left Hatton and wingers Ernie Adams and Hartburn outjumped and outmuscled by taller opponents.

Inside-forwards Don Mills and George Stewart put in the effort but were unable to help provide a cutting edge.

Wing-half duo Ivor Powell and Bert Smith tested the visitors with their solo runs and accurate, incisive passing.

Rangers' first opportunity fell to Hatton early on and Parry only grabbed his long-range drive at the second attempt. Stewart fired just wide after a goalmouth melee before forcing Parry to tip over. Hartburn could have completed a hat-trick either side of the interval, shooting over, just missing an Ernie Adams cross and heading directly at Parry.

The Swans reduced the number of chances Rangers were able to create after the interval due to solid defending but Hatton and Hartburn flashed efforts wide with Parry beaten.

And the visitors almost spoiled the promotion party late on when Ray Powell got by Jefferson and Ridyard but ballooned over with just Allen to beat.

Shortly afterwards the Super Hoops could finally celebrate. Mangnall addressed the excited crowd from the directors' box, telling them how crucial their support of the team had been.

The fans wanted to see the team and when the players emerged from the dressing room to walk along the front of the stand they were congratulated by demonstrative supporters.

Ivor Powell was picked out for a special cheer from the crowd when he responded to their plea for him to stand on the directors' seats.

Club captain George Smith told the happy throng, the *Kilburn Times* reported, 'It's been a pleasure to play for you. Thank you very much and next year we shall do the same into the First Division.'

Unfortunately, Rangers were unable to live up to Smith's pledge, no doubt said amid scenes of delirium, but a mid-table finish in their first season in the second tier was far from a disgrace.

12 v Grimsby Town 7-1

Football League Second Division. Loftus Road
30th September 1950. Attendance: 16,241

QUEENS PARK RANGERS:	GRIMSBY TOWN:
Gullan	Chisholm
Poppitt	Moody
Heath	Fisher
Nelson	Johnston
Chapman	McMillan
Farrow	Duthie
Wardle	Lloyd
Mills	Squires
Addinall	Briggs
Hatton	Cairns
Shepherd	Hair

Referee: Not known

THE LOFTUS ROAD crowd love a player who is different from the run of the mill. Stan Bowles and Rodney Marsh spring to mind immediately and, down the years the likes of George Goddard, Tommy Cheetham and Adel Taarabt are others who have had that ability to introduce a little extra into the mix, to build themselves a reputation as an entertainer as much as a footballer.

And Ernie Shepherd is among them. The chief ingredients he added were pace and a talent for bamboozling an opponent with his ball skills.

Let's deal with the pace. It was electrifying. His speed off a standing start was breathtaking. He had forever been able to fly home in sprints while serving with the Royal Air Force prior to building his football career. Shepherd had even been able to earn a bob or two by being asked to show off his jet heels at invitation athletics meetings.

Then there was his close control and ability to conjure up deceptions with a feint to the defender's left or right and leave them for dead. He had a box of tricks which left many an opponent looking baffled and foolish.

Shepherd hails from Wombwell, a small, former mining town in the borough of Barnsley known mainly in sport as being the last resting place of Manchester United centre-half Mark Jones, one of the eight Busby Babes to perish as a result of the Munich air disaster in 1958.

But Shepherd, who began his career at Rangers as Jones was starting his at Old Trafford, certainly helped put his birthplace's name on the map as far as the R's faithful were concerned. Most notably as he helped Queens Park Rangers produce their biggest win in a four-season stay in the Second Division in the late 1940s and early 1950s.

His hat-trick and overall performance in a 7-1 dismantling of Grimsby Town at Loftus Road on 30 September 1950 did more than anything to establish his legendary status among those who were there and remain and younger supporters who care about the R's history.

v Grimsby Town 1950

It provided the most sunshine for the club in a roller-coaster first experience of Second Division football. There were few survivors of the Rangers team which had earned the club a place in the second tier for the first time in its history when the Mariners came to London W12 in the first autumn of the 1950s.

QPR had dipped their toes in the deeper waters after earning their first promotion and Football League divisional title in 1948.

But football, among a host of other things, is about progression. The ecstatic scenes at Loftus Road following the title clincher against Swansea Town was in recognition of what their heroes had managed to achieve that season, but even in those wild celebrations most were no doubt leaving the past behind and looking to the future.

Expectations were naturally being raised. And when club captain George Smith told them back-to-back promotions were more than a possibility in his address to them after receiving the Third Division South trophy then they had every right to assume top-flight football was just a season away as the 1948/49 campaign kicked off.

A superb start had the supporters, players and directors – for all their varying reasons – dreaming that Smith's talk was not mere rhetoric. The players seemed refreshed from a pre-season trip to Turkey on which they beat Galatasaay and Besiktas, now familiar names in top-level European competitions. Three wins and a draw from the opening four games, with Smith back leading his troops after the injury sustained at the back end of the previous term, gave cause for such optimism.

Rangers were looking down from the summit at rivals struggling to climb up. Manager Dave Mangnall had kept faith with the squad which had brought glory in the previous season and it appeared to be paying off. Following a goalless draw at Luton Town, Leicester City were lashed 4-1 in the first home fixture in front of 24,200 curious fans with striker Bert Addinall hitting a hat-trick.

Addinall, establishing himself as a regular following his bit-part role in the run to the title and the sixth round of the FA Cup a term earlier, bagged the only goal of the game against Bradford to seal successive home victories.

Reality, however, kicked in as three reverses and two draws knocked R's off their perch and by the time they were pipped 1-0 by Arthur Rowe's fast-emerging push-and-run Tottenham Hotspur side – who ended up winning promotion – in front of a staggering 69,718 at White Hart Lane, it became more a question of how the pricked balloon could be repaired in time to avoid a relegation fight.

Mangnall's men spluttered on and they found themselves just four spots off rock bottom. But they kept themselves afloat and hauled themselves out of danger for a respectable lower mid-table finish, albeit four points off the drop zone in a tight-run race.

The manager tried to freshen up the squad with the £10,500 record club signing of defender Horace Woodward from Spurs, with club skipper Smith departing for Brentford, along with winger John McKay and stopper Stan Gullan moving south of the border from Scotland.

But the season turned into one of survival with Rangers twice slumping to the bottom of the table before clawing their way to safety.

It was time for more than cosmetic surgery prior to the 1950/51 season if Rangers were to be anything but relegation fodder in the upcoming campaign.

Legendary goalkeeper Reg Allen finally left with Manchester United manager Matt Busby getting his man, even if he had to pay through the nose, with the stopper costing a record fee for a goalkeeper of £11,000.

Queens Park Rangers' Greatest Games

And long-serving pair, defender Arthur Jefferson and striker Frank Neary departed, for Aldershot and Millwall respectively.

With the decks cleared, Mangnall brought in six close-season signings, including defender Tony Ingham from Leeds United (of whom more in the next chapter) and winger Shepherd from Hull City.

The left wing had been a problem position for Mangnall, one of the reasons he brought in McKay, but he hoped Shepherd would solve that particular problem.

And the Yorkshireman swiftly plugged that gap en route to becoming a crowd favourite. Swiftly, of course, being the operative word in Shepherd's case. But not immediately. Shepherd was thrown in from the opening game of the 1950/51 season but the winger, along with the rest of his new team-mates, found the Second Division road as rocky as their predecessors. Form was erratic, following a pattern of a win, loss and draw times three for the opening nine fixtures.

Then came Grimsby. Mangnall's side went into the encounter with a modicum of confidence gleaned from a one-all draw against Birmingham City at St Andrew's.

It was their first league game against the Blue Noses from England's second city, a team that had been playing First Division football the previous season.

The R's were helped by a lacklustre performance from their relegated opponents, which left contemporary observers unconvinced in their ability to bounce back to the top flight at the first attempt.

Yet, even so, a point was no mean feat, especially after QPR captain Dave Nelson put through his own goal for a second successive match to give the hosts the lead.

Addinall ensured the point for the visitors within five minutes with a 25-yard screamer which beat England international Gil Merrick, an effort hailed by Mangnall in the *Kilburn Times* as 'the best goal I've seen this season'.

And the manager kept an unchanged line-up for the Mariners clash. Omens were good with Rangers' second string having enjoyed a seven-goal romp against Luton Town the previous week when Ted Duggan had fired four with an Ingham penalty, a McKay strike and an own goal from a hapless Hatter.

The fact the first team were able to repeat the goal-fest had their supporters wide-eyed in wonderment following their indifferent beginning to the campaign.

And the club chairman Mr A. Hittinger rued the fact he had agreed to swap with fellow director Mr Baker on the morning of the match to take his turn at watching the reserves instead of attending Loftus Road in the afternoon.

The mauling of the Mariners was Rangers' biggest victory since they had slammed Swindon 7-0 in the first Third Division South season following cessation of Second World War hostilities.

And it was achieved with two goalscorers who were on target against the Robins in the romp on 21 December 1946, Don Mills and Cyril Hatton.

Indeed, it was inside-right Mills and inside-left Hatton who were pivotal in laying the foundations of the victory.

Loyal Mangnall, who had reportedly turned down the opportunity to take charge of Aston Villa the week before, revealed afterwards that the performance was the blueprint of an attacking plan come to life.

He said to the *Kilburn Times*, 'The inside-forwards were told to bring their wingers into the game more and to give them passes that cut out their backs. Today it worked perfectly and they saw the result.'

v Grimsby Town 1950

Rangers declined to hang around against Grimsby and Bert Addinall put them in front after just two minutes when he seized on a miscue from Mariners right-back Moody. The goal set the tone as the team from the East Coast fishing town were left floundering.

The Super Hoops had netted six goals by half-time. Hatton made it 2-0 following a ball from George Wardle, the experienced winger who had played in two Wartime Cup finals for Chelsea at Wembley.

Hatton, as part of Mangnall's game plan, provided the third for Addinall to complete his double after beating two defenders and rounding the goalkeeper.

Shepherd and Wardle were running riot with the help of Hatton and Mills, but they combined themselves for Rangers' fourth. Wardle crossed and Shepherd converted.

Tommy Briggs managed to pull one back for Grimsby almost immediately, but it was the only crumb Rangers offered. Shepherd bagged his second, with Hatton the architect.

Hatton netted his second and Shepherd completed his treble with the Mariners continuing to be lost at sea.

QPR could have made it 9-1. Mills went close with a drive on the turn and Addinall thundered an effort against the Grimsby post.

Rangers dominated but the visiting attack – while their defence leaked goals – maintained a consistent threat on the break with Tommy Briggs and Billy Cairns sweating buckets in Grimsby's cause.

Fortunately for the hosts centre-half Reg Chapman kept a tight rein on Briggs in a superb display, with Bill Heath and John Poppitt, playing in only his second game for Rangers following a move from Derby County the previous month, providing support.

But it was Shepherd who had won the most hearts among the home faithful. He had provided a high-point in Rangers' first spell in the second tier before relegation ended the club's bumpy ride in it in 1952. And they did not return until Rodney Marsh and his colleagues restored the status for QPR 15 years later.

v Watford **3-0**

Football League Third Division South. Loftus Road
30 November 1957. Attendance: 10,236

QUEENS PARK RANGERS:	WATFORD:
Springett	Curran
Woods	Anderson
Ingham	Bateman
Petchey	Billiington
Rutter	Catleu
Angell	Chung
Dawson	Harrop
Longbottom	Howfield
Cameron	Cook
Smith	Pygall
Kerrins	Walker

Referee: Not known

TONY INGHAM scored one of only three goals in 555 matches over 13 years as a player for Queens Park Rangers in a vital 3-0 league victory against Watford on 20 November 1957. It helped provide a crucial two points towards avoiding the reality of R's being relegated and becoming an unwanted founder member of the Fourth Division, which was being introduced by the Football League the following season.

And when you consider Rangers only escaped the drop by six points it was some contribution by their skipper, especially when you factor in just how demotion might have impacted long-term on the club. It was a rare moment in the spotlight for Ingham who smashed the club record for appearances out of sight. But it was one he never sought. The club always came first in the world of Tony Ingham, who passed away on 21 April 2010 aged 85. Loyalty is showing a strong feeling of support or allegiance. It is a quality which provokes differing views in football. In life.

There is a chap of your author's acquaintance who served a company for 35 years and was then laid off with little thanks and fanfare, let alone cash. He had put his heart and soul into the role and yet gratitude was minimal, an attitude which smacked of a lack of respect. The outlook can be carried over into football when individuals devote themselves to one club. It is viewed in some quarters of showing a lack of ambition.

Matt Le Tissier, a maverick, a magical performer who almost single-handedly kept Southampton in the top flight for a decade, was accused of it, just because the England international turned down bigger fish to stay on with Saints for his entire playing career.

On the other side of the coin, of course, loyalty is better understood, better respected. It is a sign that total self-fulfilment can come from staying where you are. That the grass is not always greener in pastures new. That respect and happiness can go hand in hand.

This is where Tony Ingham comes in, an individual who epitomised loyalty. Queens Park Rangers became part of his DNA as his family proved when they posted on the ThisIsAnnouncements.co.uk website upon his death, 'Tony was QPR through and through. This was his club and he enjoyed some of the finest moments of his wonderful life playing for the Hoops.'

And there is no question he was respected for the love he displayed for Rangers and that he was content to have spent almost his entire working life with the club as player, commercial manager, secretary and director.

Any doubting this statement should have been there the day your author saw him towards the end of his days in his final role for the club – as a director of the board.

He was standing in the shady entrance by the old press room which led up a flight of stairs, out onto the South Africa Road stand of Loftus Road.

He defied his advanced years – dapper in a white shirt and tie and smart suit and a full head of hair, greying but neatly coiffured. His body language oozed innate charm and was reflected in a natural smile as he nattered to fellow Rangers supporters, who were equally relaxed and grateful because Ingham was spending his pre-match time in their company. Ingham was in his element but without any hint of ego.

There was more proof positive when the Tony Ingham Function Room was opened at Loftus Road. Aretha Franklin, the Queen of Soul, sung 'R-E-S-P-E-C-T' and with this decision the club certainly spelt out just how they felt about their most loyal player, ensuring his name would live on.

Ingham was there as Rangers went through a tough time between their demotion from the Second Division in 1952 and their taking on the Hornets in a month which saw the release of Elvis Presley's film *Jailhouse Rock*. Certainly a period of Rangers getting out of jail after embroiling themselves in regular dog-fights in the relegation zone.

A change of manager, with Jack Taylor, a 38-year-old former Wolverhampton Wanderers full-back who guested for Watford in the Second World War replacing a retiring Dave Mangnam, did little to improve their luck.

Nor did the adoption of a new strip for the first time since the 1920s with the blue and white hoops replaced with a plain white shirt and blue shorts in 1953.

Even the introduction of floodlights in the same year – first used on 5 October against Arsenal and then against Manchester United as part of the deal which took goalkeeper Reg Allen to Old Trafford – failed to switch on more positive, upwardly mobile progress. But they were given enough motivation to at least keep their heads above water when the 1957/58 season kicked off.

Rangers went into it knowing no less than 12 clubs would lose their Third Division status by the end of it with the Football League having decreed it was doing away with the regional set-up of its third tier. That it was to be the last campaign with it split into North and South. The Third Division was 'going national' the following term.

And, as we know, QPR only managed to maintain their status by the skin of their teeth, finally ensuring it thanks to a 1-1 draw at Aldershot with Pat Kerrins scoring their goal and a last-day 3-0 triumph over Shrewsbury Town at Loftus Road, Kerrins bagging two more and Les Locke completing the scoring.

Ingham, of course, was involved in those games. After all he was in the midst of an astonishing record unbroken run of 274 appearances which began on 25 February 1956 and ended on 17 September 1961.

But the author opted for the game against Watford that season which gave an excuse to wax lyrical about Rangers' Mr Reliable; to highlight another side of a player known for being a first-rate defender, superb captain and the model of consistency, and his goalscoring 'exploits'.

Queens Park Rangers' Greatest Games

Goals are the gold currency of football so it goes that anyone capable of hitting the back of the net picks up nicknames such as Golden Boy.

The fact Ingham averaged one every 188.3 games ensured, of course, that such monikers were bestowed on others from the moment he laced up his boots in Rangers' cause for the first time, a Second Division home defeat against Doncaster Rovers in 1950, after moving from his first Football League employers Leeds United on a free transfer, to the last, a Third Division home defeat by Coventry City in 1963.

But Ingham's Golden Boy moments allowed him to shine centre stage on at least three occasions. The first provided mere consolation for Rangers as they toiled back in the Third Division South after relegation. The goal was the first, with Bert Addinall adding a second, as QPR went down 4-2 at Crystal Palace en route to a third-from-bottom finish.

His second effort had a more positive effect. It helped Rangers towards a 4-0 crushing of relegation rivals Millwall in April 1956. But he saved his best to last against the Hornets. At first it appeared it might not be Ingham's – or Rangers' day – when the guests pressured. The left-back was caught out when he was rounded by Peter Walker, but the Watford forward crashed his drive against the bar and goalkeeper Ron Springett, and without question Ingham was relieved to collect the rebound.

Rangers roared back and it was Ingham's goal which gave them the lead.

The full-back ventured upfield as the hosts earned a throw-in. Inside-forward Bob Cameron received the ball back in play and fed the advancing Ingham close to the left-hand touchline.

The defender, showing the skills and instinct of a predatory striker, wasted no time. He hit the ball early and it flew low into the bottom right-hand corner, leaving Hornets stopper Johnny Curran stunned and beaten. It might have been two years since his second goal for Rangers, but it was worth the wait.

The effort of the former electrician's apprentice from Harrogate had sparkling results. Arthur Longbottom, winger Alex Dawson and Bobby Cameron all went close as rampaging Rangers sought to double their advantage.

QPR were beginning to wonder whether it would arrive particularly as a one-goal lead, football history tells us, is far from a guarantee of victory. How many times have a side missed a plethora of chances after hitting the front and been pegged back and even beaten? But Rangers stuck to their task and Longbottom made it 2-0. Cameron and Dawson combined in an intricate move which ended with the ball being pulled back from the byline for hotshot Longbottom to swiftly dispatch it into the net.

It put inside-right Longbottom on eight alongside team-mate Les Locke on the Rangers scoring list for the season.

By the end of the campaign, the Yorkshireman had surged away from Locke to claim the title of top scorer at the club for the second season running, returning 18.

And Longbottom, who sported a skinhead hairdo during his time at the club, managed to cut his way to a third season on top of the Rangers scoring charts.

Any Watford resistance had been broken and George Petchey completed the scoring. The wing-half, with the reputation as one of the leading players in his position in the lower leagues, took advantage of a dithery, suicidal Hornets rearguard which allowed him time to roll the ball over the line at walking pace.

Ron Springett, whose relative Terry has worked in the club offices for four decades, it seems had a quiet afternoon in the Rangers goal after the early heart-in-mouth moment.

But the future England World Cup goalkeeper was fast developing his reputation as a consistent performer, agile shot-stopper and outstanding all-round individual. He is very much part of the goalkeeping tradition Rangers have built up from Allen, through to his brother Peter, Phil Parkes and Julio Cesar.

The individual who must have garnered most satisfaction from the stinging of the Hornets was Ingham. And it was not only because he had scored.

He had also been cleared by the FA that week of 'throwing the ball with deliberate intent' at referee Mr Potts after being sent off for the 'offence' during a 2-1 defeat at Shrewsbury Town two matches earlier. It would have provided a blemish on an untarnished reputation as a 'true gentleman of football' as one fan posted on the Indyrs.co.uk website in tribute following Ingham's death.

That supporter, Bernard Lambert, added, 'In my childhood days of supporting the R's from 1957 through to the early 1960s, Tony seemed an eternal figure, well established as captain in the No.3 left-back slot, just as natural as the rising of the sun each morning.

'He was a talented defender and without doubt, could have played his football at a higher level than the Third Division, but he remained loyal to QPR FC and stuck with the club until the finish of his playing days.

'Thereafter, he did much sterling work for the QPR FC secretarial/admin and commercial departments. I recall one occasion during the 1967/68 season when he called round to our house in person to try and persuade my father, a Fulham supporter, to subscribe to the QPR Pools!

'Rest in Peace Tony Ingham. They don't make 'em like you anymore.'

Another, Chris Tanner, also posted, 'About ten years ago, I was on my way home when I saw Tony Ingham come out of the local butchers shop (opposite where the Oldfield Tavern used to be in North Greenford). He walked about ten yards in front of me as we turned the corner into Horsenden Lane.

'As he was getting into his car, I drew up level with him. I then said to him, "I bought a photo of you the other day" and he replied, "You must be a QPR fan." So we chatted briefly and he then said, "Are you going to the game today?" I told him that I was so he said, "Jump in, I'll give you a lift." So there I was being chauffeured to a home game by none other than QPR's former player and still the holder of the most appearances for our club.

'It turned out that he was very close friends with the butchers, who had turned the shop into a QPR shrine with photos of all the greats and plenty of course of Tony. The shop is no more, it closed down about 6-7 years ago. Alas, neither is Tony. I never had the pleasure of seeing him play, but I will always treasure that 30 minutes I spent with him that day.'

Rangers legend Mark Lazarus told your author in July 2013, 'I played a lot with Tony Ingham. He was brilliant. So much so that when I went from QPR and was being signed by Wolverhampton Wanderers the Wolves manager Stan Cullis said to me, "I wish your left-back was a few years younger." He was referring to Tony Ingham.

'Tony was a gentleman and in my opinion one of the best left full-backs in the country. I know he was playing for Queens Park Rangers in the Third Division, of course, but I never knew a better left-back in my career. A brilliant player. And an absolute gentleman. I had a lot of time for Tony.'

14 v Tranmere Rovers 9-2

Football League Third Division. Loftus Road
3 December 1960. Attendance: 4,805

QUEENS PARK RANGERS:
Drinkwater
Woods
Ingham
Keen
Rutter
Angell
Lazarus
Bedford
Evans
Andrews
Clark

TRANMERE ROVERS:
Payne
Millington
Frith
Harrop
Jones
Charlton
Finney
Williams
Onyeali
Neill
Eglington

Referee: E.Crawford (Doncaster)

ALEC STOCK would be a regular visitor to Thorpebank Road in Shepherd's Bush. Stock would lead Queens Park Rangers to their greatest period of glittering success in the late 1960s, turning a black-and-white 1950s for the club into vivid technicolour in the second half of the following decade.

It was, of course, no easy job he inherited from Jack Taylor in 1959 but the former soldier who had played for Rangers before the Second World War was meticulous in his preparation. Attention to detail was everything and that is why he would often be seen in the local street which housed many of his players.

He wanted to make sure their lives away from the training ground and Loftus Road were beneficial to themselves so they could give of their best for Rangers.

The accommodation in the road made famous when TV comedy series *Monty Python's Flying Circus* filmed its Ministry of Silly Walks sketch, starring the inimitable John Cleese and his long legs, in it, was modest, holding rows of two-up, two-downs with the luxury of inside and outside loos in each residence.

But they provided adequate accommodation for the players and much needed revenue for the working class families on low incomes who inhabited them. It is an existence alien to players of today used to their six-figure wages and mansions behind protective gates and four-wheel drives for the trip to work.

Rangers' would-be heroes were earning more than the folk who were putting them up, but not so much they were able to afford accommodation more akin to that enjoyed by modern-day performers. Stock helped arrange lodgings for the likes of players Bobby Cameron, Peter Angell, George Whitelaw, Peter Hobbs and Clive Clark.

And the food and sleeping quarters must have agreed with at least three of them judging by the day they helped Rangers seal the biggest win in their history.

Left-half Angell, centre-forward Evans and winger Clark thrived as Tranmere Rovers were trounced 9-2 on the wet, cold Saturday afternoon of 3 December 1960.

v Tranmere Rovers 1960

People dusted off the books which plotted Rangers' history to confirm how the size of the victory compared with any previous triumph by the club. It was initially reported it had equalled the total QPR had scored against Grimsby 'after the war' and that the secretary John Smith believed it to be the biggest at home for more than 30 years.

Of course, as a previous chapter discussed, R's only managed seven in the 1950 win over the Mariners and Mr Smith, although strictly accurate, somewhat understated the achievement.

It seemed the decision to revert to blue and white hooped shirts from plain white with blue shorts in the year immediately preceding Stock's arrival as boss brought good vibes along with it.

The game also provided a goal rated as one of the best, if not the best, in Rangers' history, by a prime source with matches rarely recorded for general viewing those days – eyewitness Bernard Lambert, who was still following his Super Hoops as your author writes.

It was scored by one of the lodgers in Thorpebank Road – Clive Clark.

Mention QPR players capable of producing candidates for such an accolade and the first two names mentioned on many lips would be Stan Bowles and Rodney Marsh, not surprising as they were the top-of-bill stars of two eras commonly rated as the best since the club's formation. And there is also THAT Trevor Sinclair FA Cup effort (to be featured in a later chapter). But don't tell long-term fan Bernard.

He posted on the qprreport.proboards.com website, 'I was there ... and saw one of the greatest (if not the greatest) goals EVER scored at Loftus Road by a QPR player. Clive Clark beat five or six Tranmere players in a mazy run from the halfway line and smashed the ball in at the School End ... Rodney and Stan eat your heart out.'

Bernard began supporting the R's in 1957 when the club had a side he felt was made up largely of journeymen.

Yet, as he watched the goals pile into the back of Tranmere's net – including the Clark wonder goal – from the Boys' Pen section of the ground, after paying 'cheap' admission following a short walk from home, he was no doubt starting to believe the positive Stock effect was taking a grip.

His heroes were evolving 'under the management of Alec Stock into the nearly men of the early 1960s' (more of that in later chapters) and became the men who arrived at the back end of the decade.

Several supporters followed Lambert on the thread recalling the game. One opined, 'I was there – wrapped up in a car rug, sitting with mum. Only four ... cold!'

Another revealed standing on the School End terracing, 'Five, stuck in shorts and bloody frozen.'

But Clark's solo – and the other eight – warmed up the sparse 4,805 crowd present 'so much so' another member of it insisted 'we were screaming for double figures "we want ten".'

Rangers had made a decent start to the season – having risen to second at one point while throwing in a 5-2 win over Reading – but few could have predicted the goals avalanche which buried Tranmere.

Rangers burned with a sense of injustice following an FA Cup exit against Coventry City just seven days earlier and ripped into Tranmere with goal doubles from 19-year-old left-winger Clive Clark, Mark Lazarus, on the opposite flank, and strikers Brian Bedford and Bernard Evans, with Jimmy Andrews also on target for the hosts.

Queens Park Rangers' Greatest Games

Rangers were out for blood as the rain fell and the wind blustered around Loftus Road.

Clark and the experienced Andrews laid the foundations. The winger was unstoppable as he galloped up the left time and again, while Andrews, playing just inside him, was the puppeteer controlling the strings of most attacks.

Lazarus displayed an impressive level of physical fitness as he ripped his full-back apart in much the same fashion as Clark managed on the opposite flank.

And Evans led his opposing centre-half a torrid time with his physical strength as well as power of shot. Tranmere must have wondered what they had done to deserve such treatment with Evans's strike partner Brian Bedford equally threatening.

A Clark run resulted in Evans putting Rangers ahead with his first goal for the west London club after 23 minutes. Bedford nodded the second from an Andrews left-wing corner nine minutes later.

Clark's spectacular 'best-goal-ever' effort made it 3-0 on 37 minutes when he cut into the middle and left a series of defenders bothered, bewildered and beaten before slotting the ball beyond advancing Tranmere stopper George Payne.

Lazarus took a leaf out of Clark's book as far as cutting in was concerned for the fourth three minutes before the interval, although his shot found the net after a deflection slowed the pace of the ball which rolled languidly over the line by George Payne's near post.

The conditions were getting heavier as the pitch resembled something close to a mud heap as players' boot studs churned it up while the rain continued to fall.

Lazarus notched his second within six minutes of the game resuming after half-time. The right-winger turned provider for Clark to complete his double with a thundering finish after 61 minutes.

It was a magnificent seven six minutes later when Evans netted again following an intelligent ball from Mike Keen.

Tranmere finally got a break as inside-right Keith Williams pulled one back after the referee overruled a linesman who had flagged against the visitors.

Bedford made it 8-1 for Rangers after 75 minutes before Rovers, who tried to keep playing their football, managed a second with Elkana Onyeali guiding home a Tommy Eglington ball beyond Rangers goalkeeper Ray Drinkwater.

And Andrews completed the scoring following a scramble in front of Payne's goal – with the crowd baying for a tenth as soon as it hit the back of the net.

The goal getters, as usual, were the focus of most adoration for the majority of those among the lowest attendance of the season, with the weather and Christmas shopping clearly reducing numbers.

Clark was another capture from Yorkshire – following the likes of Arthur Jefferson, Ernie Shepherd and Tony Ingham – when he moved from hometown club Leeds United as one of the last players signed by Stock's predecessor, Jack Taylor, in 1958.

Chippy – Clark's nickname – was and out-and-out winger with pace to burn as he tore down the left-hand touchline at Loftus Road and the grounds of Rangers' opponents.

He was always ready to take on defenders and get in a cross to set up goals. He could also add bravery to his list of attributes, perhaps born of the fact he was the son of a professional boxer. And, as he proved against Tranmere, he knew how to bulge the onion bag.

It was much to the supporters' chagrin that Chippy was allowed to leave Loftus Road for West Bromwich Albion a year after his torturing of Tranmere (a move which proved ironic as you will discover later in the book).

v Tranmere Rovers 1960

He was very much the crowd favourite with his entertaining style, rather like former Rangers winger Mike Hellawell, who had been allowed to depart four years previously.

Even though Clark returned to Rangers for a short spell from the Baggies – then more commonly known as the Throstles – in 1969, the R's followers had seen the best of the winger respected by professionals as well as fans during the spell which featured his part in the destruction of Tranmere.

The Birmingham Mail quoted former West Brom team-mate Graham Williams saying of Clark in 2008, 'Chippy was an unbelievable player. He was fast, small but very, very brave and people forget that he scored a phenomenal number of goals for a winger.'

Fellow Thorpebank Road-ite Evans ensured he would be an instant hit with that goal double against Rovers.

Stock signed the burly Cheshire-born striker on the say-so of his Wales scout where Evans developed his penchant for making early impressions having taken just 27 seconds to score his first ever goal in the Football League while with Wrexham aged 17.

Lazarus had only followed former Leyton Orient boss Stock from Brisbane Road two months before his awesome twosome against Tranmere. The £3,000 paid out to the O's was to prove a snip as the winger carved out a legendary career at Rangers, as you can read further on.

Bedford arguably proved even better value for money with Stock picking him up from Bournemouth for just £750 in July 1959 as he went on to bang in 37 goals as Rangers finished third in 1960/61 before scoring even more the following term, a subject developed later.

Andrews was already 32 when Stock signed him as a light-footed, pacey winger, converted to play inside Clark against Tranmere, and would prove an invaluable addition to the backroom staff as reserves coach and, for 77 days, first-team boss with Stock general manager.

And a final word on the third Thorpebank Road lodger, Peter Angell. He had been converted from an outside-left with non-league Slough Town and Charlton Athletic to a dependable, defensive left-half. A watchword for consistency, Angell eventually amassed 460 games in 12 years on the Rangers staff, a few as club captain.

Lazarus told your author, 'It was history-making. I was on the right wing and Clive was on the left and we were literally slaughtering them. Every time we got the ball we were just going through them and scoring. We were well into the season. We scored a lot of goals that season [93 in the league].'

Bedford recalled on QPRnet, 'I remember when we scored nine against Tranmere, I think that's QPR's record win actually, we were trying like stink to get ten but it wouldn't go in.'

15 v Southend United 5-3

Third Division. Loftus Road
14 October 1961. Attendance: 10,519

QUEENS PARK RANGERS:	SOUTHEND UNITED:
Slack	Goy
Bentley	Shiels
Ingham	Anderson
Keen	Costello
Rutter	Watson
Angell	Grievson
McClelland	Wall
Bedford	Jones
Evans	Brand
Collins	Goulden
Barber	Kellard

Referee: A. Holland (York)

THE LATE television darts broadcaster Sam Waddell was known for the way he intoned '180' whenever either Phil 'The Power' Taylor or any other of the world-class performers bagged a maximum with their arrows from the oche on stage at a World Championship.

Well, if Newcastle United fan Waddell had commentated on football in the early 1960s he might well have screamed the same number in reference to Brian Bedford.

Bedford netted 180 goals in only 284 matches for Queens Park Rangers to put himself second behind George Goddard in the club's all-time scorers list.

It was an astonishing strike rate and not a bad return for a striker who cost the club £750 down with £250 to follow dependent on appearances from Bournemouth.

He just loved to score. And that was reflected when he selected his favourite matches for the R's. The 9-2 record demolition of Tranmere Rovers was one. Another was when he slammed home FOUR in one game for a second and last time during his six successive years of topping the scoring charts at the club.

Southend were on the receiving end on a Saturday afternoon in the middle of October at Loftus Road in 1961. Just four days after a volcanic eruption on Tristan da Cunha had forced the complete evacuation of the South Atlantic Ocean island, Bedford made the Shrimpers flee Loftus Road for the shelter of the Essex coast to lick their wounds despite a spirited display from the visitors.

Rangers' top marksman had chosen the day to mark his biggest goal haul in one game in a season in which his club netted a record 111 league goals.

He had already plundered five trebles and was to go on and tot up eight more hat-tricks but a quartet of strikes was clearly extra special, even for such a prolific striker.

Bedford said to QPRnet.com in 2005, 'Games that stood out for me personally were the ones when I got four. I did that twice, once against Halifax in 1961 and again the next season against Southend.'

v Southend United 1961

Manager Alec Stock was cranking up the R's. They were moving forward after the difficulties of the 1950s. A new decade and a new light was shining and getting brighter, and Bedford was holding the brightest torch.

He had tempted Stock to pick him off the Cherries with an enviable goals tally for the South Coast club, averaging close to a goal a game in more than 75 appearances, as Stock began developing a team of also-rans into one of just-maybes.

There was no guarantee Stock had found himself a pearl of a striker who would go down in club legend. But it soon became clear he was the master of all – or perhaps more accurately, most – hot shots plying their trade in the Football League Third Division.

He bettered the 27 goals he netted in his debut season for the club by ten in helping Rangers to within two points of promotion in 1960/61.

And it was clear he remained focused on maintaining breathtaking rates of scoring as he entered the following season.

By the time Southend visited London W12, Bedford had bagged goals in victories over Brentford and Barnsley and hit a hat-trick in a 6-2 hammering of Halifax Town. He was about to be a scoring wonder for a third season in a row with the Hoops.

After his awesome foursome against the rattled Roots Hall outfit, Bedford continued along his merry way for the rest of the season, bettering his personal tally yet again.

At one point in the second half of the campaign he scored in eight consecutive games in which Rangers were only a point short of a maximum return. Thirty-nine goals in 49 games must have made Bournemouth regret letting him go so cheaply.

Bedford's exploits clearly dominated the Southend game but Rangers had to come back from behind three times after gifting goals.

The home defence looked vulnerable against determined visitors. Keith Rutter and Tony Ingham appeared to struggle along with reserve goalkeeper Rodney Slack, who was beaten twice before he could make a stop and was grateful for the support of experienced Roy Bentley, the former Chelsea league championship-winning striker and captain turned Rangers right-back.

But QPR were outstanding going forward with John McClelland, Bernard Evans and John Collins, a member of the ground staff who replaced regular front-runner Jim Towers, creating a series of openings.

Southend took the lead through unmarked Ray Brand after Billy Wall beat Tony Ingham after five minutes. McClelland hit the post from close range before running down the wing to find Bedford who netted the equaliser.

Rangers trailed when Roy Goulden converted a Lou Costello ball after 20 minutes before Bedford made it 2-2 via a low cross from Mike Barber.

Rangers, though, failed to tighten at the back and Ray Brand latched on to a miscued back-pass by Keith Rutter to back-heel the ball for Ken Jones to beat Slack from 12 yards six minutes before half-time.

Bedford completed his hat-trick 45 seconds after the re-start by heading home a chipped Mike Barber ball.

The strength visibly drained from Southend and Peter Angell slammed home a spot-kick after Harry Grievson had handled on 58 minutes.

And shortly afterwards Bedford headed home a cross from Angell to complete QPR's nap hand and secure both points.

But the Southend victory, although a personal triumph for Bedford, certainly exposed a weakness in Rangers' bid to regain Second Division status for the first time since their initial spell had ended after only four seasons in 1952. They struggled to keep the ball out of their own onion bag.

Just look at the opening two games of the season in isolation. They produced 12 goals. The trouble was, from Rangers' point of view, their goalkeeper Ray Drinkwater picked the ball out of the net six times during them. It put more pressure on Bedford and Co. to come up with goals. It seemed as if the Hoops were enacting the old truism that if you score one more than the opposition victory is guaranteed.

Bedford, of course, did not let the side down. Nor did goalscoring partners such as Bernard Evans, new signing Jim Towers, Mark Lazarus, even though he spent five months of the campaign with Wolves before returning to Loftus Road, and John McClelland.

They smashed in goals for fun and between them helped Rangers produce six-goal wins against Swindon Town and Torquay, as well as Halifax. Lincoln City were lashed 5-0, while Barnsley, Brentford, Newport County (twice), Bristol City and Coventry City conceded four in reverses against a rampant Rangers.

They rattled up 62 goals by the New Year and a McClelland goal in a win over Notts County brought up the century of R's strikes with five games still left to play. Stock's men even took time out for a 7-1 FA Cup battering of Barry.

But the cause of concern was the goals against column. Their defence was leaky. Besides the six conceded in just the second game against Reading, they let in eight over the two fixtures against Peterborough. Drinkwater picked four out of his net against Portsmouth at Fratton Park. And Lincoln, Watford, Bournemouth, Bradford and Hull emulated Southend in piercing Rangers' rearguard on three occasions.

Rangers' porous defence was beaten 73 times over the league season's 46 games.

QPR were able to sustain their second promotion bid on the bounce, winning four and drawing three in the run-in, but completed the campaign three points behind Grimsby Town, who secured the second promotion spot with Portsmouth champions.

The propensity for being unable to stick a finger in the dyke had to be a factor in Rangers falling just short and it was also an indication of their ability to shred the nerves of long-suffering supporters dreaming that they were watching a team capable of going up.

Yet few can argue Stock's men failed to entertain that season, and Bedford in particular did as much as anyone.

The Welshman, who returned to Loftus Road as stadium manager through then director and former team-mate Tony Ingham, might have missed out on the glory years of the late 1960s when Rodney Marsh took his mantle as the hero of the fans. But he had a ball while he held the Loftus Road faithful in thrall.

Mark Lazarus told your author in July 2013, 'Brian was always top goalscorer. I remember the four he got in the Southend game. An absolute thorough gentleman. Never scored a goal from outside the six-yard box. Brave as you like. He got in where it hurts. If I had the ball on the wing, Brian used to have one thing in mind – to get into the six-yard box. He expected a cross from me. If Clive Clark or John McClelland had the ball it was the same.

'He was one of the best goal poachers around. You don't get four goals and three goals a game unless you are an absolute goal poacher. He scored a lot of good goals. Headed goals. He used to come off with stitches in his eyes from cuts caused by clashes. I had a lot of time for Brian.

'You never saw him pick the ball up from outside the box, beat somebody, and put it in the roof of the net. He was all about goals.'

v Southend United 1961

Bedford said to QPRnet.com's Ron Norris, 'I hope I justified the fee in the long run. I was simply an out and out striker. Alec used to tell me not to get too involved in the game, I was told to just lay it off, get in the penalty area and score goals and that's what I did.

'In those days of course you had those old-fashioned things called wingers. Strikers always want crosses and if I got a good one from a winger I'd score. It's a simple game really!

'Alec wasn't a great football technician. He wasn't one of those who could talk tactics all day. His big strength was he was a great psychologist. He was very passionate about the game and knew how to get the best out of his players. He told me the day he signed me that I'd score 20 goals a season for him and I did.

'I was lucky. Playing up front in those days meant I took my fair share of kicks and knocks but I think the longest I was ever out was for two weeks. I remember cutting open both eyes one week and then playing the next game, we weren't softies back in those days and we weren't mollycoddled like they are now.

'I remember we were due to play Scunthorpe United one week and I'd twisted my ankle in the week. I had a fitness test before the game and I had to go to Alec and say "sorry Alec I can't play, I can't even kick a ball" so he said he'd leave me out.

'I turned up before the game and wished the players good luck then settled in at the bar, I ordered a beer and I was just raising it to my lips when I heard Alec's voice scream out, "No don't!"

'I turned round and asked him what was wrong and he said "you're playing". I couldn't even kick a ball but he was short of strikers so I had to put the beer down and get changed. First tackle I got was on my ankle so I didn't have the best game!

'[Bournemouth manager] Don Welsh's method of management wasn't something I enjoyed so I requested a transfer.

'Alec Stock had seen me play for the Cherries against his Leyton Orient side a few years before he went to QPR, I think I impressed him and he remembered me. So that summer when he heard I was transfer listed he came in with a bid and I became one of his first signings at Rangers. I went up to London to meet him and ended up signing on the same day. He was a really good talker Alec!

'I didn't particularly want to go [from QPR to Scunthorpe] but I was into my thirties then so I was getting a bit long in the tooth I suppose. The problem was Alec didn't want to sell me to anyone local, I think selling me to Scunthorpe was his way of making sure that any criticism of letting me go was minimised because I wasn't playing locally. It was a shame because I was settled in the area and it ruled out joining clubs like Brentford, although I eventually ended up at Griffin Park anyway.

'Returning? Tony Ingham made me an offer to become the club's stadium manager. I'd always considered Rangers to be my club so I jumped at the chance and I loved working there. I worked there for a good few years and then I got sacked in 1992.'

16 v Hull City 4-1

Football League Third Division. White City
22 October 1962. Attendance: 18,281

QUEENS PARK RANGERS:	HULL CITY:
Drinkwater	Williams
Bentley	Davidson
Ingham	Sharpe
Malcolm	Collinson
Dugdale	Garvey
Angell	McMillan
McClelland	Clarke
Bedford	Price
Evans	King
Keen	Henderson
Lazarus	Shaw

Referee: T. Dawes (Norwich)

THERE MIGHT have been the combined width of greyhound and athletics tracks but a hat-trick from Brian Bedford and one goal by Mark Lazarus had the separated Queens Park Rangers players and spectators in party mode.

The efforts of Rangers' prolific goalscorer Bedford and talismanic winger Lazarus enabled their team to celebrate their first and biggest victory on the club's one-season return to the White City against Hull City on Monday 22 October 1962.

As befitting the occasion the 18,281 present would prove to be the biggest to witness Rangers adjusting to the new surroundings just a stone's throw from Loftus Road.

And the record gate receipts must have had QPR board members in the directors' box nodding their collective heads in a display of self-congratulation that they had made the right call to abandon their long-established home to boost the coffers.

A growth in attendances at Loftus Road coinciding with a couple of decent promotion bids and the team netting a record 111 league goals in the 1961/62 campaign had the money men believing the time was right to try and cash in by moving up the road to the 60,000-capacity venue for 1962/63, and that the demand would exceed the supply if they stayed put at their small stadium with a capacity of under a third less.

Rangers had tried the experiment once before – while Loftus Road staged second-string matches – in the early 1930s for similar reasons. Just as when the Tigers came to visit three decades later, an 18,000-plus attendance turned up for the club's first appearance in the venue built for the 1908 Olympic Games against Bournemouth on 5 September 1931. Again there must have been a positive feeling in the boardroom as they tucked into sarnies and sipped cups of tea at half-time (and perhaps something a little stronger following the final whistle, even though the Cherries had spoiled the debut by scoring a 3-0 victory).

Perhaps back-slapping rather than nodding heads might have been the chosen way of showing their belief that they had got it right. After all, Loftus Road attendances the previous season had only made five figures on four occasions with the biggest gate around 4,000 down on the numbers attracted to see if R's could put the bite on the Cherries.

Gates dropped off that term, but averaged out around 10,000–12,000, comfortably above the 1930/31 season's figure at Loftus Road as all-time record goalscorer George Goddard, until injured in January, Stan Cribb and Harry Wiles banged in goals to help Rangers to a respectable 11 wins and six draws, with just four losses in their Third Division South campaign, at White City.

And it also was the scene for a club record home attendance of 41,097 when the R's beat Leeds United in the FA Cup on 9 January 1932. It offered the management of the club sufficient encouragement to stay on for a second term, a decision seemingly justified with 24,347 turning up to see their heroes kick off the 1932/33 campaign there against neighbouring Brentford, although the attraction of the new home wore off alongside disappointing results and just 2,837 turned up for the penultimate home game of the season.

It represented the club's lowest Football League home attendance. Rangers' finances were in a parlous state – the players agreed to deferred payment of wages and the club's bank overdraft had gone up to £34,500 – before the directors cut their losses.

Yet the board in situ in the early 1960s appeared justified in repeating the experiment judging on those who had been lured to the White City for the Monday night encounter against Hull under the floodlights of the iconic Olympic stadium.

The venue had witnessed AAA Championships and top-class greyhound meetings before the Hoops' return. And it seemed as if Rangers could do well despite what happened the last time round. Certainly the supporters were intrigued. There was plenty to evoke the emotion. The history of the stadium which housed their first team for a start (the reserves and youth teams hosting their home matches at Loftus Road).

The sense of pride in its history was understandable. Rangers had moved into a stadium which had been the largest in the world with a reported capacity of 150,000 with 68,000 seated, after being built for £80,000 in just ten months and opened by King Edward VII in the April to save the 1908 Olympic Games.

It was the first all-purpose modern Games venue, hosting a host of sports including athletics, cycling, swimming and hockey (and subsequently used for rugby, boxing, baseball, stock car racing and speedway besides more athletics and greyhound racing).

Original Games hosts Italy were forced to give up hope of doing so when funds put by for it had to be diverted to help Naples recover from the devastation caused by the eruption of nearby Mount Vesuvius.

London picked up the baton to add the stadium to a project on the site known as Great White City with its white marble clad palaces and exhibition centres initially built to stage the Franco-British Exhibition. There was also, ostensibly, the luxury it provided in comparison to Loftus Road. The Hull City match programme pictured 'an interior view of White City's Olympic enclosure', a smart carpeted seated area which protected its occupants from the vagaries of the weather.

It described another 'from the outside looking in on this top value four-shilling enclosure' which could be seen beyond the athletic and greyhound tracks.

Rangers fan Paul Harris, a supporter since the late 1950s, told your author in July 2013, 'It was at the time considered by most fans as a great move in giving the club a very big morale boost, a large stadium with all mod cons, restaurants etc. It was quite something back then for a small Third Division club to have a home stadium that could hold 60,000.'

Queens Park Rangers' Greatest Games

There was high excitement in the Harris household when it was discovered Hull City were scheduled to be the first visitors to this iconic stadium.

Harris said, 'It was due to be played on the Monday evening of 1 October. It rained all day and I travelled to the White City and the game was called off at the last minute due to the pitch being waterlogged. As it turned out, the first game was a defeat against Notts County but I was delighted when we finally got to play – and get our first win there against Hull on another Monday night three weeks to the day after the first attempt to put it on.'

Rangers followers came, if not in their droves, but in substantial numbers on the night after work and school to see what their first team's new home looked like from the inside. They had passed it enough times. The dominant structure had, of course, always been in full view for anyone emerging from White City station following a journey on the London Underground's Central Line. There was no need to walk past it and up South Africa Road to gain admittance into Loftus Road via either the main entrance, Ellerslie Road, Loftus Road or Bloemfontein Road.

As twilight gave way to darkness, White City was shining bright. And like bees to a honeypot, supporters wanted to know if the experience could be sweet, as sweet as when they celebrated a goal at the stadium they first adopted in 1917 as a field once used by amateur club Shepherd's Bush FC. Their equivalents from the 1930s enjoyed the novelty before that wore off. What would it be like for them as the club gave it a second chance, or third if you count the two matches played there in 1912 in a temporary arrangement necessitated by an Easter holiday rail strike preventing many fans attending their then permanent home at the Park Royal Stadium?

Expectations were far from high going into the re-scheduled encounter against Hull. QPR had lost three on the bounce, starting with the reverse against Notts County in the eventual first White City league match referred to by Harris.

Clutching their sixpence programme, Rangers fans must have felt like tearing it up and going home early as their favourites laboured early on. QPR looked edgy, a condition brought about by confidence having been lowered due to the disappointing run they were on. The Tigers had their tails up and Rangers largely had goalkeeper Ray Drinkwater to thank for avoiding them sinking their teeth into a vulnerable home rearguard, the stopper making a series of fine saves.

Also, the R's were bedding in new signings Andy Malcolm and Jimmy Dugdale.

Centre-half Dugdale had a glittering past. He lifted the FA Cup twice with West Bromwich Albion (1954) and Aston Villa (1957), with whom he won the Second Division title (1960) and the first League Cup (1960).

Malcolm was a highly-regarded left-half known for marking big names like Jimmy Greaves, Denis Law and Johnny Haynes during his time at West Ham United, and had arrived from a relegated Chelsea in a £10,000 move having had a reported contract dispute with Tommy Docherty, a future QPR boss. But previous glories and reputations counted for nothing as the new boys struggled to adjust to their new surroundings.

Malcolm's tackling was causing the Tigers some chagrin but he slipped up to gift the visitors the lead after just short of half an hour.

The defensive wing-half was caught out as Hull inside-left Ray Henderson was first to the ball after Drinkwater parried an effort from visiting inside-right Duggie Price.

Fortunately the moans and groans of the Hoops followers were swiftly followed by salutations to the player most likely to get them out of the mire, Bedford.

v Hull City 1962

It was a typical piece of opportunism by the poacher supreme. Inside-left Mike Keen had a drive blocked by Tigers stopper Mike Williams and Bedford pounced to drive the loose ball into the net. Soon after Bedford came within an ace of putting Rangers ahead when a whisker away from converting a cross by John McClelland.

Rangers had Hull on the back foot. And the visitors were forced to re-shuffle at the interval with left-back Len Sharpe injured following a coming together with McClelland.

Also Andy Malcolm and Jimmy Dugdale were now settled into their roles as Rangers moved forward. And no sooner had the words of Alec Stock's half-time team talk faded than QPR were in front for the first time. It was, of course, that man again who struck on 47 minutes. Malcolm and John McClelland combined and Bedford hit the target with a header flicked home off a McClelland cross.

Rangers were rampant and Lazarus hit the bar with a spectacular effort from 35 yards. And the winger got his name of the scoresheet when he pounced on a Malcolm ball to make it 3-1 after 73 minutes. The last word, naturally, came from Bedford who completed his treble in the last minute.

Hopes that White City would be a cash cow for Rangers proved illusory. It might have been tempting to re-name the stadium White Elephant. Support dropped off following the early boost of beating Hull in front of a big crowd as history repeated itself and Rangers returned to the more limited confines of Loftus Road.

The White City experiment has been much derided – one description was 'suicidal' and your author recalls attending a match with his father there during the 1962/63 season with a small attendance.

As a spectator you rattled around like a pea in an empty dustbin inside a seemingly deserted cavernous arena. And the greyhound and athletics tracks ensured breathing down the necks of players, a feat entirely possible at Loftus Road, was impossible for those without super human powers. It was a struggle to create an atmosphere.

Official club historian Gordon Macey told your author, 'They didn't get the crowds. I was only a kid and I remember being so far off the pitch I couldn't see what was going on. Probably why I didn't go back there that season.' The goalscorers that memorable night against Hull have differing takes on the 1960s campaign spent at the White City.

Bedford said to QPRnet.com in 2005, 'We suffered with the move to the White City because it really hurt our home record. The trouble is the fans were so far away from the pitch compared to Loftus Road and there just wasn't the same kind of atmosphere so I was pleased when we moved back to Loftus Road.'

Lazarus told your author in July 2013, 'People say it didn't go well, but we didn't do too badly there. It was typical of Brian to get a hat-trick against Hull. I also remember that season for one of our supporters sticking one on a Northampton player for fouling or kicking me against Northampton that season!'

There has been talk of Rangers considering another move from Loftus Road to a bigger stadium once more.

It comes in the wake of West Ham United following Rangers' lead by moving from their traditional home to an Olympic Stadium, albeit one built for the 2012 Games.

Should the Hammers be mindful of the parallel with Rangers' experience of it?

Perhaps, but it hasn't stopped one supporter, with White City demolished and replaced by the British Broadcasting Corporation buildings, speculating on QPRnet.com, 'Wouldn't it be good if (owner) Tony (Fernandes) could build a new stadium on that very site as the BBC are moving.'

 **v Mansfield Town 7-1**
Football League Third Division. Field Mill
24 September 1966. Attendance: 6,262

QUEENS PARK RANGERS:	MANSFIELD TOWN:
Springett	Humphreys
Hazell	Coleman
Langley	Richardson
Keen	Morris
Hunt	McKinney
Sibley	Ferns
I. Morgan	Bruce
Sanderson	Hall
Allen	Curry
Marsh	Mitchinson
R. Morgan	Gregson

Referee: G.C. Kew (Leeds)

PETE TOWNSHEND, born and brought up close to Loftus Road, wrote that the 'deaf, dumb and blind kid sure plays a mean pinball' in the rock opera *Tommy* he wrote for The Who, the legendary band formed with two other lads, Roger Daltrey and John Entwistle, from the area.

Well, a Queens Park Rangers folk hero offered a small comparison to the character Townshend was writing about if one replaces the 'pin' with the 'foot'. He displayed near 20-20 vision and was almost as far from being unable to speak as one could imagine, according to many within earshot, albeit old club-mates or listeners to his punditry in latter years.

Recent tweets from him have the feel of an individual far from wanting to keep his opinions to himself, even if they divide opinion.

But Rodney Marsh did suffer visual problems and became deaf in one ear. They came as a direct result of a sickening collision with defender John Sjoberg while scoring the winning goal for Fulham against Leicester City on 21 September 1963.

It left the 19-year-old Marsh unconscious and being told his career was almost certainly over. His jaw had been broken and a bone had punctured a nerve in his left ear, while his sense of balance had deserted him. And he discovered in hospital that he had also suffered a haemorrhage and feared, as he revealed in his book *Shooting To The Top*, 'that I was going to die'. He cried and became introverted and was ready to call time on his football career but was persuaded by his dad and mentor, Bill, to give it another go, with the support of Fulham.

Marsh's sense of balance returned but he discovered his vision was 'very narrow' as a result of the accident.

Fortunately his eyesight restored itself to normal and he found he could head the ball without any problems and seven months after the accident he was back playing competitive football.

v Mansfield Town 1966

His revered – and permanent – place on the top table of Rangers heroes was sealed with his efforts in the 1966/67 campaign, generally regarded as the most successful in Rangers' history in terms of trophies collected, despite his hearing troubles. Two silver pots were placed into the club's cabinet within two months of each other.

By the time Marsh suffered an injury which sidelined him for five of the last seven matches, a league and cup double was all but guaranteed barring members of the Super Hoops' trailblazers unexpectedly transforming into a group of zombies.

Marsh played a starring role as Rangers secured the championship by a record 12 points from Middlesbrough.

He smashed his way to a club record 44 goals (30 in the league) in the highest of high-profile seasons which was ultimately successful, according to the legendary striker, due to three early performances away from Loftus Road, with one, at Mansfield Town, in particular providing the springboard to glory.

We will discuss how Rangers created history in lifting the League Cup in the following two chapters, but a first Football League divisional title also has pride of place in the memory banks of those with an affection for the west London club, whether a manager, coach, administrator or, of course, a player.

There had been three seasons of mediocrity following the record goalscoring league season of 1961/62 in which they netted 111.

Alec Stock might have been a gentleman manager, always well mannered and well dressed (bearings no doubt gleaned from his days as an Army officer in the Second World War), but he was heartily sick of his side under-achieving.

Stock, with the financial clout given him by new chairman Jim Gregory, began re-shaping the team with striker Les Allen costing a record £20,000 from Tottenham Hotspur, and Keith Sanderson and Jim Langley joining, plus full-back Ian Watson, while youth product Frank Sibley was added to the squad. And it provided instant results with a surge to third place.

England lifted the World Cup in the country's one and only final in the summer of 1966. Football fever had gripped the nation. And it was clear the manager wanted the nation gripped by his team.

Marsh, of course, provided the biggest spark needed to turn a side of nearly men into winners when he signed for £15,000 from Fulham in March 1966 – along with a stepped-up training programme.

Stock had gathered a fine bunch of players together. A mix of products of a prolific youth system, headed up Derek Healy, with the likes of Frank Sibley, Tony Hazell, twins Roger and Ian Morgan and Mick Leach, coming of age and mixing with Marsh, Mark Lazarus and the other imports.

Stock knew talent was not enough. He clearly felt that one major way of realising the potential of the group was to get the players super fit in mind and body.

He brought in Bill Dodgin Junior as the club's new coach and the pair left no stone unturned. It was all planned down to the last detail.

They brain-stormed and produced a series of innovative sessions. But the routines were not cakewalks.

The players trained twice a day for six weeks at their pre-season headquarters in Twickenham. Each was repeated over and over, pushing the players beyond what they thought they were capable of, albeit an exercise, a run, a drill. Even if it made them physically sick which, in some cases, according to Marsh, it did.

Queens Park Rangers' Greatest Games

Then there were the team talks, which continued as everyone ate lunch. And Stock also went round individually to players to fine tune. When he got to Marsh and Allen his message was clear, 'I want 30 goals from each of you.'

Allen had shown how capable he was of achieving the target while a member of Tottenham Hotspur's Double side, the first to win the Football League and FA Cup in the same season.

He scored hatfuls of goals for a side considered by many as the finest club side Britain had produced for the level they attained in that one campaign.

The striker, whose sons Clive and Bradley and nephew Martin were to don the Hoops, still retained the knack of knowing where the goal was and ended up with 16 in the league campaign.

But more was expected of Marsh. He hit the ground running at Rangers, due in part to his increased fitness following the blood sweat and tears put into pre-training before the term kicked off and, of course, his natural self-confidence and his appreciation of being given a 'free reign' by Stock, plus knowing Stock and Dodgin Junior with the team had devised an effective pattern of play.

To use the modern vernacular, he scored for fun that season (his manager increasing his target to 40 – and then to 50). Marsh's goals helped Rangers climb to the top of the table by mid-November after an unbeaten run of 15 games. And he continued to bulge the onion bag.

Marsh recalled in *Shooting To The Top*, 'I was having a purple patch in which everything was coming off. Take, for example, a goal I scored in our Boxing Day game with Brighton at Loftus Road. The ball, played across from the left-wing by Roger Morgan, rolled behind me about 25 yards out. I turned with it and clipped it back into the middle. The idea was a short centre.

'I fell as I hit the ball and looked up just in time to see it floating towards the corner of the net. "It can't go in", I thought. But it did, and I don't suppose there was anyone among a crowd of nearly 18,000 who thought I hadn't meant it.'

It enabled Rangers to remain leaders until the final day. It was ironic QPR sealed the crown with a 1-0 victory over Oldham Athletic on 15 April 1967 with Marsh beginning his five-match stretch on the sidelines (and his replacement Alan Wilks banging in the winner). But, as Marsh insisted, it was the trio of three early-season games away from Loftus Road, in particular the magnificent seven-goal thrashing of Mansfield, which held the key to ultimate glory.

Rangers had made a spluttering start with just a solitary point from the opening two fixtures. Les Allen and Marsh scored as what would be the lowest Loftus Road crowd of the season – 6,443 – witnessed a 2-2 draw against Shrewsbury Town on the opening day.

They struck the woodwork a couple of times and dominated for spells but they had to rely on a last-minute leveller from Marsh after an Ian Morgan effort had hit the post to ensure something out of the game.

A poor performance against Watford at Vicarage Road in the next fixture got what it deserved – nothing.

But good things often come out of bad ones as manager Alec Stock filmed the match and the video nasty was compulsory viewing for the players afterwards. It exposed where individuals had gone wrong.

Marsh, in particular, discovered he was ignoring the advice his first Fulham manager Bedford Jezzard had told him: to make sure he was in the six-yard box to pick up the bits

v Mansfield Town 1966

and pieces of chances to fall his way rather than gaining possession so deep he would have less opportunity to hurt the opposition.

The players in general were exposed as lacking cohesion, putting in the labour but lacking thought.

Rangers put right much of what was wrong at Watford with superb displays in back-to-back home wins against Swindon Town and Middlesbrough, netting seven goals and conceding just the one. The Boro victory showed Marsh how right the Jezzard maxim had been when he accidently diverted home a Roger Morgan cross before completely a treble within the next ten minutes.

But then came the season-shaping away days. It was the performances in the next three away games (during an unbeaten run of 15 matches) which convinced Marsh and Rangers that promotion would come at the season's end. They trailed Reading 2-0 at Elm Park before a Jimmy Langley penalty and an Ian Morgan strike ensured a draw.

Rangers were in a similar position against Boro at Ayresome Park with Marsh and Mark Lazarus goals sealing another 2-2 draw.

But it was the manner of their 7-1 annihilation of Mansfield Town at their hosts' Field Mill ground which most symbolised Rangers had what it took to not only go up, but go up as champions.

Stock's Rangers had left the Stags' headquarters in Quarry Lane with their tails very much between their legs two seasons before, having been pummelled 8-1. And it seemed the Stags had the sign over QPR, completing the double over their west London opponents in the 1965/66 campaign.

But the myth was blown apart – big style! Chairman Jim Gregory, who had taken over in 1965, remembered how he felt when his first season in the hot-seat was spoiled by Mansfield's eight-goal mauling of his team. He even told the side prior to kick-off, 'Let's get those goals back!'

The performance against the Stags showed Rangers were capable of consistently displaying chutzpah, with the recent record against Mansfield in the back of the collective mind of the players. The defence displayed a determination not to be breached. The fact their opponents managed to find a hole in what they believed was an impregnable stone wall wounded the individuals which made up the whole.

The display demonstrated just how firm the Rangers rearguard had become. Goalkeeper Peter Springett, young brother of the England stopper, was his unflappable self. Not flash, just consistency personified.

Full-backs Tony Hazell and Jim Langley, a partnership which epitomised the mix of youth and experience in the team, were superb.

Hazell, a product of the Rangers scouting system, provided proof of his ability to provide juddering tackles to limit Mansfield ambitions.

And Langley, signed from Fulham and, at 37, the senior member of the team, showed how age need not be a barrier on the football field.

Langley remained as fit as a flea. He seemed to run on the equivalent of Duracell batteries, knew where to position himself and be a step ahead of the opposition. He also displayed his nerve at Field Mill to convert his spot-kick. And Ron Hunt was solid as a rock at centre-half.

The QPR midfield was outstanding, again with captain Mike Keen, at right-half, unerring in his passing and Frank Sibley, on the left side, the heartbeat of the side with his non-stop work-rate, defensive abilities and skill.

Queens Park Rangers' Greatest Games

The identical Morgan twins, Roger and Ian, on each flank were a handful for the Stags. Ian, deputising for unavailable right-wing regular Mark Lazarus, was lively and Roger linked up well with Marsh on the left side.

Keith Sanderson also put in a shift at inside-right and deserved his goal.

Les Allen spearheaded the attack with the number 9 on his back. Allen constantly made himself available, either holding up the ball, making dummy runs to leave gaps and, of course, helping himself to two goals.

It seemed everything Rangers touched that day turned to gold. There was even a touch of total football about QPR that afternoon with attacks begun by midfielders from all areas of the pitch.

Vic Buckingham, the Fulham manager who sold Marsh to R's, must have cast envious eyes across west London at how one of his former players was part of a side trying to play the kind of football he helped develop in Holland while managing Ajax of Amsterdam prior to his spell at Craven Cottage.

Marsh might have netted his second hat-trick – bringing his goals total up to eight – with the season just seven games old, but he refused to take any individual plaudits.

Marsh said in *Shooting To The Top*, 'I scored another three goals but this, above all, was a team victory. I won't have it that my contribution was a mite more important than that of, say, Mike Keen and Keith Sanderson, who got through a ton of work. We left the field feeling nothing was beyond us.

'One of our chief strengths was that so many of the team had tremendous ability on the ball. They could each take on two or three defenders by themselves, and this alone destroyed a lot of sides. But we owed our success to more than this.

'We played for each other and I, for one, owed a great deal to the cleverness of players like Les (Allen), Roger (Morgan) and Mark (Lazarus) in taking defenders away from the middle and leaving things open for me.

'And when I wasn't scoring the others were. We always seemed to have at least one player for whom things were going right.

'It is difficult to say why we blended so well and why so many other fit, skilful teams never really hit it off. Perhaps it was because so many of us were good friends.

'Everybody wanted to help everyone else and, when we began winning and our confidence grew even stronger the feeling of togetherness we had almost amounted to a secret weapon.

'We could finish a game on a high note and pick up exactly where we left off when the next one started.

'We had respect for each other as professional and people, and I don't think there was a weakness anywhere in the side.'

Mark Lazarus was another hero of the championship campaign.

Marsh said, 'During out great season in the Third Division he was indispensable. He was a flier, a man who could put three or four opponents out of the game with an electrifying run, and the scorer of some goals that had to be seen to be believed.'

v Birmingham City 4-1

Football League Cup semi-final first leg. St Andrew's
17 January 1967. Attendance: 34,295

QUEENS PARK RANGERS:	BIRMINGHAM CITY:
Springett	Herriot
Watson	Murray
Langley	Green
Keen	Thomson
Hunt	Sharples
Sibley	Beard
Lazarus	Hockey
Sanderson	Martin
Allen	Bullock
Marsh	Vowden
R. Morgan	Bridges

Referee: J. Mitchell (Prescot)

CREAM RISES to the top. Queens Park Rangers enjoyed the most successful era in their history when there was enough to fill a pint bottle rather than just the gold top at Loftus Road.

And to pick out a game when their bottle runneth over is tough – to the outsider. What to choose from a time when a championship title was won, back-to-back promotions attained and an only major knockout trophy to date lifted.

To Mark Lazarus the choice is easy. It came the night R's dismantled Birmingham City, from a level above them, in the first leg of their 1967 League Cup semi-final with a second-half display he believes was as near to perfection as makes no difference.

Lazarus played 235 games for Rangers over three spells from 1960 to 1967 but to him the performance against the Blue Noses of England's second city is a standout during his time at the club; one which saw him produce one of the performances of his life.

And this is from the player who was to prove the match-winner in the first major English cup final won by a Third Division team.

Lazarus was integral to the victory which assured Rangers of a trip to Wembley for a final in which they would make history. He made one, scored one and generally terrorised Birmingham.

There was an electric atmosphere as 34,295 squeezed into St Andrew's. Anticipation climbed towards fever pitch as the gladiators strode out on the field of battle. There is always a little extra involved when a cup tie is played under floodlights, especially when a Wembley final is at stake.

Birmingham's hopes were high. They were flying high and banging in the goals left right and centre in the Second Division as they aimed for a return to the top flight after a two-year absence.

The side was packed with leading performers such as Trevor Hockey, a fearsome sight with his full beard and penchant for the crunching tackle. And the attacking force of Barry

Queens Park Rangers' Greatest Games

Bridges and Geoff Vowden, with bustling Mickey Bullock at centre-forward, was to be feared.

Livewire Bridges cost a club record fee when he moved from Chelsea for £55,000 in May 1966 after developing a reputation as a fast, mobile striker of quality with a full England pedigree.

Vowden, who averaged around one goal in three over seven years with Brum, was en route to being the club's leading scorer for the third season in a row.

Bert Murray, the winger named by Brum boss Stan Cullis at right-back, had class and experience as a Chelsea regular when he joined former team-mate Bridges soon after the front-runner's arrival in the Midlands.

And there was the dependable Malcolm Beard at left-half. As the hosts, with their vociferous following urging on their every move, there seemed every chance that they could keep their half of the bargain as far as producing an all-Midlands final against First Division outfit West Bromwich Albion, who were entertaining West Ham United in their semi-final first leg the following evening.

Surely a Third Division side punching above their weight would be unable to prevent being hit to the canvas and eventually knocked out in the second leg scheduled in three weeks time?

Rangers drew in their attacking horns to adopt safety-first tactics unbecoming for a team who had developed a reputation for bulging the nets of opponents on a regular basis.

Either a 1-0 or 2-0 deficit to take into the second leg would not be insurmountable at Loftus Road, having turned their home ground into a fortress while swatting away league rivals (and, of course, any visitors in the early stages of the League Cup).

A gung-ho approach might see Birmingham pick them off at regular enough intervals to leave the second 90 minutes between the foes a formality for Blues.

Unfortunately defensive Rangers soon came under the cosh. It seemed to be going swimmingly for Cullis's side and Rangers were repeatedly rocked on their heels in the opening forays.

Vowden was about to pounce on a diverted blaster from Hockey before the QPR defence blocked his path at the expense of a corner. Bullock belted the ball against the bar from the flag kick. It was merely a temporary reprieve for Alec Stock's team. The hosts hit the front through Bridges after just four minutes.

Vowden got his head to another corner and guided the ball to Bridges who kneeled down to re-direct it into the top of the net.

The set piece remained a concern for the visitors with Birmingham's tails very much up. Rangers stopper Peter Springett was caught out by one more corner but breathed a sigh of relief as Bridges and Bobby Thomson snatched at the ball and missed the opportunity to double City's lead.

But Springett made amends with a stupendous stop from Vowden before clawing away a Murray effort at full stretch as Birmingham continued to carve out opportunities.

It was of paramount importance to Rangers' opponents that they built up a decent lead as they were only too aware of how strong the west London side had been at home.

But Ron Hunt and Frank Sibley were steady in the middle at the back for QPR, while full-backs Ian Watson and Jim Langley gave it their all as the back four successfully protected Springett and their goal for the rest of the half.

In front of them the industrious midfielder Keith Sanderson hurried and scurried in a display of work-rate which would embarrass most about their own effort in comparison.

v Birmingham City 1967

Rangers even managed to create a chance before the interval. It fell to the inimitable Rodney Marsh, who had been unable to prevent himself scoring even if he had wanted to in a prolific season. He caught Birmingham on the break and home goalkeeper Jim Herriot was only able to claw his effort away with one outstretched hand. The hosts had been warned.

And the second half saw Rangers, in their change strip of red shirts, get to grips with their hosts all over the pitch. The attitude remained conservative but when the chances came along they were taken.

Within nine minutes of the re-start Marsh had equalised as Rangers completed a century of goals for the season. The marvellous maverick headed home a free kick from Les Allen. Bridges caused brief consternation among the visitors and their fans as he darted through but, as he went by Springett, the goalkeeper got a hand to the ball to divert it away from his goal.

And soon after Rangers were 2-1 up. Marsh sent winger Mark Lazarus scampering down the right. Lazarus, leaving his left-back Colin Green beaten, passed the ball square to the unmarked Sanderson who helped it on as a Birmingham challenge allowed winger Roger Morgan to cut in from the left flank and drill the ball beyond Herriot.

Rangers hit their third goal ten minutes later with the help of some ingenuity from Marsh. The Rangers talisman was tightly marked as he received an Allen ball. Quick as a flash the QPR icon back-heeled the ball to Lazarus who was able to draw Herriot before slipping the ball past the home stopper.

Birmingham were shell-shocked and beaten. Their only tactic had to be damage limitation but unfortunately for the hosts and their supporters they were unable to prevent Rangers hitting the target once more late on. Marsh headed on a Langley free kick from inside Rangers' own half to Allen who drove home an angled drive.

And the second leg at Loftus Road proved a formality with Rangers romping through to the final with Marsh netting twice and captain Mike Keen once in a 3-1 victory.

The team had evolved into a potent force since chairman Jim Gregory began running the club in 1965.

Achieved with a combination of astute purchases such as Marsh and Allen, from Fulham and Tottenham Hotspur, allied with the old guard represented by Mark Lazarus and graduates of Rangers' outstanding youth system such as Sibley, the Morgan twins, Roger and Ian, Tony Hazell and Mick Leach.

The League Cup run – besides the team's domination of the Third Division – reflected the sea change at the start of the Gregory era.

Marsh cracked in four and Lazarus one to crush Colchester United 5-0 in the opening round. Aldershot proved a tougher nut to crack but another Marsh goal and a Langley penalty in the replay at home was enough to see them into the third round.

The first major test of their credentials as cup winners in waiting came in the last 16 against top-flight Leicester City, who were enjoying a fine season in the First Division with England's World Cup-winning goalkeeper Gordon Banks and international Derek Dougan.

Roger Morgan put Rangers in front to send the majority of the Loftus Road crowd into ecstasy. But within a minute the visitors were level through Dougan before the Irishman put Leicester 2-1 up at the interval.

Allen chipped Banks to level for Rangers before Sanderson and Lazarus combined for the former Spurs striker to net his second goal. And Lazarus made the final score 4-2.

Queens Park Rangers' Greatest Games

The home performance had Bryon Butler in the *Daily Telegraph* writing, 'Rangers were more a force of nature than a soccer team … they had a goalkeeper, five players who were forwards and five others who fancied they were.'

Paul Harris, a Rangers fan for more than 50 years, said, 'I was amongst a very big crowd of 16,000 plus and it was the very first time I had seen our team actually compete against a good First Division team which included the great Gordon Banks as well as Derek Dougan, but the R's totally outplayed them that night.'

Lazarus was clearly coming into his own and a virtuoso display by the winger helped Marsh score a double to see off Carlisle United 2-1 in the quarter-final.

The victory even saw the right-winger provoke laughs as well as goals when he jetted off down the flank without any shorts on.

His previous pair had been ripped and as he was given a new pair the ball arrived at his feet, an action he claimed was 'instinctive' and that he had 'nothing showing'.

Lazarus told your author in July 2013, 'I always think the game against Birmingham at St Andrew's was our best performance that season. We were right at the top of our game.

'It was a big game for us. We came out and absolutely slaughtered them. We outplayed them in every department. Everyone was on song and the support we got from our fans was incredible.

'At Loftus Rod we took the mickey out of them football wise. We were back-heeling it and playing the ball around. We knew we were through to the final.

'But, in a nutshell, what happened didn't make us believe we could win the whole thing. We knew we had a good side. Many of the Third Division teams we played that season were beaten before we got on the pitch. Home or away. Opposition managers feared us. All we knew was that we had a chance.'

19 v West Bromwich A 3-2

Football League Cup Final. Wembley Stadium
4 March 1967. Attendance: 97,952

QUEENS PARK RANGERS:	WEST BROMWICH ALBION:
Springett	Sheppard
Hazell	Cram
Langley	Williams
Keen	Collard
Hunt	Clarke
Sibley	Fraser
Lazarus	Brown
Sanderson	Astle
Allen	Kaye
Marsh	Hope
R. Morgan	Clark

Referee: Walter Crossley (Lancaster)

IT TOOK a few seconds of thought for match-winner Mark Lazarus to remember a few of the words and a bit of the tune. He gathered himself and, for the benefit of your author, launched into the song he had recorded to celebrate Queens Park Rangers lifting the 1967 Football League Cup beating West Bromwich Albion 3-2 at Wembley Stadium on 4 March 1967.

> 'Who'd have thought that we'd have done it.
> 'Who'd have thought that we'd be here.
> 'Who'd have thought we'd be knocking back champagne
> 'Who'd have thought we'd have won it.
> 'Who'd have thought we'd get a cheer.
> 'When the final whistle blew we'd won the game
> 'QPR – they're the greatest.'

The vinyl single 'QPR – The Greatest' was put out on the Eyemark label after the triumph and sold in thousands to euphoric Rangers fans eager for a memento of the day Lazarus believes was and remains the greatest in the club's 130-year history.

And for Lazarus and his team-mates it meant bonus money the players could share for putting the Third Division club into football's Hall of Fame as the first team from the division to win a final at Wembley – and against premier opposition.

They became the first team to lift a trophy under the Twin Towers since England captain Bobby Moore held the World Cup aloft the previous summer.

Lazarus said to your author in June 2013, 'All the players were supposed to sing with me but didn't want to so I ended up singing it. I didn't mind. I liked to get up and sing. It wasn't a hit and we didn't go on *Top of the Pops* but it boosted the players' pool. We weren't on any bonus to win, you know.'

85

Queens Park Rangers' Greatest Games

Lazarus and the team had plenty to sing about. The bare facts were that Rangers came back from two goals down at the interval – with former team-mate Clive Clark scoring both of West Brom's goals – to win 3-2 thanks to Roger Morgan, Rodney Marsh and Mark Lazarus.

But the day – full of sunshine on the eve of the Summer of Love – was a whole lot more. It was one to touch the emotions, send endorphins flowing and provide personal lifetime memories which will forever remain in the rose-tinted mind's eye of all those of a Rangers persuasion.

Lazarus has a treasure trove of those memories so before we go into the nuts and bolts of the 90 minutes which has given cause for everlasting celebration in London W12, let us share a few the match winner possesses.

The former winger, now 74, has them all compartmentalised and on instant recall, like his insightful recollections of the build-up after battling through six tough rounds to play the first one-off League Cup Final which had been a two-legged affair for its first six years.

He told your author in July 2013, 'We had a wonderful build-up. Stayed in a lovely hotel in London. Fats Domino, the singer, was staying there. He was over from America to do a concert. I like Fats a lot and we met him, although I didn't get the opportunity to sing his big hit "Blueberry Hill" with him!

'We got up on the Saturday morning and mingled around waiting for the coach to take us to Wembley. We're on our way to Wembley! There were crowds of people lining the street. It all added to the excitement.

'You never had to calm anyone down. There were a few young players in there. I was 27. I'd been around a bit. But you also had Les Allen, Mike Keen, Jimmy Langley and Rodney Marsh.

'Tony Hazell was a young boy and he may have thought "I'm up against a very good player in Clive Clark". But he certainly didn't show it as we journeyed to the stadium.

'We were all just pleased to be in the final. There was no pressure on us. We knew we had a chance and were a good Third Division side, but we were STILL a Third Division side. West Brom were a very good First Division side who had won the trophy the year before. With players like Clive and Jeff Astle. And they had just beaten West Ham convincingly in the semi-finals. To go to Wembley and beat such a team was not realistic. Nobody could have foreseen what happened.'

The calm mood on board the coach was reflected in the laughing of Lazarus and the players which greeted the sight of four Rangers supporters carrying a mock coffin with the legend depicted on it.

Lazarus said, 'The four of them had started in Westbourne Grove and marched to Wembley. People tagged on at Willesden and by the time we saw them there were thousands following this coffin. We all waved at each other. It was wonderful.'

Then the coach drove into the stadium and parked up close to the dressing room.

Lazarus said, 'We hopped off and went into the dressing room to see our all-white kit (instead of the familiar blue and white hoops with both sides ordered to change because the strips' colours clash).

'We had a read of the programme as we stood there in our lovely blazers and trousers made for the occasion. We went out on the pitch. A few supporters were already there. It was a beautiful day. The sun was shining. People were in shirt sleeves. What a day to go out and perform in front of 100,000 spectators. We went back in to get changed.'

v West Bromwich Albion 1967

Manager Alec Stock kept his pre-match instruction brief. Lazarus said, 'Alec didn't say much just simply, "This is our final. Just go out there and show the fans what you can do".'

Unfortunately the first half went pear-shaped for the all-white R's as Clark put West Brom two up.

The noise abatement society might have been called in as Rangers took the game to West Brom. Half the record final gate roared the team in all white as Lazarus, Les Allen and Keith Sanderson had the favourites on their heels, but it was Clark who began to keep a pre-match promise of 'I'll be the fellow scoring all the goals' when he put the Throstles ahead in the eighth minute.

West Brom took a stranglehold of midfield and it was left to Clark and Jeff Astle to give the Rangers rearguard palpitations.

Even so, QPR were able to show what they were made of. Allen, who last played at Wembley when he helped Tottenham Hotspur secure the first Football League and FA Cup Double this century six years earlier, forced West Brom stopper Dick Sheppard to save. And Marsh had the ball in the net from a bicycle kick before Lancaster referee Walter Crossley ruled the effort offside.

Clark was in lively mood. He skipped past an over-committed Hazell and a covering Ron Hunt to cross for Astle to bring a fine save out of Peter Springett.

The danger signs were there and soon the holders doubled their advantage. Again Astle and Clark were at the heart of the goal. The duo combined and the winger defeated Hazell once more to beat Springett after 25 minutes.

Rangers hung on and Roger Morgan forced a corner and from the kick his captain Mike Keen had one shot blocked before hitting the rebound wide.

The *Kilburn Times* reported, 'Their most ardent supporters were almost ill with disappointment at half-time as their white-shirted heroes trooped off with their heads nodding if not quite bowed.' But there was little doom and gloom inside the Rangers dressing room during the interval.

Lazarus said, 'We thought their second goal was offside but didn't panic. There was no ranting and raving from Alec at half-time. We were two nought down but we weren't bothered. We were still confident. It was a case of everybody saying "let's go out there and show 'em what we can do".'

Expectations were low among all those outside of the room as Lazarus and his teammates reflected on the opening 45 minutes. Perhaps red-shirted West Brom were of the opinion that a wounded animal is a dangerous animal as they opted to defend what they had. Marsh had an effort saved and Allen almost beat the offside flag from a Morgan ball.

Jimmy Hagan's side, unbeaten in the First Division, got twitchy. Sheppard was unsighted as a defender ran across his path and the ball hit the stopper and deflected goalwards, forcing defender John Kaye to clear as Allen charged in.

Marsh, after picking up the pieces of a blocked Allen shot, then ballooned over. Was that the moment Rangers would be confirmed losers?

No seemed to be the answer as he extravagantly dummied right before putting Morgan clear to the left for a shot which was scrambled away.

West Brom's heads seemed to have gone bar Sheppard but he was left helpless when Rangers reduced the arrears through Morgan who headed past him after Allen had chipped a free kick over the wall following a foul on Lazarus by Graham Williams after 63 minutes.

Doug Fraser brought down Marsh as tension increased in the ranks of Hagan's fading would-be heroes.

Queens Park Rangers' Greatest Games

Clark relieved the pressure for West Brom as he broke past Hazell, Hunt and Springett but crossed into an empty area where R's left-back Jim Langley, in his final game at the age of 38, comfortably cleared.

It was as if the Baggies had breathed their last. The 'red' fire was out, and Marsh almost immediately levelled in the 75th minute. The Rangers maverick broke from midfield with a relaxed stride, finding his way through the West Brom cover before hitting the ball low into the net off the stopper's right-hand post from the edge of the penalty area's D.

Rangers went for the kill. Lazarus came close to connecting with a cross from Morgan after Marsh had put the left-winger away.

West Brom defender Dennis Clarke chipped a mis-placed back-pass over Sheppard's goal. Lazarus was hauled down by his left-back Graham Williams. The pressure on the top-flight outfit was telling.

And finally it happened as the winning goal came eight minutes from time.

Rangers centre-back Ron Hunt ventured upfield, deep into the Baggies penalty area and, as an Albion defender fluffed his kick, he went for the loose ball to try and prod it home. Simultaneously the brave Sheppard dived at the defender's feet and the ball broke. Lazarus, with the goalkeeper face down, prostrate, sprinted from the edge of the area to meet it and guided it home with his left foot from close to the penalty spot.

Post-match there was a debate about whether Hunt had fouled the keeper, but there was no visible protest from West Brom as the ball went in.

Lazarus hit the post as he attempted to make it 4-2 before the Rangers crowd celebrated and big players like Marsh burst into tears.

The *Kilburn Times* reported, 'Out of an almost impossible situation the spirit and dedication of a Third Division team brought glory. They went on to win as thrilling a second half as Wembley had witnessed.'

Captain Mike Keen climbed the 39 steps to the Royal Box to take a grip of the League Cup, turn and lift it above his head towards ecstatic Rangers supporters.

And indeed Keen dedicated the victory to the QPR fans because 'they deserved to have something to celebrate'.

When the players returned to the pitchside, Lazarus had a plan. He wanted to share the moment with the supporters among them. Lazarus was known for racing over to celebrate with the fans when he notched a goal at Loftus Road. Logistically that was possible given the fact the spectators were so close to the pitch players could feel their collective hot breath when taking a throw-in.

Wembley, however, was a different proposition. Two fences and a greyhound track separated the supporters from the pitch. Even so Lazarus did his best to join them, only stopped by hugging, happy, tearful team-mates.

The muddied heroes in white shirts soaked in all the applause in the evening sunshine of a glorious day of weather and, in Rangers' case, of achievement.

Rangers returned to the hotel for a champagne party. Lazarus said, 'I've got a picture from that party of me eating a chicken leg and Jim Langley try to steal it off me.'

As for the game, Lazarus said, 'It was brilliant to score the deciding goal but when Rodney scored our second I think West Brom knew we were going to win. Their players started doubting themselves. The longer the game went on the more that was the case.

'I also think the save Peter made from Astle inspired everybody to do what we did. If he hadn't made it we would have been 3-0 down. I always think we won because of that magnificent save. I do put a lot down to Peter.'

v West Bromwich Albion 1967

Lazarus told of a re-run the players saw of the final. He said, 'I was at a dinner with Rodney Marsh and the rest of the players and they showed a film of it. In the first half Rodney and I never got a kick. Never showed at all. But in the second half, of course, it was a different story.

'Rodney turned round to me at this dinner and said "bloody hell, I didn't know you played that well".

'I don't think I did that well, but showed a bit of form in the second half. We all upped our game then. I could have got a hat-trick.'

Lazarus is full of praise for everyone's role in Rangers' finest hour. He said, 'I was delighted for Mike receiving the cup. He was our playmaker. Kept it simple. Alec always used to tell him that when he got the ball to give it to me. I was at outside-right and he was my right-half.

'Rodney was fantastic. He scored all season. And didn't let us down in the final. People talk about Stan Bowles being the greatest Rangers player. I don't agree. There are plenty of others who are better – nothing against Stan. I know who'd I'd pick between Stan and Rodney.

'I was pleased for the manager. He'd done so much for us. He was a gentleman. Everybody played their part. It was the best team QPR have ever had helped by a fantastic group of supporters. Wonderful times.'

One of those fans was club historian Gordon Macey, then a teenager. He told your author, 'My dad went straight down Wembley after we beat Birmingham 4-1 away – before we'd played the second leg. Couldn't see QPR throwing away such a lead. You could turn up and buy tickets for cup finals in those days. The good old days!

'We'd beaten some good teams and felt we couldn't lose. When we went 2-0 down at half-time I thought "well maybe we can".

'My dad bought me a hot-dog to cheer me up. He had also got me a rattle and I painted it blue and white the night before and it hadn't had time to dry out. People around me got sprayed with the wet paint! The pitch was good unlike when Swindon beat Arsenal on it two years later. Wembley had just held the Horse of the Year Show on it!'

Marsh said in *Shooting To The Top* that the achievement was something he was 'going to boast about for the rest of my days'.

He added, 'I cried. I could not help it. The tears rolled down my cheeks and I had to use the bottom of my shirt to wipe them away. Queens Park Rangers had just won the League Cup and, suddenly, all the tension and worry and emotion which had been bottled up inside of me began to drain away.

'I know it is impossible, but I wish every player could have the experience of being on the winning side in a cup final at Wembley. There can't be anything in football to match the big red glow.'

Les Allen said to the *Kilburn Times*, 'If there's a club in the country which deserves to win a major trophy it is Rangers.'

Langley said, 'I cried, it was the greatest moment of my life', while chairman Jim Gregory added, 'It was great. Just great.'

And Stock felt Rangers would win because of the side's 'talent, fitness and mood', adding that 'football's not a question of kicking a ball around'.

Stock said to the *Kilburn Times*, 'We won didn't we. Worried? Of course I was worried but the boys showed great spirit. It takes a great team to come back after being two goals down in a Wembley final.

Queens Park Rangers' Greatest Games

'There was some doubt about that winning goal but we deserved to win because we showed greater professionalism. We wanted to win and didn't give up.'

The only downside was that Rangers were not allowed to play in the Inter-Cities Fairs Cup the following season as a result of their win. The rules stated that only teams from each country's top tier would be able to play in it.

It would have been fascinating to have seen if those premier teams from the continent would have succumbed like the one which faced Rangers on 4 March 1967.

Lazarus gave his in-depth description of Rangers' goals to your author in July 2013.

He said, 'The first? I got the ball on the right-hand side. I went passed Graham Williams their left-back and he pulled me down. Free kick to us. Les Allen took the free kick. Roger Morgan headed it in.

'Number two? The ball was played by Mike Keen up to Rodney. He turned on the ball looking to play someone else in and couldn't see anybody. He just took the ball further and further towards goal. Nobody came to him. Didn't have to beat anybody.

'He was looking to lay the ball off somewhere. But he couldn't see anybody to lay it off to the closer he got to the goal. I think he was just outside the area. He just shot and the ball beat the goalkeeper, hit the inside of the post and went in.

'My goal? Ronnie Hunt had the ball. He passed me the ball. I flicked it up in the air and expected to be pushed. Ronnie kept on running. I hit it with the outside of my foot. The ball went up in the air. It looked like a rugby ball it had so much spin on it. When it came down it was still spinning so much that when their guy tried to intercept it he missed it. Ronnie carried on running and it went towards the goalkeeper. The ball is still spinning.

'Their goalkeeper tries to grab the ball on the floor. Ronnie had carried on running and there was a collision. The goalkeeper never had the ball and Ronnie was quite entitled to go for it. But they went together for the ball. I think Ronnie got to the ball and pushed it on to the keeper's hands or body. One of the two.

'The ball came back out. I happened to be there and just hit it in with my left foot into the corner of the net. There was somebody on the goal line. I think it was John Kaye. I had to be precise in where I put the ball. I just clipped it into the left-hand corner. I did quite well!

'I could have had a hat-trick. I hit a six-yard volley from a corner which was saved on the line by a player who didn't know much about it.

'Then I picked the ball up in the centre of the pitch on the halfway line, went past a couple of West Brom players to the edge of the box, hit the ball and the keeper just pushed it on to the post.'

v Oxford United 5-1

10 October 1967. Loftus Road
Football League Cup. Attendance: 16,989

QUEENS PARK RANGERS:
Springett
Clement
Harris
Keen
Hunt
Keetch
I. Morgan
Allen
Leach
Wilks
R. Morgan

OXFORD UNITED:
Sherratt
Beavon
Lloyd
Smithson
Kyle
Clarke
Skeen
Hale
Bullock
Jones
Thornley

Referee: Eric T. Jennings (Stourbridge)

ALAN WILKS displayed a good line in self-deprecation while at Queens Park Rangers. The plaster had been removed from an injured leg and he had been advised to undertake a course of exercise to ensure there was no muscle wastage in it.

The slim, gangling striker rejected the suggestion, smiling, 'There are no muscles there to waste.'

Two decades later he revealed his innate modesty when reminded of the fact he scored a record five goals in Rangers' 5-1 League Cup victory against Oxford United under the Loftus Road floodlights.

The 'nudge' came, states a 2010 internet post from QPR fan Ian, following a charity match in which Wilks belted in a goal from 40 yards. Ian posts, 'In the bar after the game I mentioned that I was there for his most famous appearance for the R's. He looked slightly embarrassed and was suitably modest.'

It seems just as well that Wilks possesses a sense of humour and humility with the other comments flying around cyberspace ranging from back-handed compliments ('had the skills but couldn't hit a barn door apart from THAT game') to downright personal ('with that mop of curly hair, looked a bit of a tart') from a few of the 16,989 spectators there that famous night when Wilks wrote himself in the club's history books.

The affectionate reaction appears to underplay the significance to the point of flippancy, bordering on disrespect.

It must be remembered that to this day (on publication of this book), no other Super Hoop has been able to hit the back of the net as many times in one game as Wilks did as he ensured the League Cup holders took a second step in defence of the trophy.

Wilks's unruly shock of frizzy auburn hair stood out to those present, along with his loping gait; his 'elastic' legs which rode robust challenges; his feet capable of killing the ball in an instant.

Queens Park Rangers' Greatest Games

Wilks had a football brain capable of passing it around the field with pinpoint accuracy and effectiveness.

Most obviously, of course, the former Chelsea striker, signed as an understudy to Rodney Marsh, stood out because of his antennae for knowing how to find the back of the onion bag.

He had put on a man of the match performance in Rangers' previous game to snatch the winner against Bolton Wanderers in the same modest Theatre of Dreams just three days earlier.

His performance came in the match he first donned the number 10 shirt in the campaign. It was a display which persuaded Stock to keep him in the side for the visit of the U's.

His efforts had already helped promoted QPR set the pace in the league with eight wins and a draw in their 11 opening games, a run that laid the foundations of great things to come by the season's close.

And the five-goal haul against Oxford rubber-stamped his contribution to the rampant Rangers' cause.

Or as Sean Kilfeather colourfully summed up in the *Kilburn Times*, 'He [Wilks] caused as much havoc in the ranks of the pedestrian Oxford United team as a giraffe in an anthill.'

It brings to mind a modern-day striker who wore the blue and white hoops from 2000–2002. Peter Crouch, though, at 6ft 7in, was a full eight inches taller than Wilks and yet provoked comparable comments. Words like 'freakish' and 'gangling' are examples.

Because of the way a person is built it leads to assumptions. How can you be 'all arms and legs', as one QPR fan described Wilks, and yet have the capability of performing sublime on-the-ground ball skills? Yet, like Crouch, it was apparent against Oxford that 'Marsh Lite' had the techniques in his locker.

It was partly because of the person he was understudying that Wilks got limited opportunities to show he was, as John Marks says in *Heroes in Hoops*, a 'cultured, gifted and sometimes dazzling performer' and he moved on to Gillingham in 1971 and from Priestfield into non-league football.

But he certainly took on the starring role against Oxford that would have had theatre audiences on their feet clapping and roaring 'encore' if it had been enacted on a West End stage. It might even have persuaded cinema audiences to do something similar at a multiplex near you, or might have brought him either an Olivier or an Oscar depending on the performing art. As it was the player who hailed from just up the M40 from Shepherd's Bush at Slough, which brought us Ricky Gervais's comedy character David Brent, should have been given a match of a lifetime award after returning to the dressing room leaving more than contented smiles on the faces of the Loftus Road faithful who had lacked any faith in him 90 minutes earlier.

The crowd chanted 'Rod-ney' before the kick-off. They were missing their hero, one Rodney Marsh, who had been missing from the line-up since the start of the season because of a fractured foot sustained in training.

Marsh had made the number 10 shirt his own. And in turn made it synonymous as the one worn by the fans' favourite player, something which persisted through a few generations.

Mick Leach had been given the 'burden' of wearing it in the league and, as Rangers, had made a roaring start to the campaign to put themselves top and he had scored a few, so the Marsh devotees had let the forward off the hook.

v Oxford United 1967

But against Oxford the likeable Leach was leading the line with number 9 on his back. It was Wilks who had the 'Marsh shirt'.

The striker took just 90 seconds to start proving he might not be too bad a substitute.

Rangers right-winger Ian Morgan, with his identical twin brother on the opposite flank, had already forced Oxford goalkeeper Brian Sherratt into a save with the ball cleared out to the right wing. Wilks picked it up, moved forward a little and thundered home from an acute angle with his left foot.

Wilks secured his second goal under ten minutes later. He launched his 5ft 11in frame into the air to connect with a Morgan cross and his header beat Sherratt.

He completed his hat-trick with a cool finish after Les Allen, reverted to the role of goal-maker rather than taker this evening, and Ian Morgan had combined.

Rangers were swift, aggressive and fluent with the Morgan brothers at full throttle down the flanks. They appeared a class above, underlining that they were a side who had left the Third Division the previous season with no intention of returning to it.

But the goals – at least temporarily – dried up as they showed a tendency to over-cook their moves. There was a lack of final balls into danger areas, to paraphrase a modern cliché uttered by many a modern manager.

The visitors, who had a successful Third Division campaign that season which ended in promotion as champions, showed a little of what they had in a rare counter-attack or two. It might have lacked the greater sophistication of their hosts. It was more about method, muscle and courage as opposed to pace, flair and panache.

Rangers full-backs Dave Clement and Allan Harris were solid enough, but the middle of the defence was adjudged to have represented a soft underbelly by eyewitnesses. Twice home goalkeeper Ron Springett had to show his agility by keeping out efforts from the visitors.

And Springett breathed a sigh of relief when unmarked U's winger Barry Thornley headed over another opportunity created on the break by the visitors.

The writing appeared to be on the wall but was not heeded by Rangers. England international Springett could do nothing to prevent Oxford pegging back the not-so-Super Hoops a minute before the interval. Again he was exposed by loose marking and Mike Bullock, free of any tight shackles, netted.

Oxford had their tails up and dominated after the interval – until 20 minutes from time. And we all know who stepped back into the limelight, don't we?

Rangers skipper Mike Keen made a marauding run which cut the Oxford resistance to ribbons. Ever the provider, Keen opted against an attempt to put the ball into the net. Instead he gave it to Wilks for a simple tap-in.

Marsh had enhanced his reputation by equalling the club record of four goals in a game the previous season. Again it was in the League Cup. Again they helped R's dispense with another visiting United, from Colchester. And, again, it was part of a five-goal victory.

Wilks went one better, of course. Leach hit the bar – something he had done earlier – with a header and Wilks dived in to head the dropping ball into the net.

The striker had netted four in a reserve game but there is always room for improvement. And those Marsh fans enjoyed the moment their latest focus of attention did, along with many others in the crowd, as the chants of 'Wil-ksee, Wil-ksee' wafted across the ground.

Wilks's efforts might even make a couple of 'Rod-ney' fans – who predicted their hero would 'go to heaven' in a letter revealed in the match programme by club secretary Ron Phillips – allow 'Marsh Lite' to join their idol at the Pearly Gates.

Queens Park Rangers' Greatest Games

Wilks's manager Alec Stock told the *Daily Mail*, 'He (Wilks) has never scored five before nor, as far as I know, has anyone at the club. Yet it did not surprise me for he is our deadliest finisher.'

Mark Lazarus, a substitute for Rangers that night, told your author in July 2013, 'Alan looked gangly but had good ball skills and, particularly against Oxford, knew where the goal was.'

It proved to be Wilks's only appearance in the League Cup that season.

Rangers were given a bye in the first round due to their higher status in the league following promotion and the fact they were holders.

Leach kept Marsh's number 10 shirt warm to good effect as QPR began the campaign in round two. He scored as Hull City were defeated 2-1 at Loftus Road, with captain Mike Keen scoring one of his occasional goals.

And after the 90-minute Oxford odyssey, Wilks was on the sidelines as Burnley arrived in London W12 for a fourth-round tie.

Their visitors were from the First Division. It was an opportunity to see whether Rangers, with their dreams of immediate promotion, could compete in the top grade.

Burnley ran a tight ship, catching Rangers out on the counter attack. Their conversion rate was impressive. They only created three major chances.

QPR carved out double the amount of opportunities but only had a Frank Sibley goal to show for it. Ironically, Sibley, who normally adopted a defensive role, was wearing number 10.

But the player wearing the shirt in the competition for Rangers that season worthy of the biggest headlines was not Sibley. It was not Marsh. Push modesty aside and take a bow Alan Wilks.

21 v Aston Villa 2-1

Football League Second Division. Villa Park
11 May 1968. Attendance: 33,785

QUEENS PARK RANGERS:	ASTON VILLA:
Kelly	Dunn
Watson	Wright
Harris	Bradley
Keen	Edwards
Keetch	Mitchinson
Hazell	Park
I. Morgan	Chatterley
Leach	Greenhalgh
Clarke	Anderson
Marsh	Rudge
Allen	Godfrey

Referee: Leo Callaghan

ALEC STOCK told your author in 1983, 'I did my little bit.' It was an extraordinary understatement given the former Army captain's 'little bit' had guided his Queens Park Rangers 'troops' through campaigns which resulted in the longest period of sustained trophy-collecting yet experienced by the west London club formed more than 70 years before his arrival at Loftus Road as a manager in 1959.

Stock had served Rangers as a player prior to the Second World War but he will forever be remembered in the hearts of QPR supporters for the silverware, respect and entertaining football his team brought to London W12. He ensured the moniker 'super' in Super Hoops was not misplaced.

The day the R's travelled to Aston Villa and returned having been promoted to the top flight represented Stock's crowning glory.

A controversial goal from Mick Leach and an own goal with just eight minutes of a gruelling season remaining sealed a 2-1 victory at Villa Park and First Division status for Rangers more than 80 years after their foundation. And was by the smallest of margins, pipping Blackpool for the second and final spot by just 0.210 of a goal on goal average.

Rangers had become the first club to achieve back-to-back promotions into the top flight since Charlton Athletic before the Second World War.

It had been achieved through what Stock described as 'guts and club pride' more than fantasy football. There was a growing injury crisis (the runaway championship success of the previous season was with a settled side), limited outstanding displays despite encouraging results and the physical approach of many opponents, and the increased mental pressure which came with football at a higher level.

But Rangers, through it all, adopted a never-say-die attitude, even when the tension caused internal arguments, and a sense of urgency. Mark Lazarus, the League Cup Final hero who shone at the start of the campaign, told your author in July 2013, 'It was tough. Rangers managed to do it because they had fighters in the team.'

Queens Park Rangers' Greatest Games

Marsh remarked in *Shooting To The Top*, 'We managed to keep our heads when it mattered.'

The performance against Villa was far from pretty. The crowd-pleasing style from Rangers was largely absent. Nerves cramped the expansive qualities they had a reputation for displaying.

Rangers were one of three promotion contenders with none of the places yet decided and just 90 minutes of the season remaining as they kicked off at Villa Park on 11 May 1968.

Realistically it looked a two-horse race between Rangers and Blackpool for the second promotion spot with Ipswich almost certain to be declared champions barring a mathematical miracle.

Stock stoked up his players before kick-off in the dressing room by telling his team, 'We've come a long way. Let's not throw it away. It's with you now.'

And at the start it looked as though the responsibility was weighing too heavily on the 11 individuals he had just rallied.

Villa were completing a less than notable league season. On paper they had some decent players like Lew Chatterley and Willie Anderson. But their position in the lower reaches of the division betrayed the current state of a club who had spent more than a few years bathing in the sunshine of success at the highest level.

Yet it was the hosts who dominated early doors, looking more the part of a team with pretensions of becoming members of the First Division the following season than QPR.

Rangers treated the ball like a hot potato. Their passing was rushed. Their decision-making was questionable. They struggled to find a tempo which suited them.

It came as no surprise the hosts took the lead when Tommy Mitchinson pounced.

When Rangers returned to the dressing room at half-time, there were no recriminations. The players did not need to be told they had had a shocker in the opening 45 minutes.

Fortunately for R's they were allowed to take more of a grip on the game after the interval.

There did not seem to be any discernible improvement in Rangers' game but their hosts began to drop their level. It was Villa's turn to be seemingly gripped by bad nerves, even though they were limited to pride as an incentive.

The Daily Telegraph reported, 'The tension which had scattered Rangers' wits now spread insidiously to Villa.'

R's pressed but had little to show in the way of chances. And with 20 minutes left hopes of going up to face the big boys the following term were fast disappearing.

Cue Mick Leach. The striker headed a Les Allen corner against goalkeeper John Dunn and it rebounded off the underside of the bar.

As the spherical object dropped, Dunn grabbed it. Referee Leo Callaghan adjudged immediately that the ball had crossed the line for a nano-second. Goal.

It was the cause of much consternation among those in claret and blue shirts. No doubt they would have been first in the queue in calling for goal-line technology had it been available. In contrast, of course, there was much celebration in the away camp.

A QPR fan holding a transistor radio to his ear informed R's stopper Mike Kelly that Blackpool were beating Huddersfield 3-1. As it stood a draw was not enough for the Super Hoops.

The news went around the visiting players and hearts sank. Rodney Marsh was convinced the dream was over. And most of his team-mates agreed.

v Aston Villa 1968

Rangers put on a brave front and pushed forward. The minutes ticked by until eight remained on the clock. QPR struck. Or rather Rangers scored when Villa defender Keith Bradley found his own net.

Frank Clarke tried to find Marsh with a ball inside a defender from the edge of the area. Marsh moved menacingly towards the ball and was looking for a spot to plant it into the net. Right-back Bradley tried to intercept but only succeeded in deflecting the ball beyond Dunn into one corner of the net as Marsh's momentum carried him into the other.

All the nerves just evaporated. Marsh said in *Shooting To The Top*, 'It was like a ton weight had been lifted off our shoulders. Everybody was shouting, nobody was listening, and I remember thinking it was just as well our dressing room was so big because every Rangers supporter in Birmingham seemed to find his way in.'

The players' celebration was low-key, a quiet drink on the coach. When Rangers returned to the capital Stock's assistant Bill Dodgin Junior and a few members of the side went to visit the hospital where two of their injured squad members lay recovering, Roger Morgan and Dave Clement.

Dodgin and Co. wanted an inclusive celebration with a pair who had more than played their part. And their thoughts were also with others who had been crocked in the cause.

Besides Morgan and Clement, Frank Sibley, Ian Watson and Bobby Finch had endured cartilage operations. Ron Hunt was sidelined for four months following surgery on a kidney, while Keith Sanderson, Alan Wilks, Leach and Marsh, of course, had nursed their broken bones during an unforgettable season.

The road to Villa Park – in the 'lucky' coach, which had transported them to Birmingham City for their victory in the first leg of their League Cup semi-final the previous season – was literally 111 miles, but in reality it stretched back to close to the start of a rough, tough season.

Talisman Rodney Marsh, who had plundered 44 goals while helping Rangers to the League Cup and Third Division title double in the 1966/67 season, suffered a broken right foot in pre-season training which put him out for the opening 16 games.

There was also the question of priorities. What would come first? If elevation into the top echelons of football was top of the list would the defence of the League Cup and, indeed, the FA Cup campaign, act as a distraction to realising the chief aim?

Cup glory, of course, gives players an instant buzz, but for a manager the true test of a team is how consistent they can be for the entire campaign rather than a few flashes of form in knockout competitions.

True, Rangers had managed success in league and cup, but to expect lightning to strike twice seemed a tall order.

As it turned out the fact Rangers fell at the first fence in the FA Cup and saw their defence of the League Cup only last a couple of rounds appeared to focus minds on reaching the Promised Land of the First Division as the season unfolded. It seemed, though, too much would have been left on their plates.

As Marsh said in *Shooting To The Top*, 'We were already obsessed with getting into Division One when FA Cup time came around.

'Hundreds of managers and players, I know, have said it in the past, "Now we are beaten in the Cup, we are free to concentrate on the League." Well, I'm saying it again, this is exactly how we felt.'

The only newcomer to arrive at Loftus Road was left-back Allan Harris with 38-year-old Jim Langley retiring.

Queens Park Rangers' Greatest Games

Stock's faith in the players which had brought so much glory to the club looked justified early doors as Rangers, even without Marsh, made a flying start.

They were top after the first six games, dropping just a single point with an inspirational Mark Lazarus seeming desperate to ensure he could cover Marsh in terms of the experience and goals he could give the team.

Results became more mixed but, even with the cup competitions out of the way, tension was in the air. It was reflected when QPR threw away a 3-1 lead with four minutes left at Charlton Athletic on 5 February 1968.

Stock and assistant Bill Dodgin Junior conducted a red-hot dressing room inquest claiming the players were over-confident.

Inquests followed through the week as verbal mud was slung around. Rangers crashed 4-0 at Derby County a couple of weeks later. The poor performance made QPR appreciate that if they did not compose themselves and push on again they could kiss promotion goodbye.

The fight returned as Rangers scored a trio of 1-1 draws including one against Millwall which Marsh describes as including 'probably the best goal of my life' after nutmegging two Lions defenders.

Striker Frank Clarke, who Fulham had purchased to take on Marsh's mantle at Craven Cottage, was brought in and added plenty of edge and effort. And he netted a goal in a 2-0 win over promotion rivals Blackpool to help Rangers secure two points which were to prove vital as the season came to a tight finish.

The Seasiders, with Ipswich Town, had been breathing so hotly down Rangers' neck that experts stated back-to-back promotions might prove a step too far for the west Londoners.

Rangers stemmed a late run from Blackburn Rovers by beating them at Ewood Park and they overcame Cardiff City on Good Friday, with Marsh sidelined through a foot injury, to move five points clear.

Stock's men returned to earth with a bump the following day with a 3-1 loss at Middlesbrough.

Marsh pleaded with his manager to play at Cardiff on the Tuesday. With his foot strapped up, he got a kick on his injured foot as he earned Rangers a penalty. But Rangers' spot-kick expert, with his foot hurting and the home crowd jeering, asked captain Mike Keen to take it.

Keen's effort was saved. R's ended up losing the encounter and Ipswich took over the lead from them on goal difference with a game in hand. And Blackpool were just a point behind.

Nerves became shredded in the Rangers camp with players losing their tempers with each other in training.

But spirits were raised as Mick Leach scored from a free kick by substitute Les Allen – a replacement for the stricken Roger Morgan (who had lost his long-term battle with cartilage trouble) – in the last minute to earn Rangers a 2-2 draw against their other arch rivals Ipswich.

It came after the hosts had come back to lead through a Leach own goal and Ray Crawford after Marsh, ordered by Stock to resume penalty duties, had put R's in front from the spot.

But it left QPR, Ipswich and Blackpool all on 54 points. Ipswich won their game in hand and all three rivals had two games left.

All three won their penultimate games which left the promotion going down to the wire.

And, as the Rangers coach trundled up the M1, Blackpool were travelling to Huddersfield with Ipswich entertaining Blackburn.

Again all three won but, if you believe in superstition, as Stock's men travelled back to west London and the Seasiders returned to, er, the sea, QPR's mode of transport had proved the luckier. Just. Stock's team had made it.

Actor and writer Paul Whitehouse poked a little gentle fun at Stock through his comic character Ron Manager ('Marvellous isn't it? Small boys, jumpers for goalposts, enduring images, rolling the ball in dog muck and getting your friends to head it') in TV's *The Fast Show*.

And Whitehouse told *FourFourTwo* magazine in 2000, 'Ron is part Alec Stock and a bloke I used to work with on Hackney Council called Danny Wiseman. I suppose there's a bit of old-style punditry in there as well – "You know the referee with his flag, hmmm? Did he fight in the Second World War?"'

Well, Stock, who managed FA Cup giant-killers Yeovil, Leyton Orient and Roma prior to Rangers, did see action as a soldier, of course, and he saw plenty of peace-time action as a football boss.

His management style was based on the qualities of leadership he displayed in action during the war as captain and tank commander

In fact Mark Lazarus, who helped Rangers complete back-to-back promotions into the top flight, believes Stock was all about man-management rather than game plans.

Lazarus told your author in July 2013, 'Alec didn't say much. He was a manager of people. Not a football manager. He never said do this or do that. As he was a captain in the Army he knew how to manoeuvre men. He wasn't talking to boys.

'He was a shoulder to cry on. To take your troubles to. People had a lot of respect for him as a man.

'Manager-wise all he would tell us would be "run it kick it". He wasn't a Terry Venables or Dave Sexton (who later managed Rangers). Or even a Bill Dodgin Junior.

'Alec was a man-manager. A motivator. You respected him. You gave him what you could.

'He never said to Rodney Marsh "go out there and do this and do that". He never came up to me and said anything either. He just used to say "just go out and show the fans what you can do". Not a tactician. I loved him. He used to slap me around verbally, though. If we got beat, it was my fault.'

Marsh said in *Shooting To The Top*, referring to the time he was out injured at the start of the 1967/68 season, 'I became aware of the agony that every manager, every coach has to suffer. I sat next to Alec Stock and Bill Dodgin and, believe me, they are more involved in a game than any of their players.

'They never sit still. They never relax. It must be the most frustrating job in the world, because their future is in the hands of the players.'

It was a shame circumstances led to Stock being unable to lead Rangers out in the First Division.

His development of the side, using the players who graduated from the youth ranks alongside the likes of Lazarus and Marsh, and the astute stewardship of chairman and owner Jim Gregory, dovetailed to explain the main reason Rangers would be playing in the top flight for the first time in their history for the 1968/69 season.

Queens Park Rangers' Greatest Games

Suddenly the Stock-Gregory axis was split asunder for the time being, though the manager was to return as a caretaker manager and director.

A bout of asthma sidelined Stock for three months and the manager was gone before the First Division odyssey had begun.

The manager himself claimed in his autobiography *A Little Thing Called Pride* that the chairman had given him the old heave-ho for 'being ill' and that he had planned to take the reins back over from caretaker boss Bill Dodgin Junior.

Whatever happened, it was a sad denouement to the greatest of times in Rangers' history. Still, no one can ever take away from Stock that he is the only manager to guide the club to back-to-back promotions into the premier division of English football and a major domestic cup.

22 v Leicester City 1-1
Football League First Division. Loftus Road
10 August 1968. Attendance: 21,494

QUEENS PARK RANGERS:
Springett
Finch
Harris
Keen
Watson
Hazell
I. Morgan
Sibley
F. Clarke (Allen)
Wilks
R. Morgan

LEICESTER CITY:
Shilton
Nish
Woollett
Sjoberg
Manley
Cross
Bell
Stringfellow
Clarke
Gibson
Glover

Referee: K.H. Burns (Worcester)

L**ES ALLEN** scored Queens Park Rangers' first goal in the top flight and it earned them their first point at the premier level of English football at their first attempt. Substitute Allen's late strike cancelled out an Allan Clarke effort in the historic 1-1 draw against Leicester City at Loftus Road on Saturday 10 August 1968.

The outstanding striker is the patriarch of the phenomenal Allen family. His sons Clive and Bradley also pulled on the Super Hoops, as did nephew Martin.

But Les was the member of the footballing family who can rightly claim to have been the most successful. He had already been part of the historic Tottenham Hotspur side which became the first club in the 20th century to win the FA Cup and Football League championship in the same season by the time he arrived at QPR.

And since his record £20,000 signing from Spurs in July 1965 he had been integral to Rangers' back-to-back promotions and League Cup triumph with his nous, versatility (taking on striking and midfield roles), team ethic and goals, top scoring in his first season.

If anyone deserved to land the landmark mark on a landmark occasion for the R's it was Allen. It is often the case that when the going gets tough the tough get going and certainly Allen displayed his fulsome qualities against Matt Gillies's Leicester.

It was a day which had been anticipated the moment the whistle blew to end the gut-wrenching, tension-packed victory against Aston Villa on 11 May 1967.

Keith Bradley's own goal which sealed the victory required to ensure promotion at Villa Park was hailed as the most important in Rangers' history.

It was what everybody at the club had worked towards – the players, the management, coaches, the directors, the medical team, those on the ground staff, the administrators, Daphne the telephone operator, and others.

It was what they wanted for the loyal supporters who had been lifted by a Rodney Marsh-inspired side which had achieved back-to-back promotions and a League Cup triumph.

Queens Park Rangers' Greatest Games

It was like a ground floor office boy getting in the lift to the penthouse offices to join the company big wigs or like the film extra now starring in a Hollywood blockbuster; the entertainer used to the bread-and-butter club circuit in the provinces landing a gig at the 02 Arena. But once the euphoria which enveloped those of a Super Hoops persuasion having a super time after the final whistle at Villa Park had subsided, the new challenges of survival at the top level had to be faced.

Forward-thinking owner and chairman Jim Gregory wanted a stadium worthy of the top flight.

Initially he approached Brentford with Griffin Park offering a capacity of 40,000 and suggested a merger between the neighbours and erstwhile rivals.

When the idea was eventually rejected by both parties, he set about splashing the cash on Loftus Road in an attempt to bring it up to premier scratch.

The ground was certainly in need of modernisation. And Gregory set about organising a £200,000 stand along the South Africa Road side to replace the terracing and earth bank.

Organising such a project ensured a solution to the challenge of setting a suitable stage for such a high level of football.

But there were a whole raft of other challenges. There was the reality of how to manage the expectations of fans who had only known what life was like in the lower reaches of the Football League, chiefly in the Third Division, as they prepared to receive the Foxes.

Whether the playing squad was good enough to maintain their new status without the injection of fresh blood, especially as talisman Rodney Marsh was sidelined with injury for the club's debut in the league which was to become the Premier League 24 years into the future.

Perhaps most crucially of all was whether disruption behind the scenes would have a negative effect on the campaign with Bill Dodgin Junior taking over as caretaker manager in time for the big kick-off in the rarefied air of the First Division.

Alec Stock, the boss who had guided the side for close to a decade, the second half of which had put them on the glory road, had been taken unwell.

Mr Rangers, as Stock had become known, had taken a lot out of himself physically with asthma problems coming to the fore in getting his club to the Promised Land.

Rangers had proved they could cut it with the big boys. Their second-half performance to overcome First Division outfit West Bromwich Albion's 2-0 interval advantage in the 1967 League Cup Final showed that, and so did the professional job successful completed against top-flight Leicester City en route to that final.

There must have been a slight feeling of relief when the fixtures first landed on the desk of club secretary Ron Phillips and it was discovered the Foxes would be the first test of Rangers' mettle in the First Division.

Surely facing a side you had the measure of less than two years before – at a time when their vanquished opponents were pulling up few trees in the top grade that season – was preferable to journeying into the unknown against a team you only knew mainly from either *Match of the Day* or *The Big Match* on the telly? Better the devil you know, so to speak. Especially the devil you have beaten.

But overcoming higher level opponents in a knockout competition is a different kettle of fish to sniffing out a victory in the top tier. The Davids always have that extra incentive of bringing down Goliaths.

Now Rangers and Leicester were on a level playing field. Success and failure was not judged on one game but over 42 – a marathon rather than sprint.

v Leicester City 1968

All who had invested their time, energy, money and emotions in Rangers were keeping their fingers crossed it would all work out.

The afternoon of Saturday 19 August 1968 was a long one for them all. It was hot and sunny. There was a buzz around the ground. A slice of showbiz glamour was added with Terence Stamp, one of THE faces of the Swinging Sixties and boyfriend to fellow actors Julie Christie and Bridget Bardot and model Jean Shrimpton. Alongside him was Tommy Steele, the rock and roller turned musical star.

The ground was certainly rocking and rolling with getting on for 25,000 wedged in eager to see Rangers make history.

Gregory's vision of a stand was taking shape with flats and houses backing on to it remaining visible through the skeleton of its construction.

The green sward was pristine. All it needed were the gladiators to enter the arena. And they did to prolonged applause.

Leicester City had Peter Shilton in goal in place of England World Cup-winning hero Gordon Banks from the previous time the two sides had met at Loftus Road.

And the Foxes were also unveiling a new striker, Allan Clarke, who had just been signed from Fulham. Ironically his elder brother Frank was operating in the same position for the Super Hoops.

The R's also had Alan Wilks, the mercurial forward, alongside him wearing the number 10 shirt in place of the stricken Marsh.

Wilks had made his name the previous season by becoming the first Ranger to score five goals in a game. But taking on an experienced top-flight outfit is more than a tad trickier than dismissing a team from the lower leagues, even if Oxford United ended up Third Division champions. Yet Wilks was determined to give it his best shot and on another day could have emulated the total he achieved against the U's.

A contemporary report by the *Kilburn Times* stated, 'He [Wilks] had the sort of blooding in the First Division that causes most footballers to wake up in a cold sweat in the middle of the night. I've never seen a player so completely out of luck.'

Rangers showed themselves capable of matching fire with fire and finesse with finesse.

They delighted the crowd with the performance, buoyed by the confidence playing at home had given them as they had turned it into a fortress while climbing the leagues.

It was all the more pleasing because they knew the aura of invincibility they had shown at Loftus Road in the Third and Second Divisions would be sorely tested against the creme de la creme of English football.

But confidence is transitory and it began to lower as opportunities to score came and went. QPR cut through an erratic Leicester reargaurd like a knife through butter on occasion. But the visitors had what Rangers, and in particular Wilks, lacked – good fortune.

City hung on for dear life as their outfield players blocked the ball with every part of their anatomies.

Mike Keen and the returning Frank Sibley provided the source from which Rangers flowed. They fed the identical Morgan twins, Ian and Roger, who provided darting runs and a stream of crosses. Only a finishing touch was required.

Their defence was shored up with Ian Watson keeping a tight rein on Allan Clarke and Tony Hazell's crisp tackling and interceptions nipping any danger in the bud.

The enterprising Hazell, and fellow defender Allan Harris, also found time to join in the fun going forward.

Queens Park Rangers' Greatest Games

Left-back Harris almost caught out Leicester when he launched a long ball into the heart of the area only for John Sjoberg to make a late recovery and clear the danger.

Frank Clarke had a drive half-saved by a fledgling Shilton, destined to break the England record for caps in the future. The ball went straight back out to Wilks but the striker slipped and fell to the turf as he prepared to shoot.

Ian Morgan had a shot on the turn blocked after a foraging run from Sibley through a series of opposing challenges. And Shilton scrambled away a second effort from the winger from the rebound at the foot of the upright.

Wilks, showing impressive ball skills, made a fine solo run but was undone by his hesitancy in front of Shilton's goal. The hosts continued to knock on the door but City were not opening it.

Rangers' level of play dropped off on the re-start; their batteries appeared to be emptying in front of the shirt-sleeved crowd's eyes.

And with just 20 minutes remaining Leicester took advantage – and the lead.

Rangers failed to cut out a ball from the right which landed at the feet of Mike Stringfellow on the left and the winger stroked the ball to Allan Clarke to beat Ron Springett, who had returned to Rangers from Sheffield Wednesday in exchange for his brother Peter the year before. Deflation. But Rangers soon pumped themselves back up and Allen scored the equaliser five minutes later.

Wilks had yet another effort blocked and the loose ball fell to Allen, on as a substitute for Frank Clarke. The experienced striker pivoted on the ball and send it past Shilton. Rangers' first point as well as first goal had been collected. The performance, despite the absences of Keith Sanderson and Mike Kelly as well as Marsh, gave Rangers cause for encouragement as one reporter observed, 'If this admirable debut is any criterion, then Rangers are up to stay.'

In hindsight, the judgement proved wrong. They were unable to secure their first top-flight win until the 13th fixture when Ipswich Town came to Loftus Road on a Tuesday night and were defeated 2-1.

Barry Bridges, who had been signed from Birmingham City by now, and Roger Morgan, with a wonder strike, grabbed the goals on another historic occasion for Rangers.

Stock finally left the club in November 1968 when Tommy Docherty took over for just 28 days – with the Doc citing interference from Gregory for his departure – before Les Allen was handed what proved to be a poisoned chalice as Rangers finished the season rock bottom and relegated.

Ian Morgan said in an interview posted on QPRnet.com, 'Losing so many games by the odd goal was our problem. Our biggest mistake was we didn't sign any experienced first division players.

'After we got relegated Terry Venables came to the club and he would have been exactly what we needed, we signed him a year too late. The club was full of enthusiastic youngsters and we really needed someone who had been there and done it before, that's why we lost so many games I think.

'I remember going up to Old Trafford and we were 3-1 down with just 15 minutes to play and we lost 8-1, we weren't that bad and it shouldn't have happened. There were so many games where we played well but got nothing out of them.

'It was a terrible shame [Stock leaving], we were very surprised at the time and after everything he'd done for the club it was a shame that he didn't get the chance. I idolised the fella.'

v Leicester City 1968

Roger Morgan said in the joint interview, 'It was very sad to see him [Stock] go, especially when we'd known and worked with him for so long. I think we played Leicester at home in the first game and we were up against it from day one. It was never the same.

'We were so lucky to have a relationship with Alec that gave us the support we needed as youngsters. When I went to Spurs as a high priced player I could've done with the support of someone like Alec but Spurs was a very different club to QPR.'

'I remember when Tommy Docherty came in as manager, he put his arms round us and told us he'd make us the greatest players QPR ever had. Then two weeks later he's sacked and we're playing his Aston Villa team and I can hear him saying "kick them Morgans, they're useless"!'

Paul Harris, in his seventh decade of supporting Rangers, was among 21,494 when Leicester came to Shepherd's Bush. He told your author, 'It was a much-awaited experience for all Rangers fans and a very hot day.

'It was a fair result with a lot of tension and minus star player Rodney Marsh who had a foot injury for the first three months of the season.'

On the season as a whole he added, 'To be honest we were out of our depth but the success gained over the previous two years was the stepping stone for the future which built the club into being one of the finest footballing sides of the mid-1970s. I'm talking, of course, about the Bowles, Francis, Thomas, Parkes era.'

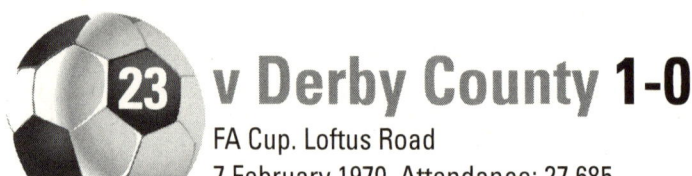

23 v Derby County 1-0
FA Cup. Loftus Road
7 February 1970. Attendance: 27,685

QUEENS PARK RANGERS:	DERBY COUNTY:
Kelly	Green
Clement	Webster
Gillard	Robson
Watson	Durban
Mobley	McFarland
Hazell	Mackay
Bridges	McGovern
Venables	Carlin
Clarke	O'Hare
Marsh	Hector
Ferguson	Hinton

Referee: Leo Callaghan (Merthyr Tydfil)

IAN GILLARD remains grateful to Brian Clough and Old Big 'Ead's captain Dave Mackay for playing a part in helping lift his relegated Queens Park Rangers out of the doldrums.

The Derby County pair combined to help present Gillard's side with a place in the quarter-finals of the FA Cup at Loftus Road on 7 February 1970; Rangers' furthest journey in the world's greatest club competition since 1948 when they also achieved promotion.

OBE's failed tactics and his skipper Dave Mackay putting through his own goal sealed the triumph which lifted Rangers' spirits following relegation from the premier division.

Gillard told your author in June 2013, 'The FA Cup run, with our win over Derby, gave us a bit of hope after being relegated. It was hard in the league.

'It had been difficult for kids like myself, Dave Clement, Gerry Francis and Mick Leach but playing with more established players in the run helped us a hell of a lot when it came to developing the 1970s era team which we were all a part of and which did so well.

'We had a run to the quarter-finals of the League Cup, losing to the eventual winners, Manchester City, to boost us that season as well.'

R's had discovered the top flight was an unforgiving environment when they slumped to rock bottom and back down to the second tier after just one season.

Manager Les Allen, who had given up playing to concentrate on the role, set about the challenge of an immediate return by signing Terry Venables from his former club Tottenham Hotspur for a cool £70,000.

The experienced midfield brought oodles of experience, know-how, ability, quick-wittedness and all-round intelligence.

Left-winger Clive Clark, who had scored twice against Rangers in the 1967 League Cup Final, returned as a makeweight in a deal which sent Alan Glover to West Bromwich Albion.

v Derby County 1970

Allen also persuaded superstar Rodney Marsh to play on at Loftus Road. A number of suitors had joined a queue for Marsh's services, hoping to take advantage of Rangers' lowered status and surmising the player's ambitions would be to remain at the highest level having had a second taste of it with QPR following his early career experiences with Fulham. But Allen and his men knew to bounce back so soon would be a Herculean task, one even beyond the divine Greek hero and son of Zeus himself.

Deflated spirit, bruised ego and a dip in confidence do not represent a combination which would provide the impetus to return immediately to an arena on a revenge mission.

New rivals would have something to say about that too, keen to show they are capable of proving themselves against a former big fish who had just plopped into their waters. A shoal of piranhas attempting to bite the big fish to death.

Rangers guided themselves through the choppy waters provided by their opponents and their lessened sense of self-worth.

A good start took them to top spot (including a 6-1 thrashing of Blackpool in which Marsh hit a hat-trick) but they flattered to deceive and, despite the acquisitions of Sheffield Wednesday defender Vic Mobley and the Aston Villa midfielder Mike Ferguson, those in the Rangers carriage on the Second Division roller-coaster took a sharp intake of breath as it descended.

They swept back up the rails before another downturn saw them grind to a halt at the end of the ride in ninth place.

But the FA Cup provided an arena of less sustained hostility for Rangers that season where decent one-off performances could provide steps towards a more realistic target.

Even though Rangers had slipped down a division, they were still able to join the competition at the third-round stage. It meant, potentially, that Les Allen could become the first QPR boss to guide his team to FA Cup glory by winning just six matches.

Rangers took the opportunity of a boost to self-esteem in their opening tie. Non-league South Shields came down from the north-east and returned having been defeated 4-1 by their Loftus Road hosts. Marsh helped himself to a couple of goals while Frank Clarke and Ferguson completed the quartet of goals netted by the R's.

A potential banana-skin had been avoided, but the fourth round saw Rangers drawing a tricky tie, one against one of those new league rivals we spoke about earlier. One of those 'piranhas'. It was a close encounter of the three-goal kind, to paraphrase the title of director Steven Spielberg's sci-fi epic as QPR pipped hosts Charlton Athletic at the Valley 3-2, with Marsh and Clarke emulating their goalscoring exploits of the previous round.

Marsh-inspired Rangers were in to the last 16. Who would be out of the hat? Staff gathered for the broadcast of the draw. The balls were fingers around in a velvet bag at Football Association headquarters, clicking and knocking against each other to provide rattling good radio before an official of the governing body pulled one out on its own.

He solemnly announced, 'Queens Park Rangers' before a delay while he hauled out a second 'will play ... Derby County'.

Brian Clough had guided the Rams into the First Division the previous season and within two years, the nucleus of the side to face Rangers were crowned champions of the Football League's top division.

And Clough and Mackay were hailed the dynamic duo (if you exclude the manager's trusted lieutenant Peter Taylor); Clough the managerial magician capable of waving his wand and turning a Cinderella club into English football's belle of the ball.

Queens Park Rangers' Greatest Games

Mackay, rated the greatest player of his era by one-time opponent Sir Alex Ferguson, was the 'ideal captain' and rated by Clough as his best ever signing.

Rangers had the good fortune to go head to head with these soon-to-be titans of football when Derby were smarting from four successive 1-0 defeats while setting out their stall in the top flight.

And the hosts were good value as they extended Clough and Mackay's unwanted run to five with their first ever win over the Rams.

Rangers dominated, each individual providing contributions worthy of being nominated for man of the match awards as they sought, although the expression might have rankled given the level they had played in the previous season, a giant-killing.

They had to be patient with the deciding goal coming just seven minutes from time.

Ferguson moved along the left wing to provide a cross into the danger area. Frank Clarke hustled and bustled his way on to it despite the attentions of Derby defenders such as Roy McFarland and shot goalwards.

The diminutive Les Green, in the visitors' goal, appeared to have the effort covered as he dived before Mackay's ill-fortune decided the tie.

Clough had converted Mackay from the midfield position which had earned him his much-vaunted reputation while starring in a team of stars during Tottenham Hotspur's glory days of the 1960s.

The Scotland superstar was a swaggering, larger-than-life, leader-of-men centre-half with Derby in what was supposedly a winding-down time in a stellar career.

But this day whatever Mackay had become, he was still prone to human frailties. He deflected Clarke's effort beyond Green and the ball nestled in the Derby goal as the Super Hoops celebrated.

The fact the result hinged on that moment was unfortunate for Mackay, because there was ample opportunity for Rangers to put the tie to bed on other occasions.

And much of that was down to how Clough had set Derby up, according to expert observers.

Clough had potent strikers like Kevin Hector and John O'Hare and other players of flair and industry in Alan Hinton and John McGovern.

But the manager appeared more concerned with keeping a clean sheet than getting a hatful of goals.

He felt that a goalless draw would suit because it would enable his outfit to take Rangers back to the Baseball Ground for a replay in which his side could express more of their attacking tendencies.

But his concentration on defence backfired as Rangers exploited holes in it seemingly at will. Barry Bridges, fit again after a training injury, used his pace to create three chances which were kept out by the over-worked but alert Green in the opening six minutes.

On the counter Mike Kelly had to save from Hector, but otherwise the Rangers stopper was well protected by a stonewall rearguard in which Gillard and Dave Clement were outstanding.

Marsh was certainly up for the occasion. He displayed his superb ball skills to torment Derby. Inevitably agitated, he attracted robust attention.

He was chopped down by Ron Webster to elicit a free-kick. But he found referee Leo Callaghan unwilling to award a penalty following a challenge on him by John Robson.

As the *Kilburn Times* reporter put it, Marsh's 'dramatic pirouette and collapse' did not deserve one.

v Derby County 1970

Marsh managed to find the net shortly before the interval, but the official's decision went against him, adjudging he had handled. Mr Callaghan's view of the incident so incensed Venables the skipper was booked for the vehemence of his protest.

And centre-half Ian Watson cracked an effort against the Derby crossbar in first-half injury time.

The cloud overhead broke up and the sun came out and shone on Rangers when Mackay inadvertently altered the direction of Clarke's drive.

More good fortune came Rangers' way when they survived a late Derby attack. Kelly handled outside the box but he just managed to save the resultant free kick as Hinton tried to chip it over him.

As a last throw of the dice, Mackay ordered his centre-back partner McFarland up front, but Rangers remained rock-like until the final whistle.

All good things come to an end. Rangers rather hoped the old adage was untrue as they took on Chelsea for a place in the semi-final.

Allen and his troops knew, despite the encouraging form shown as QPR attempted to march back to Wembley three years after the League Cup triumph, that the odds were stacked against them.

Blues were overloaded with talent everywhere you looked. Alan Hudson, Charlie Cooke and, perhaps the greatest legend to emerge from the club during that era, Peter Osgood were all included. Ron Harris, Chopper himself, was at the back in front of Peter Bonetti, arguably Chelsea's best ever stopper.

And QPR's cause was far from aided by the unavailability of Clarke through injury. But Rangers gave it a good go against their near neighbours in a derby thriller before succumbing 4-2 on a muddy surface at Stamford Bridge.

They shared possession evenly for much of the lively encounter described in contemporary reports as 'cup tie soccer at its best'.

Former Chelsea striker Bridges was determined to put one over his ex-employees as he and Ferguson attempted runs to pierce the Blue wall. Bridges found himself close in but his flick was straight at Bonetti.

And Rangers' Tony Hazell thumped a free kick just wide after Mick Leach was fouled by John Dempsey.

Marsh and Bridges forced Eddie McCreadie to clear his lines and blocked a Watson effort.

But by that time the game had turned with Chelsea going 2-0 up with two early goals in as many minutes by Dave Webb, made by future Ranger John Hollins, and Osgood.

Venables reduced the arrears with a re-taken penalty after Bonetti was adjudged to have moved to save his first effort before the kick was taken.

Leach went close to a leveller before Osgood completed his hat-trick to make it 4-1 and Bridge reduced the arrears.

24 v Nottingham Forest 3-0
Football League Second Division. Loftus Road
16 September 1972. Attendance: 12,528

QUEENS PARK RANGERS:	NOTTINGHAM FOREST:
Parkes	Barron
Clement	Hindley
Watson	Gemmell
Venables	Serella
Evans	Cottam
Hazell	Fraser
Busby	Lyons
Francis	Lyall (Robertson)
McCulloch	McKenzie
Bowles	Richardson
Givens (Salvage)	O'Neill

Referee: Not known

THE STAGE was set for Stan the Man. Stan Bowles. The living legend who took over the Queens Park Rangers number 10 shirt from Rodney Marsh claiming he 'had never heard of' the club icon.

Nottingham Forest were the visitors to Loftus Road and Bowles was about to establish himself has the new idol of the Rangers faithful in a mere 90 minutes.

He scored one, made one and shone as bright as any star you would care to mention to help Rangers overcome Nottingham Forest 3-0 on a never-to-be-forgotten QPR debut at Loftus Road on 16 September 1972.

It was a case of the king is dead, long live the king. It was the start of a reign without equal in the hearts and minds of many R's individuals from all generations then and since. Bowles had arrived at Loftus Road as a direct consequence of Marsh departing London W12.

Rangers manager Gordon Jago had reluctantly sold Marsh to Manchester City (ironically where Bowles began his playing career) for £200,000 in March 1972 as a promotion bid was falling short, by just three points as it turned out.

And history has proved how wisely he used that money, buying Don Givens from Luton, Dave Thomas from Burnley and, most crucially, Bowles, from Carlisle United.

He added the trio to the mix of youth and experience already there – graduates of the club's youth set-up, who had largely been found for R's by chief scout Derek Healy, in the shape of players such as Gerry Francis, Ian Gillard and Tony Hazell, the nous of Terry Venables and the wily earlier purchase of goalkeeper Phil Parkes from Walsall by Jago's predecessor Les Allen.

The alchemist in Jago must have experienced something of a 'Eureka' moment when Forest came to Loftus Road on the afternoon of Saturday 16 September 1972.

Thomas had yet to arrive from Turf Moor, but, as Jago watched his side, he was convinced the blend was there for the team not only to be promoted but to establish

v Nottingham Forest 1972

themselves in the top flight and go one better than Alec Stock's team in terms of league status if not silverware collecting.

The purchase he must have been most pleased about from what he saw in the 3-0 victory against Forest was Bowles.

If ever a player was destined for greatness at Loftus Road it was Bowles. It was love at first sight. The faithful adored Marsh and any successor might have expected a long courtship with them before winning them over.

Not Bowles. He headed his goal and laid on a Don Givens goal with Andy McCulloch getting the other – and the first line of the legend had been written.

It was three years before Brian Clough took over at Forest (Matt Gillies was in charge of the visitors on this occasion) but the manager who would one day buy him for the club and fall out with him – after Bowles had ruled himself out of the Forest team before the 1980 European Cup Final, upset at having been omitted from a testimonial for City Ground winger John Robertson shortly before the squad left to face Hamburg in Madrid – would have been appreciative.

A performance he might either have spotted on a television highlights programme or read about in the newspapers which could well have sown the seeds in Clough's mind that Bowles was his sort of player.

Bowles made an instant impact on a mild, sunny afternoon at Loftus Road. The pitch had been softened up by rain, but it seemed ideal conditions to show R's fans why their club had forked out £112,000 to sign him from Carlisle United.

He found himself out on the left wing with the ball in the second minute. Spotting Don Givens he guided over a precision cross which was headed beyond Forest goalkeeper Jim Barron by the Republic of Ireland forward.

Bowles scored his debut goal when he headed home a cross from McCulloch on 33 minutes.

Rangers' defence was barely troubled by Gillies's outfit that included two vital members of the Forest team which conquered Europe under Clough, Martin O'Neill and John Robertson.

But the R's midfield was buzzing with Gerry Francis leading the way. In fact Bowles and Francis hit it off immediately as they formed a triangle with Givens which left Forest reeling. And the hosts deserved their third as McCulloch completed the scoring after 77 minutes.

Mancunian Bowles had led a nomadic life in the game up to that point. He had frustrated Malcolm Allison and Joe Mercer at Manchester City enough to be shown the door. Allison believed Bowles was good enough to keep company with his all-conquering side of the late 1960s.

But he felt the player lacked intensity in his training and hung around in 'bad company', what Bowles referred to as the 'Quality Street Gang' ('who are all probably either dead or in prison now').

Bowles moved on to Bury where he lasted three weeks because he didn't get on with the manager whom he felt played him out of position.

After time out, he was given a trial by Crewe Alexandra and played for them in the Fourth Division before hooking up with Carlisle United.

When QPR came knocking he was delighted. He wanted to move to London because he was convinced it would be where he would be able to settle and make a name for himself.

Queens Park Rangers' Greatest Games

Jago knew what he was getting in terms of ability; a skilled, quick witted, two-footed, well balanced, mobile footballer with an out-of-this-world first touch, a quick turn of pace over the first five or ten yards and ability to leave one or more defenders for dead by feinting either to the left or right.

Bowles was also a team player who knew when to pass, as he quickly proved with the likes of Terry Venables and Gerry Francis, and when to go solo. He had an eye for goal having top scored for Carlisle the previous season.

Bowles had displayed all these attributes when he caught the manager's eye as his Carlisle side were being thumped 3-0 by Rangers at Loftus Road in the penultimate game of the previous season, 1971/72, a month after Marsh had moved to Maine Road.

Bowles also possessed a self-confidence which he went on to admit could have been seen as arrogant. And he was devoid of nerves, no matter what the occasion, what 'sledging' he got from opponents, what verbal abuse opposing fans spat in his direction.

The only question mark by the uninformed was whether he would achieve his true potential given the presumptions made about his personal life – his 'dodgy connections', his gambling, his lack of reliability.

True, he loved a bet and continued the habit at the William Hill branch by Loftus Road up to 15 minutes before a home kick-off, by his own admittance. But the supporters who spotted him in the shop studying the odds were unconcerned 'as long as I put in a performance in the game'.

And he admits he got into one or scrapes soon after arriving at Loftus Road. Once, he reveals in his autobiography, he was arrested with fellow Ranger Don Shanks, his best pal, mistakenly suspected of armed robbery after a day at Hackney dog track (transformed into a pink and blue hockey stadium for the 2012 Olympic Games).

They had parked in the same spot two weeks running in a Ford Transit which had been involved in an armed robbery in a previous life.

Shanks peered into a shop as he waited for Bowles to buy an evening paper. As Bowles writes, the police 'had put two and two together' when the pair had just re-visited a Wimpy bar 'to spend a tenner' of their £1,600 winnings on a burger each.

Gordon Jago turned up after the arrest 'white-faced and horrified', according to Bowles.

But generally Jago revealed Bowles was fine to deal with and he had no problem dealing with the club's swiftly appointed talisman.

It was not difficult to see why. Bowles has revealed how an investigative reporter from the *News of the World* followed him around away from the club and discovered his life was dull rather than scandalous and went away minus any juice for a double-page exposé.

The truth is that while Bowles infatuated his followers at Loftus Road as an idol beyond idols for the seven years he spent as a player at the club, he perceived himself away from the public gaze as largely just a typical down-to-earth bloke who liked a gamble on either the gee-gees or greyhounds and banter with the supporters over a pint in the Springbok pub next to the ground.

I got to know Bowles during my years as the sports editor of the *Ealing Gazette*, a bi-weekly newspaper which covered QPR and Brentford, reporting on his exploits with both clubs.

He lost his rag on occasion on the pitch but off it was ALWAYS easy-going and laid back with a constant twinkle in his eyes. He was always approachable, never precious.

He once asked me to give him a lift to a new wine bar he was opening with a business partner in nearby Notting Hill. I agreed and he hopped into my white Morris Minor. He didn't need either a 4x4 or a big red Ferrari to make a big impression when he turned up for the launch.

Affection is something Bowles never displayed to me. Our conversation flowed naturally about football, families and whatever the current affair was occupying the nation's attention before I dropped him off. He was easy to talk to and easy on the eye when he wore the blue and white hoops with the number 10 in red on his back.

Stan Bowles was the consummate entertainer on the pitch and good company off it. And he was one who genuinely loved the club with whom he will forever be associated.

That was obvious to those who witnessed the *joie de vivre* and ability he displayed when he first earned the respect of his new followers from west London.

Bowles said in his autobiography, 'I was 23 when I joined Queens Park Rangers in September 1972 for a then club record fee of £112,000.

'Rodney Marsh, the hero of the fans, had just been sold to Manchester City for £200,000. Rodney had made the number 10 shirt his own and, since he moved, no one wanted to touch the thing – it was taboo, nobody wanted to wear it.

'The shirt thing didn't seem a big deal to me. I hadn't really heard of Rodney Marsh, so I just shrugged and said, "If no one wants it, I'll wear it." They couldn't give it to me quickly enough – it was my fault that I hadn't heard of the great Rodney Marsh.

'However, as luck would have it, I scored one and made another for Don Givens in my first game against Nottingham Forest on 16 September 1972. We won 3-0 and the fans seemed to take to my style of play, which to them was like Rodney's.

'The fans had seen me previously when I was playing for Carlisle so that might have helped a bit, maybe they knew what to expect.

'As far as I know the QPR chairman (Jim Gregory) tried to buy me then. I'm certain of one thing, though: volunteering to wear the number 10 shirt was the best thing I ever did.

'The fans desperately want to have a hero wearing a particular shirt – think of Newcastle fans and that number 9 shirt – and if you do a good job while you are wearing it, they'll love you forever.

'Mess up, though, and they'll never let you forget it. I was lucky, getting off to a flying start and eventually I became the crowd's favourite.'

25 v Cardiff City 0-0

Football League Second Division. Ninian Park
18 April 1973. Attendance: 11,958

QUEENS PARK RANGERS:
Parkes
Clement
Watson
Venables
Mancini
Hazell
Thomas
Francis
Leach
Bowles
Givens

CARDIFF CITY:
Irwin
Dwyer
Bell
Phillips
Murray
Morgan
Reece
McCulloch
Woodruff
Vincent (Hoy 50)
Anderson.

Referee: R Matthewson (Worsley)

IT SEEMS ironic that a team which had spent the season entertaining crowds home and away with the style, panache and cutting edge of their football should finally seal promotion with a point gleaned from a goalless draw against Cardiff City at Ninian Park on 18 April 1973. And in front of one of the lowest crowds of a spectator-attracting term.

There were a ton of examples in that campaign where Gordon Jago's rampant Rangers produced enough sexy football to satiate the most demanding of appetites.

In the case of the match against Cardiff the significance of the result was greater than the entertainment value provided for those who had made the 300-mile trek from west London expecting their heroes to realise the dream.

Taking the day off work, or just a half day, with or without their employers' knowledge, they did not want to miss out.

They wanted to be there so they could tell anyone in their orbit (and unable to join them) how they were there the night QPR re-joined the big boys.

There were echoes of the day Rangers last played a team from Wales to secure elevation in status, when Swansea Town came to Loftus Road in 1948 (see earlier chapter) and neither side could find the net.

Then as against Cardiff, though, the precious point was all that mattered for Super Hoops followers.

The fact QPR were unable to find the target was not down to lack of effort. They had turned themselves into promotion contenders by playing bright, attractive football that was easy on the eye.

On a firm pitch practically devoid of grass, Rangers laid siege to the home goal for the opening 45 minutes.

The problem for the R's was the resistance of Bluebirds goalkeeper Billy Irwin. It seemed as if it was the 11 players of Rangers versus the young Irishman.

v Cardiff City 1973

Terry Venables had total control of midfield as he instigated wave after wave of attacks. And the west London side showed they were determined to exploit his astute promptings especially with the support of the knife-cutting-through-butter runs of Don Givens and Dave Thomas. The final ball mostly found a Ranger hitting the target.

Stan Bowles must have believed he had put Rangers in front after eight minutes until Irwin pulled off a wonder save.

Don Givens had a go. Not once, but twice. And on both occasions he was denied by Irwin. Thomas tried. Same result. Irwin must have had his manager Jimmy Andrews purring in admiration of his stopper's performance if not apoplectic with the displays of the defenders in front of him who were supposedly protecting the raw recruit.

The pressure was 'unrelenting' on the hosts until the interval, Dennis Busher reported in *The Sun*.

Rangers should have been sitting in their dressing room, either sipping a cuppa, sucking an orange or whatever else in an area which was then an inner sanctum rather than a free-for-all for reporters, commentators and television cameras, and talking about how they could build on a substantial lead or shut up shop.

The fact it was goalless left Rangers susceptible to having their promotion party spoiled. Andrews replaced Johnny Vincent in midfield with former Tottenham Hotspur player Roger Hoy five minutes after the re-start and it resulted in the influence of Venables waning and the Bluebirds beginning to take off.

Gil Reece and former Rangers striker Andy McCulloch went close for the hosts, with QPR right-back Dave Clement being forced to kick one of their efforts off the line.

The Rangers supporters present had their hearts in their mouths. Surely their heroes weren't going to pay for their first-half profligacy and about to surrender both points? Surely promotion wouldn't have to wait for another game?

As the final whistle blew there was a little relief mixed in with the joy. Manager Gordon Jago was emotionally moved by the sights and sounds he witnessed at Ninian Park following the whistle.

He later said to QPRnet.com, 'It was an unbelievable day (at Cardiff), we had finally made it and the atmosphere in the dressing room was electric. Our coach Bobby Campbell was a great motivator and his enthusiasm was incredible, he led the cheers that day and rightly so for he had played a major part in helping me to bring about the success that we all wanted.'

Rangers, as we know, went close to going up at the end of the 1971/72 season with Rodney Marsh leading the charge until his March departure to Manchester City for £200,000. Having money is all very well, the key is how you spend it. And Jago clearly spent it wisely with the likes of Don Givens, Dave Thomas and Bowles fusing with those already there to light the blue and white touchpaper.

The debut of Bowles in the 3-0 home win over Nottingham Forest early on in the campaign gave an indication that Rangers could progress from being nearly men.

But could it be sustained? What separated the good from the successful is the ability to maintain a high standard on a consistent basis, for as many of each 90 minutes as possible.

And Rangers proved they were no flashes in the pan only capable of hitting the bullseye against a strong Forest team from the Land of Robin Hood.

There were plenty of smiling faces at Loftus Road, which now boasted a sparkling new Ellerslie Road Stand to replace the structure which protected its occupants from the vagaries of the English weather with a tin roof. And with good reason.

Queens Park Rangers' Greatest Games

Rangers moved from tenth to second with five wins on the bounce, just a point off leaders Burnley at Turf Moor. Bowles and Givens were having a field day in the goals department as 13 were netted during the run with just two conceded.

After a temporary blip, Rangers got back on course as 1973 unfolded. They stormed back up to the second promotion spot and did not ease their grip of it for the rest of the season.

Both in attack and defence they were on top form. They only let in a single goal while going unbeaten for six matches in the opening two months of the year, including a crucial 2-0 home win against Burnley which pegged back the leaders. They extended the run to 11 games.

By the time they visited Cardiff their season had featured five-goal thumpings of Swindon Town – with the irrepressible Stan Bowles managing his first hat-trick for the club – and Portsmouth. Awesome foursomes did for Sheffield Wednesday, Carlisle United and Blackpool.

A 1-0 win over Millwall at The Den three days after the draw at Cardiff confirmed their elevation. There had been a mathematical miracle required to keep Rangers down as they entered the mouth of the Lions. The equation added up to Rangers losing all their remaining four games and Aston Villa winning all theirs 'by a cricket score'.

Givens ended any remote technical quibbles with the winning goal with a header from a Dave Thomas cross five minutes from time, an early Phil Parkes save aiding Rangers' cause in a lively derby in which Bowles also hit the post.

There was still the question of whether Rangers could go up as champions. They did their best by ending their season with a flourish; three more wins without conceding a goal. Brighton and Hove Albion and neighbours Fulham both succumbed 2-0 in back-to-back home victories for the hosts with Bowles scoring in each of them.

But on the day QPR overcame the Cottagers, Burnley drew 1-1 with Preston North End to complete their fixtures on 62 points. It was enough to give their Lancastrian rivals the title as the R's trailed Jimmy Adamson's side by three points with just one game left in a time when victory only earned two instead of today's three.

It meant, of course, QPR's final game was for pride on both sides. But it did not stop Rangers putting on the style and reducing the gap between themselves and Burnley to just one solitary point.

They outclassed Sunderland at Roker Park just four days after their hosts had stunned hot favourites Leeds United to lift the FA Cup (the Ian Porterfield goal, the Jim Montgomery double save and the joyous crossfield gallop of manager Bob Stokoe et al).

The trophy was on display and a cheeky Rangers player – either Bowles or Tony Hazell depending on whether you believe either Stan the Man or Jago and club historian Gordon Macey – successfully knocked the treasured silver pot off its plinth accidently on purpose to the ire of the Mackems present.

Rangers defender Ian Gillard, who played in the promotion season, told your author in June 2013, 'The mood created during the 1972/73 season was super. The place was buzzing because things were going right. You could see the change in the team. In the way we were playing. I was in and out of the team so my recollection of the games was sparse, but I can still remember how upbeat it was.

'[Manager] Gordon Jago helped bring all that about because he brought stability to the team by bringing in good players like Terry Venables, Dave Thomas, Don Givens and Stan Bowles.

v Cardiff City 1973

'Gordon was a good PR man. Very good at organisation. Concentrating on getting players in and out while leaving the coaching to Bobby Campbell [who in recent years has played the role of unofficial football advisor to Chelsea billionaire owner Roman Abramovich].

'He was influential to me. He brought me back into the team during the 1972/73 season and within five weeks I was playing for England Under-23s.

'That was a big change around for me. My career was developing with all these sort of things happening to me thanks to Gordon.'

The architect of Rangers' promotion in 1972/73 was an urbane individual. Gordon Jago would have seemed more at home running his own public relations company than managing a football team.

He had easy charm capable of smoothing over most bumps in the road along the way. He dealt with strong and maverick characters in the dressing room and boardroom.

Your author knew Jago, while at Rangers, as always approachable and willing to be quoted because he had the intelligence to say the right thing.

Jago said, 'This has been such a good season and my job has been made easy because I have such good players. Our promotion has been achieved not on 11 players but a good squad and with some of the seniors out of the side the reserves who have come in have done a fine job. We were badly hit more than most with injuries. We used 21 players during the year.

'I suppose our most vital game was against Burnley at the end of January, which we won at home.

'Every match, of course, is important but as the season draws to a close encounters become more vital. We had just lost Terry Venables and Phil Parkes and it was necessary to keep open the chance of promotion.

'Burnley held a three-point advantage and a loss at this stage would have been almost too wide a gap to close with our rivals not far behind.

'Our best all-round performance was our 1-0 success at Villa Park back in the middle of October.'

Talking to the *Kilburn Times*, he added, 'Our chances of remaining in the First Division? Well, not only are we going to stay up but be very very successful.

'Our FA Cup tie against Derby County gave us a good insight. We were overawed in the first half but we came into the match in the second [eventually losing the fifth-round encounter 4-2].

'We're not just going to consolidate our position next season. We have achieved our promotion and are going to be successful as a First Division side.'

He said to QPRnet.com, 'There was a great atmosphere around the squad and there was a confidence that we were a good team. As well as that they had a huge desire to play First Division football. They were a great group of players all with one objective to succeed.

'Promotion was the aim for sure but we were disappointed that we did not finish as champions but all credit to Burnley for they were also a very good side.'

He also gave an insight into the key transfers which sparked the promotion, revealing the part played by chairman and owner Jim Gregory.

He said, 'After the sale of Rodney we finished the season in fourth place. We were so near to promotion that I was concerned that without him we would struggle to do even better. We needed to strengthen our attack and with £200,000 in the bank and a chairman who wanted success we had the opportunity to buy new players.

Queens Park Rangers' Greatest Games

'The key was to sign the right players. When I asked the chairman to buy Don Givens he was not that keen but he allowed me to spend £40,000 on him as our first summer buy.

'The chairman was keen on Stan Bowles as he had played so well against us just before the end of the 1970/71 season so we were able to beat Crystal Palace for his signature from Carlisle for a fee of £110,000. So we spent a total of £150,000 and signed two excellent goalscoring forwards.

'We were playing well and had won six, drawn six and only lost once when Martyn Busby broke his leg at Fulham. We had a very young reserve team and there was no really experienced player to bring in.

'The meeting the next day following Martyn's injury was incredible; Jim Gregory called the meeting to discuss what action we should take to continue our aim for promotion.

'Derek Healy, our chief scout, and myself were suggesting a number of players in the £40,000 to £50,000 range when the chairman suddenly suggested Dave Thomas. I had seen Dave a number of times and knew that he was a good player.

'Leeds were making talk of a £200,000 bid for Dave and I thought he was way out of our range having already spent £150,000. Regardless I called Jimmy Adamson at Burnley and told him of our interest and we put the two chairmen together on the phone and they eventually agreed a price of £165,000.

'I then got back on with Jimmy and had him contact Dave and get him on a train to arrive in London that night telling him to make certain that he brought his boots!

'Derek met Dave at Euston Station and drove him to my house in Kingston to meet myself and club secretary Ron Phillips. Twenty minutes later Dave had signed subject to a medical on Friday morning. We had secured a third top-class forward and he played the next day against Sunderland.'

v Liverpool 2-0
Football League First Division. Loftus Road
16 August 1975. Attendance: 27,113

QUEENS PARK RANGERS:	LIVERPOOL:
Parkes	Clemence
Clement	Neal
Gillard	Jones
Hollins (Leach)	Thompson
McLintock	Cormack
Webb	Hughes
Thomas	Keegan
Francis	McDermott
Masson	Heighway
Bowles	Toshack
Givens	Callaghan

Referee: John Yates

THORNLEA FRED'S RED was of great pride to pigeon racer Gerry Francis. It won a national prize for its owner. Francis, rather more well known for his sporting endeavours in football, collected another countrywide award in the 1975/76 campaign for the Goal of the Season on the BBC's *Match Of The Day*.

The Queens Park Rangers superstar and soon-to-be-appointed England captain, a true local hero having been raised just up the road from Shepherd's Bush in Chiswick, scored it on the opening day of his club's greatest top-flight campaign against the most powerful team of the times, Liverpool.

Francis has enjoyed the success of the pigeons he had 'broken' in at his 'lofts' over the years.

But the feel-good factor of any of those flights-of-fancy triumphs was given a run for its money with his wonder goal in front of The Loft end and the rest of Loftus Road on the sunny day Rangers announced they had the potential to be genuine title contenders.

He also made the second goal, for Mick Leach, which sealed Rangers their first ever win over Liverpool on Saturday 16 August 1975.

The Reds had an air of invincibility about them going in. It often had teams defeated before they even left the dressing room. After all, they had already begun their domination of English and continental football in the 1970s and 1980s with a domestic title and an FA Cup (going on to lift a total of six crowns, three FA Cups and four European Cups).

And they had collected together an awesome group of players in the Bill Shankly era before moving into Bob Paisley's time when they visited London W12.

The 11 players who started that day were all legends or soon-to-be legends of the Anfield giants: England goalkeeper Ray Clemence, Phil Neal, Phil Thompson, Emlyn Hughes, Joey Jones, Terry McDermott, Peter Cormack, Ian Callaghan, Steve Heighway, John Toshack and, of course, Kevin Keegan.

Queens Park Rangers' Greatest Games

But Rangers had not been doing too badly since manager Dave Sexton took over the reins from Gordon Jago the year before.

Jago had got most of the players together and achieved promotion and, unlike the team of 1968/69, managed to more than survive the season as they maintained top-flight status with the addition of Frank McLintock, the 24-going-on-35 Double-winning captain of Arsenal.

Eighth spot in the 1973/74 season represented the highest position Rangers had ever attained in the Football League.

Rangers suffered a nightmare start to their second season back in the top flight. And even when Sexton took over from Jago in October 1974 it was not immediately obvious that things were getting better as they lost their first game with him in charge – at home to Liverpool.

Sexton believed in deploying inventive coaching and tactics influenced by a study of Holland's Total Football, which required players to be able to be capable of adapting to whatever position they found themselves in on the pitch.

It was clear the players were capable of implementing Sexton's bright ideas with four wins in the next five.

As it was a work in progress, Rangers had to settle for a mid-table position by the season's end. But with talented players playing a system they loved and one which entertained the crowd, hopes were high for 1975/76.

The big kick-off is cause for excitement whatever season it happens to be for any club as it brings the smell of freshly mown grass, the endorphins induced by the rays of sun (if you are lucky) and the return of something missed all summer.

But if your club has been touted as one with the potential to achieve honours it adds more than a frisson of anticipation.

That was how supporters of QPR felt as the gladiators of both sides entered the arena to high-decibel roars which drowned out most sounds around the Bush and its environs.

QPR's would-be heroes had underlined the growing potency enriched in the previous season or two in a pre-season tournament when they comfortably defeated West German champions Borussia Monchengladbach and Portugal's Benfica.

Sexton had developed a side which could unlock the tightest defences no matter how big a club it seemed. And they did not come much bigger than Liverpool.

A fluid approach akin to Johan Cruyff and Co, with fresh attacking ideas, left Liverpool having to find the answers rather than ask the questions.

Don Masson, an early Sexton signing for £100,000 from Notts County in December 1974, pulled the strings, lying deep in midfield. The accuracy and range of his passing oiled the Rangers motor.

The Scotland international completed almost all his passes, short and long, to either feet or for a team-mate to run on to with or without breaking stride such as when wingers Dave Thomas and Don Givens were haring down the flanks.

Givens proved himself versatile with his heading ability. The Republic of Ireland international brought to the club by Jago from Luton Town also displayed his willingness to sacrifice himself for the team by putting in the blood, sweat and tears so others could sparkle.

Mick Leach, a striker put into midfield in place of the injured John Hollins after 30 minutes, signed in the summer from Sexton's former club Chelsea, also put in a shift.

v Liverpool 1975

The defence provided a solid base. McLintock showed why Sexton had signed him from the Gunners in the month he took over. The manager of course knew McLintock when he coached Arsenal and was convinced the veteran Scotland international converted from midfield would add experience and stability.

Liverpool's dynamic duo up front, Keegan and Toshack, got little change out of McLintock and his partner in central defence, fellow veteran Dave Webb, the FA Cup-winning veteran who arrived from Chelsea in July 1974.

The visitors had a stellar midfield, of course, with Heighway, Callaghan, Cormack and McDermott behind their front runners, so it meant it was all hands on deck to display a calm assurance when Liverpool did come forward.

Dave Clement and Ian Gillard, the full-backs who had come through the ranks, provided their older colleagues in the back line with enough help to ensure the more-than-capable goalkeeper Phil Parkes could keep a clean sheet.

Stan Bowles, the magician who had lit up Loftus Road since taking over the number 10 shirt from Rodney Marsh three years earlier, was on his game, displaying his delicate ball skills, pace and inventiveness. And Francis was a powerhouse with a deft touch, surging through midfield, often instinctively linking up with Bowles.

There was no finer example of that understanding than when Francis put Rangers ahead with his wonder goal shortly before the interval.

The move began deep in Rangers' half over on the right with Dave Clement in possession. Don Masson moved towards the full-back requesting a pass. In plenty of space with Terry McDermott holding off from closing, the midfielder turned and curled an inch-perfect 15-yard low ball to the centre spot towards Bowles.

Liverpool skipper Emlyn Hughes tried to close in on Bowles, who was facing his own goal. But the Rangers icon was unflustered. Without seeming to even glance across he gave the ball the lightest of touches into the path of Francis running in behind him to his left.

The midfielder, in acres of space, galloped forward and, with Phil Thompson in close attendance, pushed the ball to Givens. The Irishman had his back to the defence and could see Francis continuing his diagonal run left to right between Thompson and Phil Neal. Givens clipped an angled ball which pierced the defence and Francis picked it up again behind the beaten defenders.

He now had Ray Clemence to beat. The Rangers number 8 maintained his composure and drew goalkeeper Clemence at the near post and guided the ball into the far corner from 16 yards.

He turned towards the right-hand touchline to celebrate with the ecstatic Rangers fans with his right arm raised and his right index finger pointing skywards. As he was about to receive the congratulations of team-mates Dave Thomas and Dave Clement he levered both arms up and down. A broad smile spread across his face.

The home crowd had to wait until the last eight minutes before both points were secured. And again they had Francis to thank. The inspirational midfielder crossed and Leach headed home.

The mighty Liverpool had been sunk. Deservedly, by a confident, rampaging Rangers. Sexton's men dared to dream. So did their supporters. Would this be the season the club won the top title for the first time? The expectation was realistic judging by the way they outshone Paisley's usually mighty Reds.

As Dave Luddy reported in the *Kilburn Times* it was realistic to consider 'dreams of glory with glittering prizes on the far horizon'.

Queens Park Rangers' Greatest Games

Francis appeared essential to making them come true. He scored again as Rangers drew their next home game against League Cup holders Aston Villa three days later.

And he helped the R's thrash 1975 champions Derby County 5-1, with a hat-trick from Bowles and one goal each by Dave Thomas and Dave Clement.

The tone had been set – and Francis was at its heart. Francis, whose uncle George had turned out for Rangers in the early 1960s, had arrived as a youngster to train once a week at the club each Tuesday.

He had been limited to playing for just a social club in a Sunday league as he attended a school which played rugby rather than football. But he impressed enough to be given an apprenticeship.

And when he made his league debut as a 17-year-old in a home defeat against Liverpool at Loftus Road, little did anyone realise it would lead to a day he and Rangers fans would never forget.

It would herald a title charge which went to the wire – on more than a wing and a prayer for the pigeon fancier from west London.

Francis said to Phil Shaw in *Backpass*, the retro football magazine, 'We knew we were a good side and felt we could go on and win things.

'The way we outplayed them – a fantastic side who were going to be title contenders – gave us a massive lift.'

Left-back Ian Gillard told your author in June 2013, 'That's the game that stood out for me that season at Loftus Road. That was a hard fought game. But we kept battling and trying to play.

'Liverpool weren't used to playing against a team the way we were playing them that day. They had their chances. We took ours. The overall pleasing thing was that we actually beat Liverpool who were at that time THE top team.'

27 v Leeds United 2-0

Football League First Division. Loftus Road
24 April 1976. Attendance: 31,002

QUEENS PARK RANGERS:	LEEDS UNITED :
Parkes	Harvey
Clement	Reaney
Gillard	F. Gray (Lorimer)
Hollins	Bremner
McLintock	Madeley
Webb	Hunter
Thomas	Harris
Francis	Cherry
Masson	Jordan
Bowles	McKenzie
Givens	E. Gray

Referee: W.J. Gow (Swansea)

'I'M GOING to get drunk. What are you doing Gerry?' That is what a disconsolate Stan Bowles said to his captain Gerry Francis after the dynamic duo had watched Liverpool defeat Wolverhampton Wanderers to seal the title and deny Queens Park Rangers their first top-tier Football League crown from a London television studio.

Ten days earlier Rangers had ended their season at the summit thanks to a 2-0 victory over Leeds United at Loftus Road amid scenes of joyous pitch celebrations.

But a fixture pile-up due to European commitments had given the Reds the advantage of knowing exactly what they had to do at Molineux to leapfrog the 'best team never to win the Football League' – either a victory or low-scoring draw.

Rangers got to within 13 minutes of the championship when a John Richards goal for Wolves was cancelled out by one from Kevin Keegan. And, as news reached the ground that Birmingham City had drawn at Sheffield United to relegate Wolves, the Midlanders collapsed and Bob Paisley's side completed a 3-1 win thanks to additional goals from John Toshack and Ray Kennedy.

But the power, panache and guts of the 2-0 dismantling of Don Revie's Leeds proved a testament to why Queens Park Rangers were rated the best side in England in the hearts and minds of the nation, even though the official title went to Merseyside.

It was a testament to their manager Dave Sexton, who sadly passed away in 2012.

Those are the beliefs of the team's loyal stalwart Ian Gillard.

Gillard remains mightily proud of his side, late manager and his own contribution as they combined to reflect just why he considers that side the greatest team in QPR's history on a sunny afternoon in front of 31,000 fans shoehorned into an arena that was rocking.

He said to your author in June 2013, 'The atmosphere was electric. Absolutely. It was a very hard fought game. They had Billy Bremner and all those sort of top players, but we just kept going and going and the result came right for us.

Queens Park Rangers' Greatest Games

'We knew we had to wait ten days before knowing if we'd win the title or not but it was fantastic after the Leeds game. All the players went up into the directors' box and were applauded by the fans.

'We were QPR's greatest side because everybody fought for each other. There was a great team spirit. We had our little blips, different results and all that, but we all stuck together.

'I'm a great believer in that it takes a team to win. You can have your individuals, which we did with players like Stan and Gerry. But you also have to all pull together and that's what we did.

'That's how we beat Leeds. Dave [Sexton] did a marvellous job. He made one or two changes, brought Don Masson in for £100,000 from Notts County, got in a couple of 'frees' and blended the team together.

'He used to go to training camps in Holland and studied German football. He got us to play in a more continental style with players rotating positions and we adapted to it.

'When myself and Dave Clement used to bomb on from full-back midfield players would drop in. The manager was so advanced in his techniques and coaching. He got us playing the way he wanted us to play and he proved a point in the 1975/76 season.

'It was a choker that we missed out in the end. But a lot of people, not just QPR, thought we deserved to have won the league that year. We worked our socks off. We reached a pinnacle for the club.'

Rangers refused to be distracted by a sense of injustice – over the timing of Liverpool's final fixture – as they set about Leeds.

They were able to lift themselves up, puff their chests and say to Liverpool and anyone else within earshot, 'If we are going down we are going down fighting to the last drop of blood. You have got to rip this trophy from our grasp. We ain't letting it go.'

Their fantasy football was on display alongside grit and determination for all to see as a season's-best crowd recorded gate receipts of £34,718 as Revie's Leeds came to town.

The supporters were ready to hail their heroes as champions. That in itself could have put pressure on the players who knew defeat – and most probably a draw – would gift the title to their Merseyside rivals.

But Rangers dug in against a team who rivalled Liverpool at the top of English football in the 1970s.

Leeds had a formidable line-up made up of most of the players which had forged their reputation as a force in English football.

They had Norman Hunter and Paul Madeley at the back with Paul Reaney and Frankie Gray at full-back, experienced skipper Billy Bremner and Trevor Cherry in midfield with talented Eddie Gray out wide and Joe Jordan, a battering ram of a centre-forward alongside the mercurial skills of Duncan McKenzie. And Peter Lorimer, known for his rocket-like shooting, was on the bench.

They had made a decent fist of a title challenge too and went in boasting the best away record in the league bar Liverpool in the season, having taken maximum points on eight occasions.

But Rangers took the game to their Yorkshire visitors. Bowles drew a foul from Bremner with the Leeds player believing his opponent had dived. Don Masson took the free kick which marauding defender Dave Webb, in echoes of his winning goal in the 1970 FA Cup Final against Leeds while at Chelsea, headed towards goal before being denied by visiting goalkeeper David Harvey.

v Leeds United 1976

Don Givens had a drive which cannoned off Leeds defender Paul Madeley.

The hosts almost hit the front with a beautifully worked move involving interplay between Don Masson, John Hollins and Don Givens who squared it for Gerry Francis to hit a volley from the edge of the box which Harvey saved low to his right.

Francis, resplendent in his bushy side-burns, had an effort blocked following a Dave Thomas cross from another Masson dead-ball kick by Harvey.

Masson had a shot charged down before Rangers thought they might have been awarded a penalty by referee Bill Gow.

Another well worked move between Thomas, Hollins, Masson and Frank McLintock put Bowles in possession in a central position on the edge of the D of the penalty area.

Bowles used his left foot to control the ball and his right to skip by Norman Hunter in a flash before crashing to the turf under a challenge from Carl Harris before Mr Gow waved away appeals for at least a free kick.

It was suggested Bowles might have dived, although a replay showed he was caught by Harris – a few inches OUTSIDE the box.

Tension rippled through the ground before Hunter relieved it for a few seconds by splitting his shorts and putting a new pair on after exposing his underpants.

Webb headed away a rare Leeds raid but Rangers continued to press. Another sweeping move saw McLintock, Bowles and Francis combine to create another opportunity. It ended when a Bowles shot took a deflection off a Leeds defender and a touch close in from Francis but the alert Harvey saved.

Patience was a hard quality to find but Sexton knew his side had to find it and keep plugging away as Mr Gow sounded the half-time whistle.

It seemed as if it would pay off with another superb movement when Bowles and Francis worked a one-two down the right to leave Leeds left-back Frank Gray chasing shadows before Bowles lifted the ball high towards the far post. Dave Thomas nodded the ball back across for Francis who was unable to make full contact with a bicycle kick and the ball went just wide.

Leeds gave Rangers a reminder they were not there just to make up the numbers as they threatened on the break and giant Rangers keeper Phil Parkes, who had received the Player of the Year trophy from boxer John H. Stracey before the kick-off, saved twice from Duncan McKenzie and once from Trevor Cherry.

Harvey then had to save bravely at the feet of Don Givens after the Republic of Ireland international had latched on to the ball following a slip-up from Leeds centre-back Paul Madeley dealing with a long Frank McLintock ball.

Finally QPR got their breakthrough when Dave Thomas put them ahead. Givens headed on a McLintock ball from the right and the diminutive Thomas nodded into the net at the far post unopposed. Francis drove just wide and energetic midfielder John Hollins headed over as Rangers searched for a second.

Again Leeds threatened on the break and substitute Peter Lorimer blasted wide from 20 yards, then McKenzie forced Parkes to save. And the QPR goalkeeper grabbed the ball on the line after a goalmouth scramble with Bremner left appealing to the referee, apparently either insisting the ball had gone over the line or that a Rangers defender had handled.

QPR allowed the tension to flow out of their bodies with their second goal. A superb long ball with the outside of his right boot by McLintock to Bowles on the right wing set it up.

Queens Park Rangers' Greatest Games

Bowles cut in, bamboozled Hunter and, with Francis screaming for a pass, elected to guide a left-footed shot into the far corner off goalkeeper Harvey's despairing hands.

Bowles looked almost embarrassed in his celebration as Dave Clement hugged him and one group of supporters waved their 'Bowles is God' flag.

But when the slight, shaggy-haired figure so beloved of the Rangers faithful returned to the centre circle he gave a wink to those offering congratulations close by.

He almost created a third goal when he turned Trevor Cherry inside out before crossing but Clement was unable to get over the ball and his header sailed over the bar.

Shortly afterwards the match was all over. Rangers had done something unique in their history by finishing their season top of the top division in English football for the first time having collected 27 of a possible 30 points in their last 15 games, and they had remained unbeaten at home. The fans rushed on to the pitch jumping up and down and chanting 'champions'. Premature, clearly. But who was going to begrudge them?

The race for the title developed into one which saw the emergence of shock contenders. Liverpool, reigning champions Derby Country and Leeds United, the 1974 winners, made up the usual suspects for a challenge. Aston Villa, under Ron Saunders, had been tipped to make a bid but it was another promoted team which shook up the favourites. Manchester United did so well they looked odds on to be crowned before their bubble burst in March.

Rangers, of course, were the other surprise package to the wider world outside London W12. Dave Sexton's team had been damned by faint praise by those who tipped who would do what during the season.

One pundit reckoned they were 'the best looking team in London', which was not saying much as north London rivals Tottenham Hotspur and Arsenal almost went down the previous season with West Ham United, although the Hammers had lifted the FA Cup, and were not that far away from the danger area themselves.

Sexton had instilled his tactical nous and adventurous approach, reflected in adopting Holland's fluid Total Football concept, into a team largely got together by his predecessor Gordon Jago, with the Stan Bowles-Gerry Francis partnership its axis.

And after Rangers' opening day performance against Liverpool (as described in a previous chapter) the world, or at least the Football League First Division title, seemed their oyster.

Gerry Francis, appointed England captain in September, was bullish about their chances as the gladiators gathered their weapons for the battle. He said at the time, 'We can beat any team in the country. If we can get consistency into our game there's no reason we can't be in the top three.'

Rangers were top by the end of September after reaching the summit of the top division for the first time in their history during the month when a Mick Leach goal secured a 1-0 win over Leicester City.

But they suffered their first reverse when Leeds came back from a Stan Bowles penalty to beat them 2-1 with a slip-up from Frank McLintock letting in Allan Clarke before Peter Lorimer hit the winner. But R's bounced back to top spot with a five-goal win against Everton, yet slipped to fifth before regaining momentum as they embarked on an astonishing record-breaking run when John Hollins and Francis fired the goals which defeated Aston Villa 2-0 at Villa Park on 31 January 1976.

They proceeded – during mild weather which kept pitches in good condition and allowed R's to play their free-flowing football – to extend an unbeaten sequence to 12 matches in which they won 11, netting 27 goals and conceding only seven.

v Leeds United 1976

They battered Wolverhampton Wanderers, Spurs at White Hart Lane, Ipswich Town, Coventry City, Everton and Middlesbrough and were too strong for Leicester City, Stoke City, Manchester City and Newcastle United. The only point dropped was in a goalless draw against Sheffield United.

The Bowles-Francis partnership thrived with their 'telepathic' understanding and their attributes as individuals. Francis put his foot in and offered a creative spark to earn him a comparison to footballing great Dave Mackay, who also had similar qualities which were rarely combined by others.

And Bowles insists he felt 'invincible' as he destroyed opponents with his skill, pace, flair and goals, while entertaining the crowd.

His private life, as Bowles admitted in his autobiography, caused Sexton grief. His gambling habits, time-keeping and regular transfer requests were three reasons.

He revealed how the habits constantly left him short of cash, leading him to seek win bonuses BEFORE games, a fashion shoot with a naked 'stunna', made-up 'exclusives' for the tabloids and turning up less than 15 minutes before the kick-off after watching a bet go down the drain.

Bowles told how chairman Jim Gregory indulged him with regular cash handouts and the loan of a house rent free (though Bowles sold the greenhouse in it to team-mate Dave Thomas to fund his gambling).

And Sexton, also, largely tolerated the lifestyle of his star player who was able to perform to his optimum on the field for the sake of the team.

The back unit – which mainly consisted of full-backs Dave Clement and Ian Gillard with veterans Dave Webb and Frank McLintock in the centre – was tight in front of giant stopper Phil Parkes, while displaying a taste for getting forward. Webb was often seen in opposing penalty areas causing havoc and seeking a goal.

In the middle, Don Masson, in front of the back four, had the skill and passing ability to get the team on the go before the likes of Francis and Bowles weaved their magic along with super-fit Dave Thomas and goalscoring Don Givens on the wings, supported by the versatility of Mick Leach. It was no wonder Bowles thought they were worth a £400 punt for the title. It was not a question of charging into the title equation, it was a case of turbo-charging into it.

Even Liverpool, during a decade synonymous in football with their dominance of it, looked up rather than over their shoulders after the Boro drubbing which featured a goal double from Francis and one apiece for Bowles and Don Givens in a 4-2 romp.

Rangers were back on top and the title was in their hands. If they won their remaining three fixtures it mattered not a jot what their Anfield rivals did.

Then came a defeat Rangers supporters will forever bemoan, a surprise 3-2 reverse against Norwich City at Carrow Road on 17 April 1976.

It was an encounter which justifiably could have made the final cut for this book such was its significance, but one your author felt might be too uncomfortable to dwell on for too long, especially for R's fans who went to East Anglia that day.

Dave Thomas scored a goal which rates among the best of any of the 67 Rangers eventually scored from their 42 games that season as he weaved through the home defence in a blur.

But there was no consolation to be had for the Hoops because the destination of the title had been ripped from their grasp by the mid-table but on-song Canaries and the fact that Bob Paisley's Reds had stuffed Stoke City the same afternoon.

Queens Park Rangers' Greatest Games

It meant Rangers not only had to win both their final games, but hope Liverpool slipped up in at least one of theirs.

Frank McLintock and Gerry Francis popped up with the goals as QPR pipped Arsenal at Loftus Road on Easter Monday.

Anxious Rangers fans tuned in transistor radios to see how Liverpool had got on against Manchester City at Maine Road that same afternoon. The news was bad. City were not the force they were at the end of the 1960s and the Reds had romped in.

And then it was down to the last fixture. Francis said to *Backpass* magazine in 2011, 'We had a great team and ought to have won it, really.'

Of the ten-day delay, Francis said, 'That would never be allowed to happen now; the last matches would kick off simultaneously. It was out of order because it meant Liverpool knew what they had to do.

'Give Liverpool full credit. They were always up there, decade after decade. They were a big club, a buying club rather than a selling club like QPR.

'We were still a small club really. So they were able to build on winning the league, which they did. That season, though, I honestly thought we were the best side.'

The understanding Francis and Bowles had was a big part of that. Francis said, 'We had such an understanding. Telepathic. I could play things blind and he could do the same. Really, really enjoyed playing together.'

Bowles said, 'Gerry and I hit it of straight away. Terry Venables said right away when we played together on the first day in a five-a-side at training – we'd never met each other before but just hit it off straight away. I loved playing with Gerry.'

They got on off the field too, although Francis recalls the relationship had its moments.

Francis said, 'We were sitting down eating our lunch and there was a knock at the door. His wife at the time answered the door.

'It was the bailiffs. They came in and took the table we were eating on, the chairs we were sitting in and the television we were watching. After they'd gone we looked at our plates of food – they were on the floor. So that was life with Stan Bowles.'

Francis said of watching Liverpool beat Wolves 3-1, 'It was sad to watch 90 minutes of football and see your whole season go up in flames.'

Reds captain Emlyn Hughes, now passed away, said at the time, 'QPR had come from nowhere. Suddenly it's "whoops we're challenging for the title". And it gets into a player's mind thinking "are we capable of winning the league title?" It gets into your mind. We knew if we just hung in that we'd eventually win it.'

Rangers' 1908 squad which won the Southern League and faced Manchester United in the first FA Charity Shield match

QPR squad which completed a second Southern League title and FA Charity Shield runners-up Double

Rangers all-time leading goalscorer George Goddard who netted four in record 8-3 win against Swindon Town in 1930

Tommy Cheetham who struck a treble in Rangers' record 8-1 FA Cup win over Bristol Rovers in 1937

Goalkeeper Reg Allen who helped seal 1948 Third Division title against Swansea Town

QPR flying winger Ernie Shepherd who hit a hat-trick in 7-1 second-tier win over Grimsby Town

Dave Mangnall's Rangers squad which clinched the 1948 Third Division South title

QPR hotshot Brian Bedford who scored twice in the 1960 record 9-2 win over Tranmere Rovers, fired four against Southend United and hit a hat-trick in the White City win over Hull City

Tony Ingham, Rangers' all-time appearance maker who scored a rare goal in a 1957 victory over Watford

Roger Morgan heads the first goal for QPR in the 1967 League Cup final

Rodney Marsh scores the equaliser in the 1967 League Cup final

Mark Lazarus (No.7) celebrates after scoring the winner in the 1967 League Cup final

QPR celebrate their 1967 League Cup triumph at Wembley. Back row (left to right): Mike Keen (captain), Tony Hazell, Ron Hunt, Mark Lazarus, Les Allen, Frank Sibley and Jim Langley. Front row: Peter Springett, Roger Morgan, Rodney Marsh, Ian Morgan and Keith Sanderson

Rangers chairman and owner Jim Gregory with the 1967 League Cup and Third Division championship trophy

QPR thwarted by Leicester City goalkeeper Peter Shilton during Rangers' first ever top-flight game, at Loftus Road in 1968

Gerry Francis, Frank McLintock and QPR manager Dave Sexton celebrate finishing their 1975/76 season top of the First Division table following victory over Leeds United

Gerry Francis scores one of his two penalties in the 1976/77 UEFA Cup quarter-final victory over AEK Athens

QPR beating Slovan Bratislava on way to 1976/77 UEFA Cup quarter-finals against AEK Athens

Rangers captain Glenn Roeder introduces Princess Anne to the team before the 1982 FA Cup final

Gary Bannister scores for QPR in the 5-5 draw with Newcastle United in 1984

Alan McDonald, who shone in the 1986 League Cup semi-final against Liverpool at Anfield

Rangers goalkeeper David Seaman who shone in 1990 FA Cup win over Arsenal, his next club

Rangers striker Dennis Bailey who hit a famed hat-trick against Manchester United at Old Trafford in 1992

Ray Wilkins who took part in QPR's 1990 FA Cup win against Arsenal, the first ever win in 1991 at Liverpool and the 1992 league win at Manchester United

Les Ferdinand who wrote this book's foreword and shone in Rangers' first victory at Liverpool in 1991 and hit a second hat-trick over three days against Everton

Trevor Sinclair who was famed for his Goal of the Season bicycle kick against Barnsley in the 1997 FA Cup

Ian Holloway's Rangers' 2004 promotion squad

v SK Brann 7-0

UEFA Cup first round. Brann Stadion
29 September 1976. Attendance: 11,527

QUEENS PARK RANGERS:
Parkes
Clement
Gillard
Hollins
McLintock
Webb
Thomas
Leach (Busby)
Masson
Bowles
Givens

SK BRANN:
Not known

Referee: Jan Kelzer (Netherlands)

STAN BOWLES blew hot in the cold. Bowles the Goals, as he was neatly and appropriately dubbed by the media, had promised a repeat of the hat-trick he had scored in the first leg.

And he kept it as Queens Park Rangers defeated part-timers SK Brann 7-0 in Bergen to complete an 11-0 aggregate victory over the Norwegians as his side made a successful bow in European competition.

The only away result in Rangers' history to match it came when they summarily dismissed Bristol Rovers 8-1 in a first-round FA Cup tie in 1937.

Bowles, the free-scoring footballer with the fear of flying, steeled himself for a flight around the Arctic Circle to the city in an area known as the Seven Mountains.

And the trip to Bergen, on the west coast of Norway and dubbed the Gateway to the Fjords, afforded an extraordinary experience for Bowles, his team-mates and the Rangers supporters' club members who had booked the same Dan Air flight out of Gatwick at £89 per head inclusive of accommodation.

Stan the Man kept his promise of netting a treble and QPR celebrated their first away match in a European competition with a record 7-0 victory – with Don Givens (two), Dave Webb and Dave Thomas scoring – to complete the first-round victory.

And Bowles and the rest of the Rangers party got to know a little of a part of the world known for reindeer, fjords, being a sea cruise away from viewing the Northern Lights – 'nature's fireworks' – and the Midnight Sun. And vast empty spaces.

As one fan, Robin Haldane, who posted his recollections on the Indyrs website, discovered on a three-hour walk around his hotel when he did not see one other human being, 'a far cry' from what he was used to around his home in Earlsfield, south London.

Around 150 supporters made the trip and they were rewarded after Rangers took to the field. Despite its proximity to the Arctic Circle, Bergen is known for its mild winters thanks to the warm Gulf Stream.

But temperatures have been known to dip to minus 13.3 degrees centigrade and it was a trifle parky when QPR kicked off.

In fact it was so cold full-back Ian Gillard told your author in June 2013, 'There was a doubt about it going ahead.'

The first leg against SK Brann had been an event. Rangers had faced European opposition in friendlies under Sexton, who was keen to compare the progress he had been making with his continental approach at source.

And generally the experimental games brought success, although one such match against SK Brann had resulted in a 1-0 defeat.

But dipping a toe in the water of European competition was a whole other ball game. It was the litmus test. How would Rangers fare in this new arena?

Stan Bowles had invited George Best, whom he knew from Manchester, and the Rangers icon certainly turned it on in front of the world icon under the Loftus Road floodlights.

Rangers swiftly took a grip on the game but the fans, baying for a goal to kick off their continental experience in style, had to remain patient as the Norwegian visitors hung on.

Bowles put the home faithful out of their misery by putting QPR ahead by converting a Dave Webb pass after 29 minutes. Stan the Man struck once more four minutes later as he made it 2-0.

He secured his treble after 64 minutes before Don Masson wrapped things up on 85 against a club rated as a premier force in their own country but not, it seems, beyond, its borders (although Tore Andre Flo came from the club to make a good fist of a career with Chelsea in the English top flight in the 1990s).

The comfortable nature of the victory took the pressure off for the second leg. But Rangers were entering a whole other world in the away match.

It could have been a whole lot different moving into an alien environment – and perhaps one or two of the natives were restless over some history between the English and Norwegians back in the 14th century when a ship from our shores docked in Bergen and inadvertently spread the Black Death!

But Rangers, though, swiftly adapted to unfamiliar surroundings at the Brann Stadion to cruise into the second round.

Dave Webb put them ahead after just two minutes. The veteran centre-back, ignoring a bone-hard surface, dived forward in heroic fashion to connect with a ball in from out wide by Dave Thomas and head the spherical object beyond Brann goalkeeper Jan Knudsen.

The hosts had the temerity to cause Rangers discomfort a few minutes later. And Rangers stopper Phil Parkes warmed himself up in the freezing cold with a couple of decent saves.

It got worse before it got better for the visitors when versatile Mick Leach was removed from the action after suffering a knee injury following a challenge from midfielder Larsen midway through the opening half.

It was clear Leach, feeling the whack he had just received, would not be returning to the field of play for the remainder of the 90 minutes as Thomas and Rangers' club trainer-physiotherapist Richard Roberts helped him limp to the sidelines. He was replaced by Martyn Busby.

Rangers' fortunes veered back towards good when they doubled their lead on the night and made it 6-0 overall eight minutes before the interval when Don Givens managed to squeeze an angled drive home.

v SK Brann 1976

The screw on the helpless hosts was tightened even more after-half time. It was torture by a thousand cuts for the hosts as Rangers came down on SK Brann like a knife through melted butter.

But the visitors had to wait until the 68th minute before they added to their total. Bowles netted his first of the game to make in 3-0 after 68 minutes when he diverted a Don Masson cross into the net.

Within two minutes Givens had scored his second from a Thomas ball and Rangers led 8-0 on aggregate.

Any resistance from the Norwegians evaporated. It must have seemed mission impossible from the outset for a group of players who earned their livings in other walks of life. Their lack of full-time training combined with a lowering of any spirit which was lying at the bottom of the barrel. Their experience at Loftus Road had left them a mountain – if not seven mountains – to climb.

And if there was a place below the foothills, they were in it with Rangers dominant and hungry for more. Brann remained on the hook and the visitors made them suffer.

Brann conceded three more goals in the final ten minutes. Thomas had proved a constant thorn in Brann's side as a creator of goals and finally turned one in himself after 81 minutes.

Bowles secured his treble four and two minutes from time then Dutch referee Jan Kelzer ended Brann's agony to leave Sexton and his troops ecstatic.

Rangers earned praise from the members of the press corps who joined them for their Norwegian experience.

The Times reported, 'Bowles completes annihilation of amateurs', and that the Brann defence was 'cut to ribbons'. The *Daily Mirror* splashed the headline, 'Bowles Blitz'.

And some of the supporters who made the trip recalled how a Bergen newspaper printed a picture of Bowles shrugging his shoulders as if apologising to his hosts for having the bad manners to bang in three goals against them once more.

The caption read 'Jeg er let meg Brann', which, translated into English means 'Sorry Brann'. Hopes had been high that Rangers would enjoy success on their debut in European competition.

Manager Dave Sexton had been influenced by the adventurous and entertaining Total Football methods adopted by the Dutch and the superb technical skills to be found within the West German system.

And it reflected in the performances of Queens Park Rangers in the 1975/76 season. It was, as you have discovered by now, a style which English football fans took to their heart.

The 'best team never to win the Football League' – as Rangers have been dubbed in the title of an official club DVD of that momentous season – seemed ready-made for the UEFA Cup.

Their manager, as we know, had even got them used to playing continental opposition with the series of winning friendlies against Red Star Belgrade, Moscow Dynamo, Benfica and UEFA Cup holders Borussia Monchengladbach.

Sexton must have salivated at the thought of competing against those who had given him ideas which put him in advance of most coaches in the domestic game.

What better vindication could he have than taking on his mentors and others to prove the pupil had become a master of what they had taught him.

For the players, it would be a chance to help the manager who had done so much for their careers. He had inherited a decent team from Gordon Jago with the likes of

Queens Park Rangers' Greatest Games

Bowles, Dave Thomas and Don Givens, and moulded them into a team which finished the 1975/76 season top of the pile in arguably the greatest league in the world.

And for the fans it would be an opportunity to collect a bundle of life experiences which could be placed in the compartment of the memory banks on quick and constant recall.

Visits to countries merely seen in an atlas to experience new cultures, cuisine and soccer. Being part of glory glory nights under the Loftus Road floodlights as visitors from across the English Channel came to call.

And owner and chairman Jim Gregory would be able to reflect on another unique step on the journey he had taken them – rescuing them from close to extinction to competing in Europe with the hope of financial rewards to be gleaned from the higher profile.

It was a win-win situation for the football club formed in Paddington when two youth club teams, St Jude's Institute and Christchurch, combined in the 1880s.

UEFA Cup fever swept through London W12 and its environs the moment a runners-up spot in the First Division confirmed their entry. The European Cup would have been good but no one was getting greedy down the Bush.

The first round was most certainly an example of an experience to be re-told to children and grandchildren and passed on down through the generations.

R's went into the Brann tie with their tails up. Rangers were two points off Liverpool in the race for the league title and making headway in the League Cup after overcoming Cardiff City 3-1 at Ninian Park thanks to goals from Bowles, Thomas and Dave Clement before a 2-1 home win against Bury, with Frank McLintock and Don Givens hitting the target (the start of another decent run in a competition they had won ten years previously – more later).

They might have been without their Captain Fantastic – Gerry Francis – due to injury but it seemed they were making up for his absence judging from their demolition of Brann.

Gillard told your author in June 2013, 'It was exciting to be in Europe. We wanted to try and do well, but if you ask me what our first experience of it abroad was I would use one, maybe two, words. Cold or very cold. It was freezing.

'We didn't even think we'd play the game. It was minus whatever. We adapted to the pitch and played some decent football. The scoreline showed the difference between full-time and part-time players.'

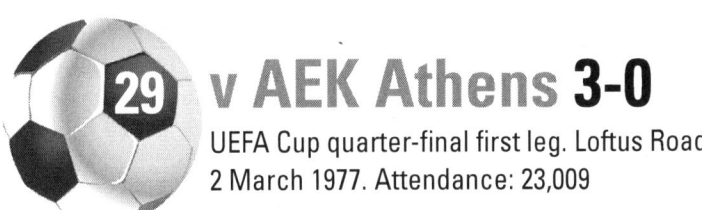

29 v AEK Athens 3-0

UEFA Cup quarter-final first leg. Loftus Road
2 March 1977. Attendance: 23,009

QUEENS PARK RANGERS:	AEK ATHENS:
Parkes	Stergioudas
Hollins	Nikolaou
Gillard	Ravoussis
Kelly	Intzoglou
McLintock	Theodoridis
Webb	Tsamis
Thomas	Papadopoulos (Tasos)
Francis	Nikoloudis
Masson	Papaionnou
Bowles	Wagner
Givens	Mavros

Referee: Ole Amundsen (Denmark)

STAN BOWLES, voted Queens Park Rangers' all-time cult hero in a BBC poll in 2004, broke the individual scoring record for a British player in one season of European competition when he struck 11 goals to beat the marker laid down by Manchester United's Denis Law during the 1976/77 campaign.

And his 11th goal helped Rangers overcome AEK Athens 3-0 at Loftus Road on 2 March 1977 to put themselves in the box seat for a place in the semi-finals of the UEFA Cup.

Bowles's goal added to two penalties from Gerry Francis to ensure R's would go to the Greek capital for the second leg of their last-eight encounter at the 70,000-capacity Olympic Stadium confident of getting through in their first season of continental competition.

And full-back Ian Gillard vividly recalls Stan the Man showing why he was the hottest of the UK's European hotshots on an evening packed with unforgettable memories.

Gillard told your author in June 2013, 'Stan was good that night. He had a great campaign overall and we all enjoyed it too.'

The atmosphere at Loftus Road on a European glory night is arguably better than an equivalent occasion at Old Trafford, the Nou Camp, the Bernabeu or even the Allianz Stadium in terms of in-your-face action as the floodlights blaze down surrounded by a pitch-black sky at Rangers' compact home.

Squeezed-in spectators, 23,000 of them when AEK came to London W12, standing and sitting shoulder to shoulder, are so close to the players their roars of encouragement for their Heroes in Hoops, to borrow the title of a book by John Marks, are close to ear-splitting. Their verbal fire and brimstone towards opponents is of a comparable decibel level. And any performer close to the touchline had best be advised to wear earplugs. The venue is intimidating, particularly against visiting teams used to a big stadium in which the atmosphere can be more diluted.

Queens Park Rangers' Greatest Games

The trouble for QPR, as you have probably guessed, is that such nights are as rare as rain in the desert given the club have yet to develop a reputation as perennial campaigners on the European stage.

They were denied the opportunity of competing in the UEFA Cup on account of them being too low down the pyramid of English football on winning the League Cup in 1967. 'We can't have oiks from the Third Division lowering the standard' was, we guess, the private thought of individuals who ran Europe's governing body.

Nine years later, in 1976, UEFA could not argue against Rangers' inclusion. Dave Sexton's side were not only firmly established in the top division of the Football League but had come within one or two points of qualifying for the association's big one.

You know, the one Alfredo di Stefano and his original Galacticos in all-white representing Real Madrid won when the Bernabeu giants ruled the competition in the 1950s and early part of the 1960s.

The one the likes of Lionel Messi's Barcelona, Sir Alex Ferguson's Manchester United and Arjen Robben's Bayern Munich have taken such a shine to in more recent years. The European Cup.

And the visit of AEK Athens illustrated how suited Sexton's men were to the continental competition.

Gillard recalls how he guessed every resident in London with a link to the Greek capital, its mainland or islands in the Aegean, seemed to be present that night.

He pondered on whether Mediterranean restaurants owned by members of the capital's Hellenic communities were either closed for the evening or being run by a skeleton staff of non-football fans serving up dishes such as moussaka and grilled fish.

It was decades away from Greece winning the 2004 Euro tournament. But AEK Athens were a useful outfit, the oldest club in their city (formed in 1896) and the first team to complete a national league and cup double as they established themselves as one of Greece's most successful and famous clubs.

They had finished runners-up in the Greek League two years in a row under Frantisek Fadrhonc, who was appointed manager by new chairman Loukas Barlos in the wake of leading Johan Cruyff's Holland to the 1974 World Cup Final.

Sexton would have been impressed with Fadrhonc, being a student of the Dutch game, and approving of the fluid style of football he had got his Greek team to employ.

AEK also included several players brought to the club by their Dutch boss with right-sided forward Walter Wagner arriving soon after Fadrhonc came to the club.

And for the 1976/77 campaign right-sided forward Thomas Mavros, left-sided striker Takis Nikoloudis, central defender Petros Ravousis and reserve goalkeeper Nikos Christidis (who was to play a vital role in deciding the tie – more later) were all added.

The visitors had also become battle-hardened in the competition having disposed of Moscow Dynamo with a penalty from Tasos Konstantou in the last minute of extra time in the second leg.

AEK then saw off Derby County, which led to the sacking of the English club's Dave Mackay after a league title, two top-four finishes and an FA Cup semi-final in three years.

Red Star Belgrade blocked their path to the last eight, but they overcame the Yugoslavians on the away goals rule thanks to a Walter Wagner strike after Mimis Papaloannu and Thomas Mavros goals and a clean sheet saw them through the first leg.

The pedigree of the visitors made Rangers' victory and the absence of banned Dave Clement all the more impressive.

v AEK Athens 1977

Equally impressive was the fact Rangers were able to turn on the magic despite a poor pitch with mud patches, one extending almost the entire middle area between the edge of the centre circle to the edge of the penalty area on one half of it, and stretches of sand all over it.

QPR were very much aware of the state of the surface and had tried to delay the game 24 hours so it could be staged at Wembley, but AEK declined the offer perhaps as the green sward of the national stadium would suit Rangers' free-flowing style.

But Rangers were fortunate in as much as the Greeks on the night bore gifts, clearly caught in the floodlights.

By 11 minutes Rangers were two goals in front with AEK conceding two penalties.

The first came in the seventh minute. Bowles chased a headed clearance, took a touch and jinked towards the byline to get the ball across. AEK defender Tsamis, no doubt a believer in the justified goalscoring reputation of the talisman who was side on and facing away from goal, appeared to put his body into the player of slighter build. Bowles went flying and ended up face down.

Francis stepped up and visiting goalkeeper Lakis Stergloudas moved before the midfielder connected with the ball and was off his line leaning to his right as Rangers' spot-king put it to his left. Francis converted his second four minutes later in almost a carbon-copy face-to-face, though this time the stopper ventured even further forward as the QPR ace maintained his composure to plant the ball into the same corner of the net that his previous effort had nestled.

The award came about after Don Givens had latched on to a Don Masson ball and rounded a defender before the covering defender Petros Ravoussis was adjudged to have caught the Republic of Ireland international who was one-on-one with the goalkeeper.

AEK had arrived intent on a containing game and decided they needed to start venturing forward to claw back at least one away goal, which would count double if the aggregate score was even. But they were caught out on the counter with Masson again a central figure as Rangers netted their third goal shortly before the interval.

Frank McLintock arced a long ball forward to Bowles who, with his back to goal on halfway, guided it out to Rangers' right with a first-time touch to Masson.

Bowles began a run towards goal and he met a Masson cross first time to side-foot home from the six-yard line with the yellow shirts and black shorts of the opposition nowhere and Stergloudas helpless.

Any thoughts of an AEK comeback faded when the superb Papadopolis was injured. Mobile Mavros took a few tricks out of his bag to try and get something back for the visitors but Rangers remained locked tight at the back.

Masson went close to a fourth but Rangers believed three goals and a clean sheet would be enough to see them through.

That Loftus Road was such a hotbed that night was largely because the Rangers faithful had been revved up by the exploits of Sexton's side earlier in the competition following their record-smashing 11-0 battering of Norwegian part-timers SK Brann in the opening round described in an earlier chapter.

Rangers put on what has been described as one of their greatest ever away performances as they took on Slovan Bratislava in the next round.

There are a few other contenders for that accolade, such as the five-goal thrashing of First Division champions Derby County in 1975, overcoming Liverpool in 1991, Manchester United in 1992 and Everton in 1993 (the last three featured in later chapters).

Queens Park Rangers' Greatest Games

But the display against the boys from Bratislava comfortably rivals all those efforts when you bear in mind their opponents included seven of the Czech team which had just become European champions by defeating World Cup holders West Germany after overcoming Johan Cruyff's Holland in the last four. They included Jan Svehilk, who scored in the final.

It was witnessed first-hand by about 50 Rangers fans in a 40,000 crowd. The supporters had endured a two-day coach journey via Frankfurt and Vienna to be there but those few were left with lifetime memories.

Bernard Joy, the former Arsenal player turned *Evening Standard* reporter, wrote, 'QPR's performance ranks among the finest I have seen from an English side in away ties since European competitions started in 1955.'

And their rivals' coach Michael Vican was quoted as saying, 'Rangers do not play like any other English team.'

Vican picked out Bowles and Thomas for special mention, but the architect of Rangers' effort was manager Dave Sexton, using his knowledge of continental football.

Bowles and Givens put Rangers ahead after the hosts had taken the lead. Bratislava bounced back to lead 3-2 before Bowles levelled in a thriller. And Givens (three), Bowles and Clement scored in a 5-2 win in the home leg.

FC Cologne were edged out in the following round. Givens, Dave Webb and Bowles scored in a 3-0 first-leg victory at Loftus Road. And preventing Cologne from scoring proved crucial.

Don Masson scored early to quieten a vociferous 40,000 crowd in the return leg. But the wheels began to come off the QPR wagon as the hosts hit three before the interval after Clement got his marching orders for violent conduct and the hosts made it 4-1 on the night. But a series of superb Phil Parkes saves ensured QPR went through to face AEK Athens on the away goals rule.

It looked, as we know, as though Rangers were on the march into the last four, but the soccer Gods declined to look down on them favourably as it all unravelled at a half-full, still-lively Olympic Stadium as they lost the second leg 3-0 against AEK before exiting the tournament after losing a penalty shoot-out.

Mavros rifled home the first from the edge of the area as the Greek supporters waved their banners and let off flares.

Rangers were caught out by a breakaway goal as the hosts moved towards a goal of levelling the aggregate.

Again it was Mavros who pressed the acceleration button when he turned and drifted by a challenge in his own half. Rangers temporarily blocked his progress 20 yards out but a deflection presented the ball back to him and the forward drove beyond Phil Parkes from just inside the box. AEK made it 3-0 on the night and 3-3 overall when Mimis Papaloannou headed home a cross.

Drama unfolded in the penalty shoot-out as AEK missed the target when Takis Nikoloudis rolled his effort wide of Parkes's right-hand post.

But Frantisek Fadrhonc had already pulled what proved to be a master stroke. Three minutes before the end of extra time he substituted the erratic Stergloudas, who seemed unable to cope with penalties, with Nikos Christidis. And it was the reserve stopper who emerged the hero for the Greek side.

With the shoot-out score standing at 6-6, Chrisitidis dived to his right to keep out a well-struck effort from David Webb.

v AEK Athens 1977

The European odyssey had ended for Rangers and the crowd went crazy with delight as the hosts made it to the semi-finals where they lost to eventual cup winners Juventus of Italy.

But for Rangers it was like sport imitating life; it was about the journey.

QPR, who disappointed in the league, had been boosted in their efforts with a parallel path in the League Cup, the dream of emulating the team of 1967 ended by Aston Villa over three matches in the semi-final.

Rangers' international defender Ian Gillard told your author in June 2013, 'I remember that night we beat AEK at Loftus Road well. There were a lot of Greek football supporters in London and we were swamped with them. But we absolutely paralysed their team and we were delighted for Stan getting the goal record.

'Unfortunately when we went out there the same thing happened to us. It would have been great to have played Juventus in the semi-finals. A real downer.

'The Slovan Bratislava away game sticks in my memory. I had to mark a guy who taught me a few lessons when I was playing for England against Czechoslovakia. A quality player. It was a great game. But we beat them convincingly in the second leg.

'Cologne absolutely battered us after we went 1-0 up in the first ten minutes. They thought it was going to be extra time after they'd beaten us 4-1 and the aggregate scores were level. We knew that we were through thanks to our away goal! That was nice.

'I enjoyed the League Cup run but Villa battered us in the third game. Our league form was shoddy but not because we had one eye on Europe. It was the fact we had a small squad so injuries made it difficult.'

Bowles said in his autobiography, 'The Greek manager had said in the press after the game [the first leg against AEK Athens] that the ref had been very biased towards us and that I had scored an offside goal. He implied that we had bribed the referee with gifts and money.

'They moaned about the penalties as well. In the directors' box things had got very heated. Jim Gregory [the Rangers chairman and owner] had welcome the AEK Athens officials in traditional hospitable style, exchanging gifts, kissing each other on the cheeks, and all that business.

'But by the end of the match the two lots of club officials were squaring up to each other, as the Greek contingent got very excitable. Jim threw them all out of the box.

'One Greek official's parting shot to Jim was, "When you come to Greece we will slit your throat." Jim replied, "I've got news for you, I'm not going to Greece. Now f*** off." A couple of days after the game I started to receive death threats. It didn't bother me.

'(For the second leg) we had to contend with a very hostile crowd. The fans were throwing huge rotten apples on to the pitch before the game had even started.

'When we arrived at the ground in the team coach we came through a narrow entrance near to one of the stands. The Greek supporters were up there pissing down all over us.

'I had to time most of my runs down the wing using the linesman as a human shield. After a while the crowd ran out of apples and began tossing tomatoes at me. The referee was obviously terrified of the crowd.

'We were the better side but with three of our best players missing we had struggled. We had gone down fighting but that defeat in Athens was very hard to accept. It was one of the most disappointing moments of my career.'

Club historian Gordon Macey said, 'Those European nights under the floodlights in 1976/77 were special.'

Queens Park Rangers' Greatest Games

David Luddy, who covered the game for the *Kilburn Times*, remembers a hostile atmosphere inside and outside the Olympic Stadium in Athens.

He told your author in July 2013, 'I was in a coach with other journalists such as Donald Saunders of the *Daily Telegraph* and Victor Railton and their fans were throwing things at it.

'Inside we took our place in the press box behind a thin plate of glass. I saw one of their fans and it looked as though he was going to put his fist through the glass.

'And as he did I pulled Donald back out of the way and there was blood on his copy paper as he wrote his report. There were no laptops in those days.

'I was also friendly with all the players partly because I used to be allowed on the coach for away games in England with them as the local reporter.

'Anyway, we were in Greece and Victor Railton said to me, "I'll give you two fives if you can get Stan Bowles to say whatever it was" – nothing too controversial – so I agreed.

'I knew Stan and got him to say what Victor wanted him to say. Then I slipped the copy under Victor's hotel door and the next morning I received an envelope with two fivers in it. Big money for a local reporter in those days.'

30 v Coventry City 5-1
Football League First Division. Loftus Road
28 April 1979. Attendance: 10,950

QUEENS PARK RANGERS:	COVENTRY CITY:
Richardson	Sealey
Clement	Coop
Gillard	Holton
Hollins	Roberts
Howe	McDonald
Roeder	Hutchison
Busby	Powell
Shanks	Blair
Walsh	Wallace
Goddard	Nardiello (Gooding)
Allen	Hunt

Referee: Not known

CLIVE ALLEN has a cutting from the sports pages of the *Ealing Gazette* newspaper from west London stored among his memorabilia. It is a pastiche of the front page of the *Roy of the Rovers* comic with the cartoons cut out and replaced by pictures of him scoring each of his goals while completing a hat-trick on his full debut for Queens Park Rangers against Coventry City at Loftus Road on 28 April 1979.

It is an idea your author thought would reflect the instant hit the 17-year-old had made during his time as sports editor of a bi-weekly series which covered Rangers.

It clearly struck a chord with Allen with the mere fact the clipping remains in his possession more than 30 years later

Allen told your author in July 2013, 'I remember that *Roy of the Rovers* page. I've got a copy of it at home in my scrapbook. It is a fond memory of a fantastic day for me, really.'

Rangers had to come back from behind when Coventry took the lead through Ian Wallace after nine minutes. The striker, who signed for European Cup holders Nottingham Forest the following year, headed against the bar before pouncing on the rebound to beat Rangers goalkeeper Derek Richardson.

Allen levelled with his first goal in the 19th minute. Its execution was to prove a rarity among the hundreds he went on to score. The striker, who developed a reputation as a fox-in-the-box when it came to hitting the target, slipped his marker to drive the ball beyond Coventry goalkeeper Les Sealey from outside the penalty area.

He was closer in to put Rangers in front a minute after the re-start. The hosts began the move from the back with Martyn Busby carrying the ball through the field before supplying the striker who was Johnny on the Spot, rifling beyond the helpless Sealey.

Six minutes later Don Shanks made it 3-1 to QPR with a header from a left-wing cross by Republic of Ireland international striker Mickey Walsh, who was to make his name with FC Porto where he appeared in the UEFA Cup Final, after being fed the ball by midfielder Martyn Busby.

Queens Park Rangers' Greatest Games

Allen's strike partner Paul Goddard missed a golden opportunity to pile on the misery for the visitors.

But soon after Allen completed his treble when he seized on a defence-splitting through ball from Busby to fire home.

Rangers were unstoppable and five minutes later they completed their scoring when Mick Walsh converted a penalty after Coventry defender Bobby McDonald appeared to punch the ball clear under pressure. The over-worked electronic scoreboard flashed up 'goal' and QPR had secured a result which belied their plight.

Those who came to give the last rites to the club's First Division status were left wide-eyed in wonderment. The result came out of the blue and was a diamond in the rough – and it allowed its most shining jewel to shine a month short of 18 years old.

Clive Allen's name was not on the team list for QPR in the match programme but it was certainly up in lights by the time the final whistle sounded.

He said to your author in July 2013, 'I remember having to claw the game back. The goals are difficult to recall vividly in detail from this distance. I do remember the first one was from outside the box if I remember right.

'The pitch was really, really heavy. A muddy pitch and Coventry wore a horrible chocolate brown strip. Certain things stick in your mind.

'I couldn't have dreamed of anything like that. It was a dream come true. It really was. I was told on the Friday I was starting on the Saturday. It was one of those. Like falling asleep dreaming of something like that was happening, but never imagining it would happen.

'In a way it was the innocence of youth, I think, helped me. I was very fortunate because I was born into a footballing family.

'I'd been in and around QPR as a football club since I was five or six years of age. It was like a second home for me. The magnitude of a debut, although it was special, it wasn't that great.

'It wasn't something I was going to be overawed by. It was almost like it was my destiny that this was my time. My chance. And I felt really comfortable with it all.

'The manager just said "go out and play and enjoy yourself". Do what I'd been doing. Nothing brain-storming. I'd scored goals through the youth team and reserve team. I think he identified the talent.

'I felt very relaxed. Obviously nervous, but felt comfortable doing what I wanted to do. Fantastic.

'I maintained my perspective. I was never allowed to do otherwise. My dad told me to keep my feet on the ground. It was "now you've scored a hat-trick you've got to go and do it again the next game, the next week". I was never ever allowed to get carried away with what I did that day.'

It seemed as if manager Steve Burtenshaw felt the injection of Allen's youth was needed to give Rangers a lift as they fought relegation (in an ultimately doomed bid to survive in the First Division).

The campaign had been a traumatic one even before it kicked off. Boss Frank Sibley resigned and was temporarily replaced by Alec Stock, who had guided Rangers to the 1967 League Cup and back-to-back promotions into the First Division, before Burtenshaw was appointed Sibley's full-time replacement.

Burtenshaw instigated a shake-up. Many members of the team, some of whom had given the club sterling service, like Don Givens, a key member of the great Rangers team of the mid-1970s, were shipped out.

v Coventry City 1979

Republic of Ireland winger Givens departed to Birmingham City, Wales international flanker Leighton James to Burnley and Brian Williams ended up at Swindon Town.

Burtenshaw signed ball-playing centre-back Glenn Roeder from Leyton Orient, who experts felt could become the next Bobby Moore with his skilled, calm approach.

He also bought Crystal Palace crowd favourite Rachid Harkouk, a forward nicknamed Spider, to try and spread his web for the benefit of Rangers and a young striker in Billy Hamilton from Northern Ireland.

And, most tellingly, Allen was taken on as a professional following an apprenticeship.

Burtenshaw's tenure saw Rangers struggle despite the new faces.

A five-goal hammering against Arsenal, who the manager had coached in succession to Don Howe, saw them prop up the First Division. It was their third reverse in four.

There was a brief reprieve when Peter Eastoe and Harkouk scored to record the side's first victory of the season, which came against Middlesbrough on Teesside.

Like London buses, when one arrives so does another and Harkouk was on target with the solitary goal it took to defeat Aston Villa at Loftus Road seven days later. A mixed bag of results saw them edge up to 13th. They would go no higher and they slid into the mire, hovering just above the relegation zone at the turn of the year. It got worse with five defeats on the bounce following a hat-trick of deadlocks.

Now the problem of hanging on to their best players enveloped the R's. Top performers want to perform at the top. That is logical and it seemed QPR were heading for a support slot in the Second Division.

Rangers' prized assets attracted attention and a couple were lost. Striker Eastoe was sold to Everton and, most significantly, West Ham United swooped for Phil Parkes. Rangers were able to cash in with the £550,000 paid being a world record fee for a goalkeeper.

But the giant stopper had been an outstanding servant, one of the stars of Rangers' super side earlier in the decade. It was a massive hole to fill.

Reserve Derek Richardson, who had arrived as cover from Chelsea in 1976, did his best, but was placed in a difficult position trying to establish himself in an ailing first team short on confidence.

Results got worse and Rangers were in the zone. The relegation zone. And their chances of escape lessened as their nearest rivals Wolverhampton Wanderers pulled clear. Rangers trailed the Molineux club by four points and had played two games more.

The sun was setting on Rangers' time in the First Division as the season drew to a close and another managerial change took place with Burtenshaw sacked and replaced by Tommy Docherty.

Owner Jim Gregory's decision to bring back the Doc was a stunning one, given how his new manager had walked out on the club after 28 days claiming board interference.

Your author met the flamboyant Docherty to ascertain whether he was the manager to revive Rangers' fortunes. We met up for a relaxed chat at the Kensington Hilton Hotel on his arrival and for a more frenetic natter, due to his time constraints, in his car on the A40 between the club's Greenford training base and Loftus Road. He was certainly charismatic, voluble and full of positive ideas.

And his personal attributes clearly won over the players, who were ready to give the Second Division a bash. The Doc's persuasive tongue also managed to talk promising goalkeeper Chris Woods to move from Nottingham Forest, along with David McCreery, who played under the manager at Manchester United, and the outstanding Tony Currie, from Leeds United, to help Rangers return to the top flight at the first attempt.

Queens Park Rangers' Greatest Games

And the wheeler-dealer in the Doc also got in centre-backs Steve Wicks and Bob Hazell to bolster the bid while selling club icon Stan Bowles to Brian Clough's European Cup holders Nottingham Forest, who were to retain their trophy in 1980, with Hamilton and Richardson also departing to balance the books.

Most importantly of all he had a prolific teenage striker to call on in Allen as Rangers made a decent fist of trying to get back in the big time although they wobbled in the immediate aftermath of Bowles's departure.

Allen, now 18, bagged a staggering 30 goals in his first full season, another stepping stone to a stellar scoring career and six-figure transfers. The treble had clearly been no flash in the pan.

And establishing a regular place in the Rangers first-team line-up had vindicated Allen's decision to follow his dad Les's advice to sign for the club.

He told your author, 'I had the chance to sign for Ipswich as a schoolboy and also Spurs. Dad had looked at the QPR team. It was quite an ageing one with a few older players who weren't going to go on forever.

'So the way we looked at it was that if things went well and I did well enough going there at 16 by the time I was 18 I could possibly be in the first team. Luckily that's the way it worked out.

'It was good I was able to prove I wasn't just a flash in the pan and was able to sustain my goals record over the years.

'That was something I realised. My dad had drummed that into me. That was very much a part of the education I was fortunate to have growing up as a kid. People said you were a professional at 17. I said, "I was probably a professional from six or seven years of age."

'The messages that were being sent out. The way I trained as a kid. Played as a kid. Like a professional. What I was doing with QPR was a continuation.'

Allen's jet-speed take-off to a 17-year playing career was aided by his partnership with Paul Goddard, who played alongside him as Coventry were put to the sword.

Allen said to the club's website, 'We struck up a really good relationship. He was a fantastic target man. I think we worked particularly well together.

'We had the opportunity to play through the youth ranks. We won the Southern Junior Cup, got to the later stages of the FA Youth Cup as well and then broke into the first team at the same time.

'It was a smooth transition coming through the reserves and then into the first team with Paul.'

31 v Luton Town 1-2
Football League Second Division. Loftus Road
1 September 1981. Attendance: 14,176

QUEENS PARK RANGERS:
Burridge
Gregory
Fenwick
Currie
Hazell
Roeder
Flanagan
Francis
Allen (Gillard)
King
Stainrod

LUTON TOWN:
Findlay
Stephens
Aizlewood
Horton
Saxby
Doughty
Hill
Stein
White
Antic
Ingram

Referee: Alan Robinson (Portsmouth)

TERRY VENABLES published a book entitled *They Used To Play On Grass* in 1970 when he was a Queens Park Rangers player. The story, as you would think, is about how synthetic pitches had replaced the natural green stuff in football.

Venables's work of fiction became fact for him and Rangers when a plastic pitch, with the brand name Omniturf, was installed at Loftus Road for a cool £350,000 for the start of the 1981/82 season.

The manager's club had dug up the grass surface at London W12 following a five-goal victory on it against Cambridge United at the end of the previous season.

And on 1 September 1981 Rangers hosted the first fixture to be played on an artificial surface since the Football League was formed 93 years earlier.

It ended in a 2-1 victory for Luton Town after QPR forward Andy King had netted the first ever goal on the surface.

It proved, though, that momentous days in the history of football clubs are sometimes not always linked with the winning and losing of a trophy, the winning and losing of a match, the flash of individual brilliance to leave you with an indelible picture in your mind's eye.

Rangers that Tuesday evening took to the revolutionary road in an attempt to change the face of football for the better with the whole of the game looking on; to improve players' techniques on a true surface, to add extra, and in most cases, much needed, revenue streams. It was the first opportunity to collect data on whether the Omniturf experiment would be a success.

The cover of the match programme against Luton had Rangers striker Clive Allen, re-signed from Venables's previous club Crystal Palace in the summer, being pictured using a broom to 'sweep' the new low-maintenance surface.

The symbolic message, one guesses, was that a new broom was sweeping clean in London W12 and across football.

Queens Park Rangers' Greatest Games

Venables, one of the game's deepest thinkers, was confident he had collected together a team during his ten months since replacing Tommy Docherty in November 1980 that would have little trouble adapting to the surface and launching a promotion bid.

He had made Simon Stainrod from Oldham Athletic, a big character and the latest successor to Rodney Marsh and Stan Bowles in the number 10 shirt, his first major signing.

Venables also plundered Palace to bring in Terry Fenwick, Mike Flanagan, goalkeeper John Burridge and former QPR skipper Gerry Francis.

They all lined up against the Hatters alongside Allen, another close-season capture, John Gregory from Brighton & Hove Albion, Docherty signing Andy King and 18-year-old Gary Waddock, representing a thriving youth set-up, with the classy centre-back and captain Glenn Roeder a calm authority at its heart, alongside Bob Hazell.

It was packed with players who were comfortable on the ball, sharp of brain and, particularly in the cases of Allen and Stainrod, with an eye for goal.

Venables told your author prior to the kick-off, 'We're looking to get up there in the top three. It's a healthy situation with the second team very strong and putting pressure on the first-team players.'

Rangers seemed to settle on the alien surface quicker than the David Pleat-managed visitors.

Francis, with his intelligence and ball control, and Flanagan, a versatile forward played out wide, maintained a supply of balls up to Allen and King with Stainrod cutting in from the left as the hosts overran their Bedfordshire visitors.

Allen and Roeder forced Luton stopper Jake Findlay to pull out fine saves as Rangers maintained the pressure and moved the ball around well, being careful to hit it to feet on a bouncy surface.

Allen thought he had doubled QPR's advantage before Findlay blocked his effort from close range.

King wrote his name in football history when he put the Super Hoops ahead ten minutes before the interval. The goal stemmed from an unlikely source. Centre-back Bob Hazell had ventured forward to supply a cross for King to head home.

The Hatters finally got to grips with the pitch and their confidence grew, creating a series of swift one-touch counter attacks and they levelled 20 minutes from time.

Rangers keeper John Burridge got caught off his line as the ball bounced off the pitch from a Ricky Hill right-wing cross and Mark Aizlewood half-volleyed a lob over him.

QPR were unable to bounce back and Hill crashed home the winner after Gerry Francis had been hustled by visiting duo Steve White and Aizlewood.

The questions afterwards were all about the surface, of course, and it got a general thumbs-up.

Roeder told your author after the game, 'It's early days, but the pitch surface was no problem. You've got to play it to feet otherwise it could race away from the man you are passing to.

'As a defender I tended to stay on my feet a bit more. It cuts out slide tackles. Instead I jockeyed my opponent and closed him down.'

Venables also told me, 'I feel defenders will learn to defend better and more skilfully. Passing has to be made with care. There were no injuries caused by the new surface. It will lessen the chances of ligament type injuries because the surface is even and not bumpy.'

Pleat, whose side were eventually promoted, added, 'We enjoyed it. Skilful players will benefit.'

v Luton Town 1981

But any flutters of QPR hearts caused by the reverse were soon settled as Rangers eased to their first win on the plastic against Newcastle 3-0 four days later with Andy King, Glenn Roeder and Simon Stainrod supplying the goals.

Home proved sweet for Rangers that season, when they even managed a 7-1 win over Bolton Wanderers after sand had been added to the surface to deaden the high bounce of the ball.

The jury, though, remained very much out on Omniturf. Like most things which break the mould, it met with resistance. Many do not like change and feel suspicious, cynical and positively hostile towards anyone or anything that might lead to it.

There are cases throughout history in every area of life where this applies. Galileo was convicted of being a heretic when he insisted the Earth orbited the sun and was not the centre of the universe in the 1600s to quote a left-field example!

Football was populated by many with similarly conservative, if not openly as extreme, views.

People loved their natural surfaces. With the right choice of footwear, players thrived on it whether the ground was heavy, firm or frosty, they argued.

Skills had been developed sufficiently to cope with the variables turf threw up, whether it was either slick, muddy, or pristine. If it ain't broke don't fix it attitudes were common.

But in truth something did need to be done. Rangers' natural surface often resembled a cloying pudding more than a flat surface on which the run of the ball was true.

And that was a common, perennial problem, even at the biggest clubs as visitors to the likes of Old Trafford and White Hart Lane would testify back in the day.

Just a look at the *Big Match* re-runs on ITV will show you. How Spurs managed to play possibly the best football ever seen in the English game during their march to the Double in the 1960s is quite remarkable.

So where was the harm in trying to find another kind of stage on which the surface would remain consistent beyond the first match of the season?

A surface that would enable moments when a carefully weighted pass would deservedly find a team-mate instead of getting stuck in the mud or bobble off a divot?

Science had not developed sufficiently for groundsmen to be able to produce the near-perfect natural surfaces we see all year round today in the Premier League, or come up with the 3G artificial pitches which are fast developing towards being a facsimile of the real thing.

Venables and his club's owner Jim Gregory were merely pioneers, the next link in the chain to what we now have. They were trying to make the product look better with better footballers trying to make ball-playing skills more important than brawn.

Venables told your author in August 1981, 'When the question of floodlights was being discussed people were saying this and that. It's a false light and football shouldn't be played at night and that it'd never catch on. Now everyone's got them.

'So anything that's new will always get criticisms and so forth. But I just want to wait a reasonable period of time before we actually make up our minds about the Omniturf.

'Of course, there's reluctance to accept change. There's too much tradition.'

The motivation was, of course, also to help improve football clubs' finances to help them survive and prosper.

Certainly Gregory and the club wanted to make money. And when you have an unchanging surface no matter what the weather, you have a versatile asset. Loftus Road could stage sport events like American football, hockey, and in the case of Barry

Queens Park Rangers' Greatest Games

McGuigan's world title-winning bout against Eusebio Pedroza, boxing. Or just about any entertainment the public would pay good money to go and see.

Venables said in 1981, 'A lot of clubs are going through a very bad period and they might even struggle to keep their heads above water.

'I think it's got to be a viable proposition because the finances of the clubs are definitely going to be of the highest priority and if that sort of surface enables clubs to subsidise themselves and keep their heads above water it is something they've go to think seriously about.'

But overall Rangers fans did get to watch a brand of football which was largely pleasing on the eye, although far from perfect.

The experiment lasted seven seasons – during which Luton and others followed suit with their own version of a plastic pitch – but English football ultimately returned to turf with the help of the boffins.

Clive Allen told your author in July 2013, 'We had a good record on it. It was a pitch for ball players. Players who could deal with the ball. It wasn't necessarily about strength. It was about technique. Definitely the types of players we had.

'We had Glenn Roeder, a ball-playing centre-half. Two full-backs who could deal with the ball. We had pace in the team. We had the right make-up to be successful on that surface. It was something Terry recognised and built the team around that.'

Full-back Ian Gillard, who played in the emphatic wins over Newcastle and Bolton, told your author in June 2013, 'Once we got used to the pitch it was fine, especially when some of the northern teams came down.

'They trained on it on a Friday afternoon testing out what footwear they would need for the match the following day. And if it was a dry day it was more bouncy. On a Saturday morning our groundsman used to flood the pitch with water.

'They used to come out for the game with all the wrong footwear on. We knew we were a goal up before we even kicked a ball. It was good for us because we knew we had the advantage. When people say we didn't, that's rubbish.'

v Tottenham Hotspur 1-1
FA Cup Final. Wembley Stadium
22 May 1982. Attendance: 100,000

QUEENS PARK RANGERS:	**TOTTENHAM HOTSPUR:**
Hucker	Clemence
Fenwick	Hughton
Gillard	Miller
Waddock	Price
Hazell	Hazard (Brooke)
Roeder	Perryman
Currie	Roberts
Flanagan	Archibald
Allen (Micklewhite)	Galvin
Stainrod	Hoddle
Gregory	Crooks

Referee: Clive White (Middlesex)

GLENN ROEDER and Ian Gillard remain proud their careers gave them the opportunity to win an FA Cup Final medal. Queens Park Rangers have only played in one over around 130 years of existence, appropriately coming as the club celebrated its official centenary.

Many clubs and many top players have missed out on an appearance in the match rated as the ultimate football dream for UK youngsters kicking the ball around over the park or in the neighbourhood car park.

And Roeder, the captain, and Gillard, the loyal one-club full-back, pulling down the curtain on a 16-year stay with the R's, still appreciate the significance of their involvement against Tottenham Hotspur in front of 100,000 spectators at Wembley on 22 May 1982.

The fact they and their team from the Second Division held a glamorous club from the top tier that was seeking a seventh FA Cup Final victory to a 1-1 draw after extra time made their chests swell even more.

Roeder told your author in July 2013, 'Traditionally, as a kid growing up to play in the FA Cup Final at Wembley was the greatest game you could take part in. It was every potential professional footballer's dream to happen.

'And the percentage of players who achieve that is small compared to the amount of players who play. To lead the team up the tunnel and out on to the pitch with the manager in front of you made it a double honour for me.

'I enjoyed the day immensely, personally. I'm sure the other players did. It just flew by. I can remember sitting there in the dressing room afterwards thinking "crikey, where did that go? That's just flown by, that game." The sadness for me was that I was banned for the replay for being sent off at Luton a few weeks earlier.

'[Manager] Terry [Venables] did magnificently for me. He fought very hard with the FA to get me a Cup Final medal, which he did. So the Cup Final medal I've got is not a winners' one, but it is not a losers' either.'

Queens Park Rangers' Greatest Games

Gillard treasures his souvenirs and memories of his swansong as a Ranger after more than 480 appearances in a first-team career stretching back to 1968.

He said to your author in June 2013, 'Getting the medal was nice. It meant and still means a lot to me. Not too many players get to play in a Cup Final. The club also gave us a little souvenir of a small statue of a footballer with our names inscribed. That was nice too.

'It was an emotional match for me and one thing in particular I will always remember was something Brian Clough said to me as I came out of the tunnel. He must have been there doing some commentary and he said to me, "I hope you get yourself sorted with a good club."

'I thought that was really nice. For someone who was a big name like Brian Clough to do that meant a lot. He didn't have to do that. He knew I played for QPR and that I'd played against his teams. That was it. But for him to say that was really special. Very touching.

'Apart from the game, which was important for us to win, from a personal point of view for him to say that was really nice. He knew it was my last game.'

Gillard had been at Wembley as a youth player with the club watching Rodney Marsh, Mark Lazarus and Co. seal the 1967 League Cup in a season which also saw the R's promoted.

Gillard had debuted during the club's first ever season in the top flight (1968/69) and, while the likes of Stan Bowles and Gerry Francis grabbed the headlines, was largely the number 3 of choice in the 1970s side which became the nation's favourite as it came within a whisker of the English premier title for the first and only time and stormed Europe.

If ever a player deserved centre stage for loyalty and consistency it was Gillard. And he relished at least being part of a superb defensive performance, alongside Roeder, who oozed calm, cool and fine leadership qualities, Bob Hazell and Terry Fenwick, which helped keep a Spurs side packed with glittering stars at bay for 90 minutes and force extra time. The likes of Glenn Hoddle, Steve Archibald and Garth Crooks had helped the White Hart Lane outfit lift the trophy the previous season following a final replay against Manchester City rated one of the best games to decide the winners of the Cup since its inception.

And the winning goal from Ricky Villa brings little argument in many circles as the finest seen during the denouement of the world's greatest domestic knockout competition.

Rangers and Spurs would have had to go some way to rival the excitement, drama and goal quality displayed 12 months previously, but there was no question David was standing up to Goliath. Venables had set up Rangers to be solid with Gary Waddock designated to shackle the wonderfully expansive skills of the world-class Hoddle – and doing a world-class shackling job. The tigerish Republic of Ireland midfielder proved just what kind of talent could be produced through the club's youth system under Chris Gieler.

And he had 6ft 4in goalkeeper Peter Hucker, the 22-year-old who had begun the season as understudy to John Burridge, in fine form whenever Spurs were able to pierce their resistance, although the profligacy of Archibald and others also helped.

Rangers' effort was all the more impressive because they had lost the attacking outlet of Clive Allen – with his replacement Gary Micklewhite putting in a double shift – who became a passenger when he was injured after just two minutes.

Even when Rangers finally conceded after 109 minutes of football there was more than a hint of good fortune for Keith Burkinshaw's Lilywhites.

Waddock was inadvertently impeded from tackling Hoddle by referee Clive White before Graham Roberts broke with the loose ball to put it square to the Spurs midfielder

v Tottenham Hotspur 1982

on the edge of the D of the penalty area and his low right-footed effort took a deflection off Currie to wrong-foot Hucker. Waddock, who went on to manage the club in 2006, said to your author, 'The referee accidentally got in my way when Glenn and I went for the ball. Glenn won it and I was flat on my face. The next thing I knew they'd scored.'

And Currie told your author, 'I thought I'd done enough to block it.'

With the dyke breached, whatever the circumstances, it seemed Rangers might get flooded out. After all they had expended a lot of energy to stay in the game. But their spirit remained intact and Venables's collection of men, and boys who became men, equalised.

It was Fenwick who scored the goal. He became the first full-back in open play to net a goal in the FA Cup Final when he came in at the far post to head past Spurs goalkeeper Ray Clemence after Bob Hazell had flicked on a long throw from the left by Simon Stainrod to the near post. Fenwick, who clenched both fists into his chest in celebration, said to your author, 'The feeling was absolutely brilliant.'

It was no more than Rangers deserved in a display which showcased their talent going forward even minus the threat so often posed by Allen.

The arrival of Gary Micklewhite, who eventually replaced Allen, saw the substitute carve a golden opportunity but John Gregory was unable to convert his header.

Currie's creative brilliance going forward gave Waddock and Mike Flanagan chances but both efforts were off target.

But Spurs striker Garth Crooks fired over and Hucker saved from Archibald, Spurs skipper Steve Perryman, born up the road from Shepherd's Bush, and Hoddle, with Currie now roving in front of the back four to support the Rangers rearguard.

Stainrod forced a stop from Ray Clemence as the game went into extra time.

Hucker tipped over a long-range drive from Spurs substitute Garry Brooke at the beginning of the second period of it before the two goals which took the final to a replay for the second year in a row and only the third time since Wembley had begun staging it.

And Venables said your author, 'It was just the dress rehearsal.'

Rangers gave Spurs a hard time again in the second game but they were undone by an early goal which gave Spurs a 1-0 victory.

Stainrod, under pressure from Hoddle, gave the ball away in the centre of the field. Graham Roberts latched on to the ball, beat Gregory and kept running. Hazell came in to challenge but was held off as Roberts moved deep into the 18-yard box where he fell under a challenge by Currie, captain in place of the suspended Roeder. Hoddle beat Hucker from the penalty spot with a strike so quick the television cameras only just caught it.

Rangers fought hard for the equaliser inspired by man of the match Waddock, who left nothing out on the field with his running, tackling and all-round energy.

Rampaging teenage defender Warren Neill, called up in Roeder's absence, put in two superb runs, one only ended by handball from Spurs defender Chris Hughton and the second saw Flanagan shoot wide from his pass.

Two minutes before the interval Micklewhite netted but the 'goal' was disallowed with Flanagan having been adjudged to have handled. They then had a penalty appeal turned down when Fenwick was grounded by a challenge from Crooks.

Rangers maintained the pressure and Stainrod forced Clemence to go full stretch before Waddock had an effort saved by the busy stopper.

A John Gregory chip hit the bar and Stainrod headed wide as QPR created a series of chances before the referee's whistle ended their onslaught on the Spurs goal and quest to win the FA Cup.

Queens Park Rangers' Greatest Games

There was no skulking off to the dressing room to shed tears as the Rangers braves saluted their fans. There had been heroic performances again from the likes of the departing Gillard, Hucker and Micklewhite. Spurs had the silverware but QPR took the plaudits.

The Rangers camp spoke freely to your author, who covered both games for the *Ealing Gazette*, on the night. Venables said, 'I am very proud of my team. It was a moral victory for us.' Neill said, 'We lost in style. I feel choked.' Micklewhite said, 'I think we must have won a few friends out there tonight.' Hoddle told your author, 'QPR played very well – in the second half especially.'

Gillard was sad it was all over and that he had to pick up the pieces of his career at Aldershot the following season. But he will forever recall the before and after, although the during bit is harder.

He said to your author in June 2013, 'It feels wonderful to have played in a Cup Final. We gave a really good account of ourselves and got another bite at the cherry.

'You hadn't got time to think during the 90 minutes and 30 minutes of extra time. It was unbelievable how quickly it went. There's the atmosphere with 100,000 but the time just goes. The first game was THE event. THE occasion, with royalty there and what have you. The replay was not the same. They've done the right thing by changing it to extra time and penalties for the first game in the event of a draw.

'The build-up to the first game was fantastic. We stayed away at a hotel for a week in the Crystal Palace area. That's where we did all our training in the week leading up to it. We went into town one night to see a film to relax.

'We transferred to the more central Royal Lancaster, did all our press bits. On the morning of the match we went over to Hyde Park to train, had a pre-match meal. Then it was in the coach and off to Wembley. There was a bit of music but it was quiet with everyone thinking about the game. Getting our minds on the game.

'You feel you were in this position because you'd achieved something. And we had. And we wanted to achieve a bit more! As soon as you hit Wembley Way and see the Twin Towers it hits you. It is a special moment.

'The big gates shut behind us as we went into the stadium by the dressing rooms. We went out on the pitch in our blazers to get a taste of the atmosphere.

'When we got back into the dressing room and changed, Terry went round giving his instructions. Getting everybody sorted. He had his serious side but also a jolly side. He'd tell a few jokes to ease the situation. You don't want to be too tense. He had a good rapport with us and was as bright as a button.'

Allen, whose dad Les won the competition with Tottenham Hotspur in 1961, said to your author in July 2013, 'I injured my ankle in the second minute of the first game. I was a passenger until half-time. I should have come off at half-time but it was the FA Cup Final, so I got strapped up and tried to carry on.

'I lasted for another five minutes before I had to come off. Then I went into plaster the following day and obviously didn't make the replay on the Thursday.

'My first appearance in the Cup Final was a real disappointment but I scored in my second one for Spurs against Coventry in 1987. That was fantastic. And ironically I got it in the second minute.' The march to the final began with two ties which went to replays.

Teenage defender Warren Neill was the unlikely hero when he headed the deciding goal in a 3-2 replay victory against Middlesbrough at Ayresome Park after the hosts had pulled back a two-goal lead given to Rangers by Simon Stainrod, who netted in the drawn first game at home.

v Tottenham Hotspur 1982

Allen rattled in four goals as Fourth Division side Blackpool were overcome 5-1 at Loftus Road after a goalless away draw.

Stainrod made it five in four Cup ties in a 3-1 dismissal of Grimsby in London W12 with Allen and centre-back Ernie Howe on target.

Allen fired the only goal of the game to seal a semi-final date with First Division West Bromwich Albion, the club they had defeated in the 1967 League Cup Final, at Arsenal's Highbury. It provided the opportunity for dreams to come true in front of 45,000 for the likes of England international Tony Currie, who had lost three last-four showdowns in his illustrious career, and wide-eyed youngsters such as Gary Waddock.

Dynamic duo Allen and Stainrod, who had scored 11 of Rangers' 13 goals in the run, had the chance to keep on scoring.

Rangers could also score their first win at the ground since their debut triumph in 1930. And all of those chances were taken as Allen scored the winner off his knee as Baggies defender Ally Robertson tried to clear.

Currie and Waddock were in tears. Currie said afterwards, 'It has been a long time coming but it feels fantastic. I've finally made it to Wembley. After the final whistle I went a bit mad. I saw Garry Waddock crying and it got me choked up a bit as well. It is a marvellous feeling. It hasn't hit me yet – but it will.'

Allen, who had joined and left Arsenal without playing a competitive match, said to your author in July 2013, 'It was really a case of the ball hitting me on the knee, which is quite ironic. Obviously after the experience I'd had at Arsenal to end up scoring the winning goal in the semi-final was special.

'The day? Very big deal for QPR. But Venners had got it absolutely right tactically. I always remember big Bob Hazell played Cyrille Regis out of the game. He had an unbelievable day. We did a job. They were a top team, West Brom. The fans hadn't had much to shout about in reaching major finals [his dad Les was in their only previous one, the League Cup success in 1967].'

Roeder said, 'The goal? Ally Robertson went to clear the ball and Allen put his leg up and it hit his kneecap and went in. They all count. The West Brom team of Cyrille Regis, Brendan Batson and Statham was a good one. A top-tier team versus a second-tier team.

'We were playing very well under Terry Venables, the best coach I ever worked for in every facet of being a coach and a manager. He set us up to be well organised defensively. We worked hard at that in training. On the day we restricted them to hardly any chances at all. It was a question of whether we could get one at the other end.

'Clive Allen did, of course. Clive would have been as good a finisher as any I played with and against [for Newcastle United]. His goal won't rank as the best in his life but it will probably rank as one of the most important goals he scored.

'To score a goal in the semi-final to take your team to Wembley is something of great importance. Something he'll never forget.

'Tony [Currie] was a superb midfield player. You would hear or read people say he was a lazy midfield player, strolling around. Impossible to be lazy if you want the ball all the time. He never hid. He did look as if he was strolling because he wasn't particularly quick.

'He was so physically strong. People couldn't get the ball off him when he was on it. He used to play lots of short passes. You certainly wish England had one of those players today in their team.

'He could play the short game and he could hit stunning long accurate passes to his own team-mates on the run. He was an important player on the day.'

33 v Fulham 3-1

Football League Second Division. Loftus Road
2 May 1983. Attendance: 24,433

QUEENS PARK RANGERS:	FULHAM:
Roberts	Peyton
Neill	Parker
Dawes	Lock (Reeves)
Waddock	O'Driscoll
Hazell	Brown
Fenwick	Gale
Wicks	Davies
Sealy	Wilson
Stainrod	Coney
Flanagan	Houghton
Gregory	Lewington

Referee: Not known

WARREN NEILL joined former Queens Park Rangers team-mates on the field at the interval of Rangers' Premier League match against Newcastle United on 12 May 2013.

It was to celebrate the 30th anniversary of the season Neill and Co. ensured the club's promotion to the top flight for the first time as champions.

The full-back, Tony Currie, Gary Micklewhite, Bob Hazell and Steve Wicks were given a warm reception as they waved to a crowd in need of cheer with Harry Redknapp's Rangers completing their home fixtures after being relegated a fortnight earlier.

A reminder of good times past can work two ways in the present. It makes the cynic compare negatively, despair and yearn without hope for the camaraderie and spirit instilled by Terry Venables into his 1983 disciples in blue and white hoops and still clearly visible in the body language within the group as they smiled, greeted and chatted unstiltingly to each other.

Conversely the optimist compares positively, having faith that the feel-good factor wafting around Loftus Road will motivate a return to happy days, that the glory of 1983 will be repeated and the right chemistry, balance and talent found to enable that to happen. Even, perhaps, as soon as the following season.

Neill said to your author in July 2013, 'We all enjoyed the day Rangers invited us back. The banter between us was great. We always had that fantastic camaraderie to go with a good mix of experience, youth, pace and enthusiasm. And Terry was so organised, paid so much attention to detail and was such a good motivator and man-manager. There wasn't a manager who lived up to him as a man-manager.

'It all combined for us to follow up getting to the Cup Final with the promotion. And it was a bonus to do it as champions."

Rangers sealed the title with three games still to play with a west London derby win against Fulham in front of Loftus Road's biggest crowd of the season, 24,431, on 2 May

v Fulham 1983

1983 after clinching promotion two games and ten days earlier before that with victory against Leeds United.

And the season ended with QPR ten points clear in a race they dominated, having not been outside the top two since the previous November.

It was a triumph for Venables and his players. And a poignant one for Jim Gregory, the self-made millionaire car trader who drove a dying club into a thriving one, who had announced he was stepping down as chairman and owner after 18 years and hoping his manager would take over the running of the 'football side' of the club.

Venables was a man with a plan the moment he took over from Tommy Docherty in November 1980 and went close to guiding the club to promotion in his first full season in charge despite the distraction of a run to the club's first FA Cup Final in 1982.

Yet the side still needed tweaking to ensure it was consistent enough to sustain a bid to earn elevation to the premier division as he prepared his players for the 1982/83 season.

He had sufficient confidence in the players he had been moulding into a successful unit to not feel the need to bring new players in while Ian Gillard, Ernie Howe and John Burridge departed. He had plenty to call on; the experience of Glenn Roeder, Bob Hazell, Steve Wicks and Mike Flanagan, the growing maturity of Terry Fenwick, the youth of Neill, Gary Waddock, Gary Micklewhite, Peter Hucker and Ian Dawes, the speed, effervescence and goals of Tony Sealy (another signing from Crystal Palace), the sharpness and sharp-shooting of Clive Allen, the self-confidence, skills and net-finding radar of Simon Stainrod and the all-round abilities of John Gregory.

Venables worked on them all while it came together – big-time – and any L-plates were swiftly discarded. Rangers became a well-oiled, fully-functioning steam-roller which flattened almost all before them as the season progressed.

He got his strikers to play wide, just inside the opposing full-backs, and cut inside when the opportunity arose.

It was a ploy which often left centre-backs – and indeed full-backs – bemused as to who they were marking and enabled the likes of Flanagan and Allen to avoid the bumps and bruises often inflicted by tight marking. The tactic gave Rangers more players in midfield to dictate play.

Venables instructed the defence on how to remain tight and bright-minded. It became a mean machine and constantly caught opponents offside by either squeezing them high up the pitch or winning the ball back and breaking to create a chance.

Neill said, 'I remember Leeds moaning up at Elland Road when we beat them 1-0 when we caught them about 50 times. It was said that it was up to the Leeds forwards to make better runs. We were, generally, well marshalled when it came to offside. In fact George Graham, who was our youth manager, took that on to Arsenal and did exactly what was being done under Terry. We had a formidable back line. Very rarely did we get beaten by lots of goals.'

Another whinge by opponents was that Rangers' Omniturf was giving Venables's outfit an unfair advantage.

QPR blew that theory out of the water as they thrived as much on the natural surfaces of their opponents, scoring ten wins by the time they overcame Leeds in the promotion clincher, and completing four draws on their travels by the close of the campaign.

Captain Glenn Roeder said, 'The lads enjoyed playing on the Omniturf but also enjoyed playing on grass more. It was a double whammy for Terry and the club. We were nearly unbeatable on the plastic because we knew how to play on it.'

Queens Park Rangers' Greatest Games

Rangers were pipped 1-0 at Newcastle by a goal from new signing Kevin Keegan, soon to be hailed a footballing messiah on Tyneside, in the opening game of the season.

They got motoring, even with Roeder and Steve Wicks sidelined through injury, as youngsters like the solid Neill, dependable Dawes and determined Gary Waddock stepped up to the plate, establishing themselves among the front-runners.

And they stepped up a gear after being knocked out of the FA Cup in the third round by West Bromwich Albion, avenging the semi-final reverse against QPR the previous term.

Venables's side won ten of 13 (including a 6-1 mauling of Middlesbrough with Clive Allen hitting a hat-trick), gaining 32 out of a possible 39 points going into the home fixture which rubber-stamped their passport back into the top flight after a four-year absence.

Leeds United were not the force they were when Stan Bowles and his fellow Super Hoops overcame Don Revie's team to go top of the table in their final match of the 1972/73 season.

But the Yorkshire side, now managed by Revie's wing wizard Eddie Gray, were none too shabby, having had a decent season just behind the clutch of main promotion candidates.

It proved a game which might have left a connoisseur of the sport far from satisfied, but Rangers put the tips they had received on pragmatism from Venables to good use and did what it took to get the three points required to secure promotion. Neill and Mike Flanagan combined before Leeds centre-back Paul Hart, to become Rangers manager in 2009, diverted the latter's shot into his own net after nine minutes.

The celebrations, though, were worthy of the occasion. The champagne flowed in the dressing room with Neill joining Micklewhite, Sealy, Stainrod, Wicks and Gregory in an impromptu linked-arms *Cancan* and singing the chorus a la Dexy's Midnight Runners' version of Van Morrison's 'Jackie Wilson Said', a record released coincidently as the season kicked off. Nothing complicated you understand, merely 'der-der-der-der-der-ded-der-der-der-der-der'.

But after the bottles were emptied and the final steps completed there was a feeling that the last waltz had yet to be danced.

Rangers had won the championship in moving up from the third to second tier in 1948 and 1967.

But their previous two elevations into the top flight – in 1968 and 1973 – had come after finishing as runners-up.

Venables's Rangers wanted to make it third time lucky and join the big boys by finishing top of the pile.

Neill spoke for the camp when he said to your author after the Leeds game, 'Great, innit? But now I want a championship medal. You don't get anything for second or third.'

They had plenty of leeway, having charged to an eight-point lead over nearest rivals Wolverhampton Wanderers prior to the encounter with Leeds.

They had five matches left after Gray's men returned to Elland Road defeated. Those games were tantamount to five match points in tennis.

Well, Andy Murray had close to the same number before beating Novak Djokovic in the 2013 Wimbledon men's tennis final and become the first Brit to do so since Fred Perry 77 years previously.

The question for Rangers in their quest to make history was whether they could close out and achieve the goal they had set themselves.

A journey to one of the furthest outposts of the Football League earned them nothing. Rangers fielded the same team which had overcome Leeds, but they returned from Carlisle

v Fulham 1983

having lost 1-0 in front of a mere 5,000 spectators at the club which sold Stan Bowles to them back in the day.

But a showdown closer to home produced the ace which gave them the trophy and prestige they desired.

Fulham, managed by Malcolm Macdonald, had offered a spirited challenge to obtain top-tier football for their fans. They were only four points down on Wolves in the third promotion slot prior to Rangers' Leeds win.

They were packed with decent players such as prolific Wales international striker Gordon Davies and solid midfield performer Ray Lewington, who became their manager and joined ex-Cottagers boss Roy Hodgson in the England set-up in 2012.

But Rangers were in an irrepressible mood. It took just four minutes for the hosts to take the lead. Versatile John Gregory latched on to a long ball, raced between two Fulham defenders and as one came in to tackle and goalkeeper Gerry Peyton rushed out to dive at his feet, Gregory coolly slid the ball home from the edge of the area.

Tony Sealy made it 2-0 on ten minutes. QPR had tried to deaden the exaggerated bounce of the ball by adding sand to the infill worked into their polypropylene fibre Omniturf surface.

But it was a feature that still seemed very much in evidence as Sealy raced on to a high ball. He managed to control the ball with his chest and hold off a strong challenge to his right before lobbing a volley over Peyton.

Fulham struggled on the 'plastic' with mis-hit crosses and an inability to create chances.

And it was unsurprising Rangers got a third goal three minutes after the re-start. Fulham, presumably, had not done their homework on an oft-tried set piece thought up by Venables.

Somewhat of an oversight as Rangers had used it in front of 100,000 Wembley spectators and a worldwide television audience of millions during the 1982 FA Cup Final when Terry Fenwick had nodded home a headed flick from Bob Hazell at the near post from a long throw from the left wing by Simon Stainrod.

Against Fulham, big defender Hazell took up the same position to await a left-wing corner which swung over and the centre-back headed on as the rushing Peyton left his goal unoccupied to challenge, an action which allowed Stainrod, in a central position and unmarked, to nod in.

Rangers continued to press and Sealy was within a bootlace of converting a low right-wing cross which fizzed across the area.

If Macdonald had any thoughts his side could climb Mount Impossible they were soon banished when Lewington clattered into Stainrod from behind, sending the Rangers striker sprawling on the controversial surface which the club laid while exploiting a loophole in the rules which did not specify what surfaces were allowable for playing football on.

It turned out to be close to 30 years before Rangers were able to overcome Fulham again when Redknapp's side pipped the Cottagers 2-1 in December 2012 as they fought the campaign which eventually saw them fall through the trap door (read about that later).

From Margaret Thatcher to David Cameron. From David Bowie's 'Let's Dance' on MTV the 'Gangnam Style' getting one billion hits on YouTube.

But the victory that came when it mattered in 1983 will forever remain 'toppermost of the poppermost', to quote John Lennon when predicting the rise of the Beatles, to the true Super Hoops who experienced it. And give the current supporters hope of a repeat in the not too distant future.

Queens Park Rangers' Greatest Games

Glenn Roeder said to your author in July 2013, 'We carried the form and the success of getting to a cup final into the season. Started it well, which is key, and we never looked back. We were over the hill and gone pretty quickly.'

The Rangers heroes at the time were effusive in their praise of the achievement to your author in 1983.

Club captain Terry Fenwick said, 'To get to the Cup Final was nice, but this feeling is much better. I'm chuffed.'

Waddock said, 'I'm only 21 yet have played in the Cup Final, played for Eire and won promotion as a champion. I thought my season was going to be a disaster when I suffered a cartilage injury but since I've come back everything has gone so well.'

Gregory said, 'Gary said early in the season before one game, "Let's go, for the first 90 minutes." The boss liked that and so did we and it has reflected in our play this year.'

Stainrod, who wrote a weekly column for the *Ealing Gazette*, said with a smile, 'I'm as sick as a parrot!'

Assistant manager Allan Harris, a member of Rangers' 1968 promotion team, said, 'We wanted the championship.'

And chairman Jim Gregory announced his intention to call it a day and naming Venables as his preferred successor.

Gregory said to your author at the time, 'I feel it is time to hand down to a younger man. It's a young man's game. I did everything when I was young. I was only 37 when I became chairman.

'Now the time is right. It's something I've been thinking about for about four years so it is not exactly a surprise.

'I'm amazed Terry is the first manager to be offered the chance of running the club. Terry's got first refusal and I hope he takes it up but I'll be selling the lease whatever happens.

'It's good to know Terry is the one I've offered it to – he's well suited to be a good businessman. It's very simple and logical that Terry should run the club. If you work for a fish and chip shop you hope to own it one say. The same with Terry.'

Venables told your author then, 'I've got £1m to find and, although it is going to be a bit of a problem, I'm confident of raising it. It's a very exciting prospect. I believe I can combine being a team manager and running the club. I'm flattered to be offered the chance.'

34 v Newcastle United 5-5

Football League First Division. Loftus Road
22 September 1984. Attendance: 14,234

QUEENS PARK RANGERS:
Hucker
Neill
Dawes
Fereday
Wicks
Fenwick
Micklewhite
Fillery (Stewart)
Bannister
Stainrod
Gregory

NEWCASTLE UNITED:
Carr
Brown
Saunders
Haddock
Anderson
Roeder
McDonald
Wharton
Waddle
Beardsley
McCreery

Referee: Not known

GLENN ROEDER shakes his head and smiles wryly when he recalls the extraordinary day he returned to Queens Park Rangers for the first time as a player. Roeder had captained QPR in the 1982 FA Cup Final and been part of the campaign which saw the club regain their First Division status in 1982/83.

The year before he led the R's out at Wembley, the classy defender had scored one of the three goals which gave QPR their first ever victory on their plastic pitch, a 3-0 win over Newcastle United. And on Saturday 22 September 1984 he was part of a match which featured one of the great comebacks from a losing position in football history as his Toon surrendered a 4-0 interval lead to draw 5-5. Roeder insists the experience left Newcastle's players cowered behind each other in the showers afterwards as manager Jack Charlton came storming down the corridor armed with a verbal shotgun.

Toon looked to have uncovered the secrets of the Omniturf which had remained a mystery in their two previous experiences of it when they had not even been able to score a goal let alone win any points. It seemed as if it would be third time lucky as Chris Waddle hit a hat-trick and laid on another goal for Neil McDonald to give Roeder's new employers a cushion which would avoid any teacup-smashing in the dressing room at the interval.

But Rangers roared back with goals by Gary Bannister, Simon Stainrod, John Gregory, Steve Wicks and Gary Micklewhite to secure the unlikeliest of points.

One could only imagine what the odds would have been for that to happen as Rangers sat shell-shocked in the adjacent changing room at the interval with Alan Mullery unable to offer a rallying cry for the second 45 minutes, according to his right-back Warren Neill.

It is no wonder Danny Baker, the comedian, presenter and writer, highlighted the match in his *Freaky Football* series with a classic piece of tongue-in-cheek commentary, with the preface, 'Now bear in mind in those days Rangers' plastic pitch gave off clouds of noxious, mind-expanding fumes which contributed to what you are about to see.'

Queens Park Rangers' Greatest Games

Roeder said to your author in July 2013, 'Chris Waddle said to me at half-time, "You must be loving this." I said, "Yeah, I am enjoying this" because, although I loved QPR, had a great time there, I wanted to win with a new shirt and a new badge.

'At 4-0 all the Geordies – Newcastle were always well supported – in the crowd were happy. But I said to Chris, "Rangers can be lucky bastards and only have to score and they'll be racing." That's what happened, of course, but we should have had enough to win!

'When we kicked off at 5-5 I said to the referee "how long to go now?" He went "we'll kick off and blow up". I said "thank f*** for that" thinking "we are going to get beaten 6-5 here" even though Chris Waddle had put on a stunning, virtuoso performance.

'I've never known any team to shoot down the tunnel into the dressing room after the game, quickly getting the kit off and all hide behind each other. Charlton was coming down the f****** corridor with his "pearl shotguns". If he'd have had them he'd have used them on us! You never saw such a bunch of cowards hiding behind each other in the shower with the manager going absolutely apeshit! Apparently the QPR owner and chairman Jim Gregory, God bless him as he has now passed on, was happy with 5-5 because he made loads of money from the running off of thousands of videos and selling them in the club shop.'

Mullery had some act to follow in June 1984 when he took over from Terry Venables, who had left Loftus Road to take over at Barcelona.

Whoever stepped into the hot-seat would inevitably be compared to the boss who worked the oracle to such an extent one of European football's giants wanted him to come up with potions which would ensure the European Cup would be finding its way to the Nou Camp sooner rather than later.

The drill soon cracked the concrete of the firm foundations Venables had laid down as he, and assistant Allan Harris, disappeared into the sunset towards Catalonia.

Jim Gregory first tried the smooth-talking Gordon Jago, who had signed Stan Bowles and sparked promotion and a top-tier title shot in the 1970s, to renovate the damage as general manager. The appointment of a team manager was top of Jago's agenda. Less than a week later Jago was sacked and David Pleat and John Lyall entered the frame to become Venables's successor. Then Mullery was appointed with your author interviewing him in his office less than an hour into the job. He was bullish.

When I asked him if the players' love of Venables made his role harder, he said, 'No, not at all. I'm probably as close to Venners as anybody is. I don't envisage any change. I'd like to get that "Terry Feel" going along. I love attacking football as does Terry.

'The chairman rang me yesterday afternoon. I knew the chairman had been in for David Pleat and John Lyall as well but I wouldn't have minded if I'd have been 91st choice.

'I'd like to improve what Terry has done. He's built the foundations with the chairman. If somebody said "would you like the Manchester United job" I wouldn't because I think this club could be as successful.'

Mullery, an experienced manager who had guided Brighton & Hove Albion into the top tier, clearly seemed undaunted by the challenge. His first task was to get a potent striker in with Clive Allen reported to be seeking pastures new to re-invigorate him.

It was thought Cyrille Regis, the strong, pacey West Bromwich Albion striker plucked from close to Rangers' back yard as a promising non-league performer at Hayes, would fit the bill. Then Mick Harford, the tough-as-teak, no-nonsense Birmingham City forward, was thought to be the answer. But any deal for Harford, who was to become caretaker Rangers manager in 2010, collapsed.

v Newcastle United 1984

Third on the list was a striker of contrasting qualities. Gary Bannister was a diminutive, mobile player who wanted a new challenge after banging in the goals for Sheffield Wednesday, having tolerated what was deemed a long-ball game employed by Howard Wilkinson at Hillsborough. And Mullers got his man despite competition from Brian Clough's Nottingham Forest and Sunderland.

Bannister seemed capable of plugging the Allen gap and giving Mullery breathing space from the 'we-only-want-Venners' lobby who appeared to want any successor's head on a plate. The 24-year-old established an instant rapport with Simon Stainrod in the opening games. His non-stop running style helped create opportunities in the first top-flight encounter of the season. Stainrod bagged two of them and Terry Fenwick added another as Regis's Baggies were overcome 3-1 on Rangers' artificial surface.

In the next game he scored his first goal to help earn Rangers a 1-1 draw against Watford at Vicarage Road. Bannister failed to score in the third fixture but Mullery was still smiling. Any time you take on Liverpool at Anfield and emerge with a point has to be good news.

But the jet-heeled workhorse was back on the scoring trail as he showed Clough what he was missing with his second goal in a 3-0 home victory over Forest, an emphatic win which saw Wayne Fereday netting twice.

A run of four matches unbeaten to kick off a managerial career was encouraging for Mullery and the R's. But the bubble was pricked when QPR visited the club Mullery served outstandingly as a player for eight years. Tottenham Hotspur took Rangers apart, handing out a 5-0 thrashing at White Hart Lane.

The pro-Venables crowd were no doubt sharpening their tongues to spit verbal vitriol at the new boss. It was unfair, but consistent with the fickle nature of those looking for an excuse to dish out turbo-charged whingeing at the earliest opportunity.

Then QPR faced an unpredictable Newcastle who had won their opening three fixtures and then lost the following three following six years out of the top tier. Newcastle also had Waddle and Peter Beardsley besides future manager Roeder.

But Rangers, despite their setback at White Hart Lane, still looked strong on paper with the team Venables had built barring Bannister.

And when Rangers went four down at the interval against Newcastle the jury was not only out but could just have been about to pass a negative judgement on the new manager who had supported the club growing up as a boy in Notting Hill.

But football is a funny old game, as Jimmy Greaves once reminded us.

Rangers went one down after three minutes when Neil McDonald headed home a towering header at the far post after Chris Waddle had jinked his way to the byline, holding off Rangers right-back Warren Neill following a huge kick from goalkeeper Kevin Carr.

The hosts had a penalty appeal turned down as Gary Bannister fell to the surface following a Newcastle challenge.

They even forced Carr into a couple of saves as they continued to look for an equaliser.

But Newcastle doubled their advantage through Waddle on 17 minutes. On the right wing, he controlled a bouncing return ball from McDonald just inside the penalty area, cut in and headed towards the near post, drawing Peter Hucker, before calmly slotting into the far corner from eight yards despite an acute angle.

Waddle netted his second five minutes later. Roeder knocked a free kick into the box which Neill headed clear. The ball fell to Kenny Wharton on the edge of the area and he caught it on the volley with his left foot, the shot deflecting on to the post via Neill.

Queens Park Rangers' Greatest Games

With Hucker having dived one way, Waddle slipped round the back unnoticed to tap home first time into an unguarded goal from six yards with his left foot. Steve Wicks had his arm up for offside but his plea was ignored.

Rangers thought they had pulled one back as Bannister looped the ball over Carr from a Stainrod delivery, but the man in black had declined to give QPR the advantage.

So instead of a goal Rangers received a free kick for a foul on Stainrod. Apoplexy reigned on the home front, and Waddle completed his hat-trick four minutes before the interval. He picked up a clearance from near Rangers' left-hand corner flag, then controlled and steadied himself, with seemingly all the time in the world, to curl a beauty high into Hucker's goal, just inside the far post from 20 yards.

Rangers, despite the mood in the dressing room at half-time, began the second half on the front foot looking for a way back no matter how impossible the mission seemed.

And two minutes after the restart Gary Bannister pulled one back. Simon Stainrod got his head to a hefty Hucker clearance and Bannister latched on to the ball and attempted to chip the ball over Carr. The stopper got a hand to it but Bannister kept his eye on the ball as it looped up and he ran in behind Carr to head home from close range.

QPR, with the encouragement of the crowd, had the bit between their teeth and Carr saved from Steve Wicks. Newcastle's first-half tempo dropped and Rangers found themselves with space and Stainrod halved the deficit on 56 minutes.

Micklewhite moved into the area following a series of passes. Roeder policed him wide and the ball ran to fellow defender Peter Haddock with his face towards the away goal. Haddock tried to thump the ball for a corner but hit Wharton flush in the face and it ricocheted off Stainrod and beyond Carr.

Wicks almost put through his own goal when he attempted a pass back to Hucker from the centre circle but the goalkeeper managed to save at full stretch before the referee disallowed a Rangers goal for the second time after Stainrod hit the target. Rangers were left bemused and angry. John Gregory closed the gap to just one goal 16 minutes from time. Gregory exploited a gap in the Newcastle defence to run on to a glorious through ball from the centre circle, waited for it to bounce and Carr to advance before chipping the goalkeeper in the far corner. Dominant Rangers, though, were rocked when Wharton scored for the visitors six minutes from time.

Again Waddle was involved. Beardsley picked up a loose ball, Waddle got on his bike wide on the right and Beardsley found him with a 30-yard pass.

Waddle's control was exemplary as he teased and beat Wicks before pulling the ball across the goal for Wharton to knock over the line for 5-3.

The revival was back on within the minute as Steve Wicks headed home a Micklewhite cross to the far post following a Gregory free kick.

Micklewhite completed the comeback in injury time when substitute Ian Stewart and Gregory combined for the midfielder to dart into the penalty area and chip Carr from 12 yards. The electronic scoreboard flashed the scarcely believable scoreline: QPR 5 Newcastle 5.

Mullery said, 'We needed a miracle and got it. The sort of game which is exciting for the fans but gives managers heart attacks.'

Charlton said, 'It was a total embarrassment.'

Neill said to your author in 2013, 'It was bizarre, fantastic. One of the greatest comebacks of all time. The 11,000 in the ground sounded like 100,000 as we came back.'

35 v Partizan Belgrade 6-2

UEFA Cup. Highbury
24 October 1984. Attendance: 7,836

QUEENS PARK RANGERS:	PARTIZAN BELGRADE:
Hucker	Not known.
Neill	
Dawes	
Fereday	
Wicks	
Fenwick	
Stewart (Burke)	
Fillery	
Bannister	
Stainrod	
Gregory	

Referee: Mr. Tritschler (West Germany)

QUEENS PARK RANGERS faced Partizan Belgrade in the home leg of their second round UEFA Cup tie at Highbury on a wet Wednesday night in late October 1984. Although Rangers had slipped through loopholes in the rules relating to the type of surface allowable to play domestic football, the European governing body had refused the club permission to use their Omniturf pitch to stage matches in the competition which bore its name.

As Rangers ran out from the dressing rooms within the Marble Halls of a ground they had borrowed for the evening from Arsenal, the atmosphere was subdued. It was light years from Rangers' debut season pitting their wits in meaningful European showdowns.

The memories of the continental glory nights under the lights at a heaving Loftus Road in the 1976/77 campaign – when Stan Bowles and Co. led the club to the quarter-finals – were either a distant memory or one to catch up on if you happened to have a VHS tape to slot into your video player. Just 7,836 paying customers – with a mere few partisans from Belgrade – thought it worthwhile braving the rain and the vagaries of the London rush hour to part with their shekels to rattle around in a stadium with around a 40,000 capacity.

The brave few of a Super Hoops persuasion were rewarded with six of the best, a record in terms of goals scored by QPR at 'home' in Europe.

The current Rangers proved like their predecessors that they could adapt to continental opposition with their continental ways.

Gary Bannister scored twice and John Gregory, Wayne Fereday, Warren Neill and Simon Stainrod once as Rangers, under new manager Alan Mullery, romped home despite off-putting antics – which included allegations of spitting and hair-pulling – from the Yugoslav opposition which incensed.

Indeed the perceived winding-up tactics of the experienced European campaigners got Neill sent off shortly after he had scored the most spectacular of a series of outstanding Rangers goals.

Queens Park Rangers' Greatest Games

Rangers had been picking up the pieces following the departure of Terry Venables to manage Barcelona in May 1984.

Venables had weaved his magic to turn a struggling club into an upwardly mobile and stable one during his four years in charge.

After returning to the club he served as a player and taking over from Tommy Docherty in November 1980, Venables took Rangers from Second Division strugglers into the FA Cup Final then the First Division as champions and into Europe in his final season.

There had even been talk of Venables taking over the running of the football side as Rangers confirmed their first ever second-tier title in 1982/83.

Jim Gregory, stepping down, said he wanted his popular, bright, shrewd manager to take over the reins.

Venables had tried to dissuade Gregory from putting an end to his 18-year reign but when push came to shove he insisted he could combine the role of team manager and overlord provided he could get a consortium together to stump up the money.

The idea fizzled out so he was free to concentrate of underlining the belief that Rangers could not just survive in the top flight but would immediately thrive and push towards the top.

Bold and brash as the prediction seemed it was clear the mood in the camp reflected the opinion of the management as it prepared for the 1983/84 season

Your author sensed it when allowed by Venables to take part in a training session for a feature to be published in the *Ealing Gazette*.

The atmosphere was buzzing as I took to the freshly cut swards of the Birkbeck College Sports Ground in Greenford, Middlesex, a few miles up the A40 from Shepherd's Bush, resplendent in my Dunlop Green Flashes and with self-deluded optimism that I could in some way earn a modicum of respect for my efforts.

The fitness levels, ball skills, speed of thought, accuracy of passing, positional sense, team play and, above all, banter and general camaraderie was indicative of a squad who shared the confidence of their manager about mixing it with the big boys.

They also had a determination to good-naturedly tease the infiltrator in their midst, with Venables himself joining in when laughingly telling me an *Evening Standard* reporter had asked for the name of his new signing.

It soon became clear that the R's were indeed more than capable of holding their own in the First Division when the serious action started.

They sustained it to such a degree that, although the title was beyond them, claiming a spot in Europe was very much on the cards as they went on a six-match winning run, with Clive Allen bagging a half-dozen goals, to ensure it.

But new manager Alan Mullery had replaced Allen with Sheffield Wednesday's Gary Bannister in August 1984 as he set about taking full advantage of the continental experience won for Rangers by Venables.

And the 24-year-old Bannister sustained the early promise he displayed in the opening games and swiftly proved a major asset.

He had scored 14 goals in his first 15 games for Rangers going into the Highbury showdown with Partizan, and formed a natural striking partnership with Simon Stainrod, despite a spluttering start to the campaign by Rangers.

The opening-round tie against Iceland's FC Reykjavik illustrated how Bannister had hit the ground running in place of Allen, who had netted 83 goals in 147 full appearances for Rangers and had joined Tottenham Hotspur.

v Partizan Belgrade 1984

Bannister netted one and Stainrod two in the 3-0 victory over the Icelanders before banging in a hat-trick, with Jeremy Charles also on target, at Loftus Road to complete a 7-0 aggregate scoreline to secure a second-round date with Partizan. So it was no surprise he continued his goalscoring streak when the Yugoslavs came to Highbury.

Partizan, formed by officers from the Yugoslav People's Army, had developed their name in European football by taking part in the first ever European Cup tie – against Sporting Lisbon in 1955 – and becoming the first Balkan/Eastern European side to contest a final in what is now known as the Champions League, when they lost 2-1 to Real Madrid in 1966 after earlier overcoming Manchester United.

And Nenand Bjekovic, another new manager keen to make an impression, brought with him to Highbury a good team, packed with technically gifted players.

Rangers took the lead through John Gregory after 12 minutes. Terry Fenwick headed the ball back into the goalmouth at the far post from a deep Ian Stewart corner and Gregory hooked it into the Partizan goal.

The visitors, though, caught QPR cold from the re-start and equalised through captain Nikica Klincarski less than a minute later.

Rangers lost possession in the centre circle and Partizan broke with pace through the middle and a superb through ball saw Klincarski guide an angled chip over onrushing home stopper Peter Hucker.

It got worse for Mullery's men as Partizan took the lead on 24 minutes. The visitors' star striker Dragan Mance, who had yet to feature in the match, announced his presence with a wonder strike rated one of the greatest in his club's history.

Terry Fenwick headed clear but Admir Smajic picked the ball up in midfield to clip the ball to the edge of the D where Mance controlled it and, as it bobbed up, struck a curling shot into the roof of Hucker's goal.

Rangers made it 2-2 through Wayne Fereday shortly afterwards. A tried and tested tactic employed by Venables seemed to have failed as two Partizan defenders ganged up on Steve Wicks at the near post as he tried to flick on a long throw by Stainrod.

But Wicks got a second bite and hooked the ball across. Gregory tried an overhead kick which was blocked and the ball fell to the unmarked Fereday who curled it into the near post from ten yards out with the outside of his right boot.

A diving near-post header from Stainrod from an Ian Stewart cross from the byline restored Rangers' lead just before the interval.

Rangers put on an irresistible second-half performance to complete a stunning victory.

Neill won Rangers' goal of the game contest to make it 4-2 ten minutes after the re-start. Gregory picked the ball up on the left and found Bannister who, despite a hefty challenge, guided the ball out to the right. As Neill and Mansa converged on the ball the home defender won out, spun round, took one touch and then cracked a screamer into the top of the net. Neill was deservedly swamped by team-mates as he smiled and arced his arm with his hand clenched in a fist in celebration.

Bannister proved his goalscoring form had been no fluke with a double to make it 6-2.

The first one came just before the hour when he made a late run to get in front of a defender after a low cross by Steve Burke, fed by Gregory, from the left.

And he bagged his second with a superb effort which challenged Neill's goal as the pick of the bunch seven minutes from time.

He intercepted a ball from the mercurial Mance with Partizan on the attack and about 25 yards from the home goal.

Queens Park Rangers' Greatest Games

The diminutive striker then sprinted down the middle, and fed Stainrod outside him on the right before continuing his run and guiding a perfectly-weighted low cross from his fellow front-runner behind the visitors' back line home on the stretch with his left foot just inside the six-yard box.

But the second leg was shades of Athens in 1977 when Dave Sexton's Rangers were unable to defend a 3-0 lead against AEK from the first leg in the Greek capital in a hostile atmosphere.

Rangers, stunningly, lost the tie on away goals when they were defeated 4-0 in Belgrade, with the home crowd equally as volatile as AEK's, to become the first side from Great Britain to depart a European tournament having held a four-goal advantage.

QPR made it through to the fifth round of the League Cup and struggled in the league in a roller-coaster season.

But no one can doubt that Mullery's season was eventful with that rainy night at Highbury a worthy highlight.

Neill said to your author in July 2013, 'I've watched re-runs of my goal since. It was lovely, especially as it was in a European competition. I challenged the fellow and as it came off him I read it, took a touch, looked up and made up my mind to hit it. I caught it sweetly. It moved like balls do now, going from side to side, and it flew in from 30 yards out.

'I remember Grego [John Gregory] grabbing hold of me and the other lads piling in. I only got seven in all my career at Rangers. That was special.

'Unfortunately I was sent off shortly afterwards. Simon [Stainrod] went down as if he'd been hammered and, as we all had such a good bond, I ran up from right-back and as I got there one of their players gobbed in my face and I pushed his face away from me and the ref sent me off and that put me out of the second leg.

'They also pulled your hair when the ref wasn't looking and dived. We felt it was cheating. We were hard but fair and all this stuff was alien to us.

'I went out there for the return leg and their fans were throwing nuts and bolts on the pitch. Unbelievable. Intense.

'Going out there 6-2 to the good you'd have thought would have been straightforward but there wasn't a happy mood at the club with Venners gone and we were playing on memory from what he told us. But it would have been difficult for any manager coming in after Terry.

'I enjoyed the European experience. It made me a better player. The football was different and we played in contrasting stadiums. The one in Reykjavik was like a school stadium and then you are in a noisy packed one in Belgrade.'

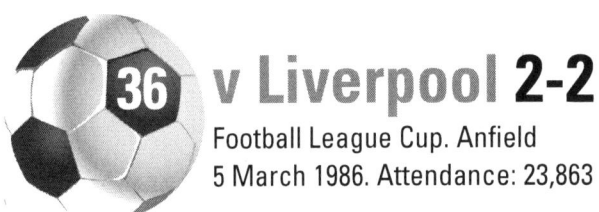

v Liverpool 2-2

Football League Cup. Anfield
5 March 1986. Attendance: 23,863

QUEENS PARK RANGERS:	LIVERPOOL:
Barron	Grobbelaar
McDonald	Lee
Dawes	Beglin
Neill	Lawrenson
Wicks	Whelan
Fenwick	Hansen
Robinson	Gillespie
James	Johnston
Bannister (Fereday)	Rush
M. Allen	Molby
Fillery	McMahon

Referee: David Hutchinson (Harrogate, Yorkshire)

ALAN McDONALD stood in front of the Queens Park Rangers supporters celebrating a famous achievement over one of football's most famous teams at one of the game's most famous grounds at the final whistle.

The towering defender had just put on a largely imperious performance to help ensure his underdogs would be playing in the League Cup Final.

The colossus of a centre-half had, typically, sweated blood for the cause in an extraordinary semi-final second leg under the Anfield floodlights on Wednesday 5 March 1986.

Kenny Dalglish's mighty Liverpool conceded two own goals in a 2-2 draw as the Super Hoops completed a 3-2 aggregate triumph.

And McDonald's first thought was for the fans and what the moment would mean to them.

He had just helped Rangers beat the team which had won the trophy four times in the previous five years, been European Cup finalists the season before and would go on to complete the FA Cup and First Division Double in Kenny Dalglish's debut season as boss.

McDonald loved the supporters and they loved him. He was an icon for a reason that went deeper than the more glamorous accoutrements which often attract supporters' affections like the swagger, the eye-popping piece of skill (although McDonald certainly displayed it on occasion), the goals-for-glory moments.

Rodney Marsh and Stan Bowles, for instance, will deservedly remain folk heroes at the club, especially those who witnessed their exploits in the 1960s and 1970s.

But into the 1980s and 1990s? McDonald won hearts because he took the followers and their club to his heart. It was a mutual love-in.

The Rangers faithful knew he would go through a brick wall for the Super Hoops every time. He was the team-mate to have in the trenches with you for the toughest of battles and the player who displayed the deepest humility, perhaps his greatest quality.

Queens Park Rangers' Greatest Games

Every time I dealt with him during the time I covered QPR for the *Ealing Gazette* newspaper in the 1980s the quality shone like a beacon, along with his innate honesty, approachability, thoughtfulness and humour.

I remember being flattered he had accepted my invitation to him and his lovely wife Tonia to attend the British Sports Writers' Association dinner in London as my guest.

To join other local sporting heroes in lower profile sports at my table. There was no lauding of his status, no 'don't-you-know who-I am' attitude. He fitted like a hand in a glove, sociable, respectful and mindful to get his round in without fanfare.

It was unsurprising when told in 2002 that he had been voted Rangers' greatest centre-half by the recommended QPRnet.com website that he said, 'They're easily pleased aren't they! A couple of friends of mine are still season ticket holders and one of them sent me a programme when they done the greatest team of all time and I was in it.

'That's a great honour for me because when people say to me what did you win, really when you look at my career we never really won anything with QPR but for me when ordinary people on the street say you're the greatest ever centre-back or you're in the best team ever, for me that makes up for not having cups and medals and all that.

'I probably was never one of the most gifted players in the world but I gave what I had and it's nice to be appreciated.

'I had some kids come up to me, about 12 years old, and say, "Oh you're Alan McDonald, my Dad used to watch you and he says you were the best player at QPR." They're 12 years old and they know me!

'So it's nice if you affect people's lives and it's a great honour for me when they do these polls. It's very humbling because when you're there you get paid and you enjoy your job and for people to appreciate what you've done is great, it's great for me.'

It is no wonder the player who turned out 476 times for the R's – putting him high on the all-time appearance list – and earned more international caps than any other while in the club's employ (52 with Northern Ireland) was dubbed Mr Queens Park Rangers.

'I'll love QPR until the day I die,' he said in 2011. Tragically he passed on a year later.

And it was no surprise there was such outpouring of grief when Alan McDonald died, aged 48, after collapsing on a golf course in his native Northern Ireland on 23 June 2012.

Chairman Tony Fernandes, who owns Air Asia, featured in tribute an image of a QPR shirt with the legend 'Alan McDonald 5' on one of his planes painted in R's colours with McDonald's widow Tonia saying, 'On behalf of myself, son Joshua and all the McDonald family I cannot thank Mr Fernandes enough for his overwhelming gesture of deciding to remember and honour Alan by naming one of his planes after him. We know Alan would have been so proud and amazed at such a generous tribute.'

Petitions were sought to have a Loftus Road stand named after him and to have a statue of him outside the ground.

There was a minute of "spine-tingling" applause for him prior to Rangers kicking off the 2012/13 Premier League season against Swansea City.

He had remained true to the club for 17 years even when the likes of Manchester United and Tottenham were linked with him, but he decided the grass isn't always greener.

Fernandes and other fans and former team-mates understood that as they expressed their feelings.

And they all appreciated his value on that unforgettable night against Liverpool on 5 March 1986 when all of McDonald's qualities were on display.

v Liverpool 1986

Anfield was not a place for faint hearts and McDonald had proved he did not possess one during the run to the last four.

McDonald had stepped up to the plate all through the competition. He helped Rangers complete an aggregate victory over Hull City in the opening round as the Tigers were left toothless as the visitors scored five goals against their Second Division hosts at Boothferry Park.

McDonald was part of the team which secured its first win against Watford at Vicarage Road in 16 years in the next round, John Byrne scoring the only goal of the game after Rangers stopper Jim Barron had saved a Kenny Jackett spot-kick for the Hornets.

And he was impressive when Brian Clough brought his Nottingham Forest side to Loftus Road for a last 16 showdown.

The tie had been scheduled to be played the previous week before a floodlight failure caused its postponement.

And it went ahead in shivering temperatures on a pitch covered with patches of sand which otherwise might have produce a few 'slipping-on-a-banana' type moments.

Terry Fenwick converted a disputed penalty early on and Rangers hung on to the lead until the manager's son Nigel netted an equaliser just ten minutes from time before Gary Bannister and Byrne fired late goals to see Rangers through 3-1, while Forest's Peter Davenport was sent off.

McDonald proved himself again as he put in a superb display at the back in a thrilling 1-1 west London derby draw at Chelsea in the quarter-finals on the plastic pitch at Loftus Road, which had the 'full house' sign up with 27,000 packed in to soak up the tingling atmosphere. McDonald almost scored the winner after Pat Nevin, in Chelsea's all-red away kit, had cancelled out a John Byrne effort.

McDonald was in stonewall mode in the replay at Stamford Bridge and popped up with one of the goals when he headed home a Robbie James corner in extra time which secured a 2-0 victory, with Michael Robinson netting the second from the halfway line into an empty net after Bannister dispossessed Chelsea stopper Eddie Niedzwiecki, who had ventured into midfield with the ball at his feet.

QPR moved into their first League Cup semi-final in six years confident but realistic with the calibre of opposition which awaited them.

Liverpool, it was felt justifiably, would be a harder nut to crack than Aston Villa in 1977. And, as the R's had exited the competition at the hands of the Birmingham outfit, they knew they had to upgrade their nutcracker.

The Reds, who had been dominant in so many competitions for the previous decade, seemed to have developed a particular liking for the League Cup, lifting the trophy four times (and going on to double that figure by 2012).

It might not be the European Cup but it certainly helped to swell the amount of silverware in the Anfield trophy cabinet.

Rangers needed something to hang on to from the first leg to take to Anfield to give themselves a fighting chance of making it to Wembley.

That meant Jim Smith's side had to try and get their noses in front, while maintaining a dam at the back which would not be breached by any Red waves crashing against it.

And they took advantage as Liverpool struggled on the Omniturf just like they had done in the First Division fixture on it earlier in the season.

Terry Fenwick, who had netted in QPR's 2-1 home league win against Liverpool, put Rangers ahead midway through the opening half.

Queens Park Rangers' Greatest Games

He got in front of his defender to divert a right-wing cross from Martin Allen beyond Bruce Grobbelaar as the ball dropped.

Rangers continued to create chances as Kenny Dalglish's side floundered. The visiting manager changed the set-up of his side which played with a high defensive line to entrap the Super Hoops in offside positions.

And when Liverpool were able to break, apart from when an unhindered Ian Rush missed a golden opportunity on the counter, the back line held firm with McDonald dominant. QPR could have done with a second but a goal advantage and none conceded gave them an edge for the second leg.

Their hosts had a strong line-up for the Anfield date with legendary defenders Alan Hansen and Mark Lawrenson in front of goalkeeper Bruce Grobbelaar, the talented and brave Craig Johnston and no-nonsense Steve McMahon in midfield and the prolific goal-getter Ian Rush.

There was also the crowd, particularly those on the Spion Kop, singing 'You'll Never Walk Alone' and providing the atmosphere which had sent chills down a multitude of opposing teams from England and all over the continent since they had taken a stranglehold on the club game early in the 1970s.

Liverpool took the game to Rangers and won a controversial penalty award when referee David Hutchinson adjudged that Ian Dawes had handled inside the box when a replay revealed him to have been outside.

Jan Molby had scored six spot-kicks in a haul of 15 goals in the season but Paul Barron got down to his right to save after former Red Michael Robinson had a word in his ear.

Rangers boss Jim Smith had urged his side to be on the front foot but the hosts forced R's back, hoping three away wins in the cup on the trot, as against three reverses in the league, would spur them on.

Rangers stood firm. Steve Wicks, Terry Fenwick and particularly McDonald stood tall in protection of their goal. And Rangers' travelling army of fans could be heard above the home crowd chanting 'QPR QPR QPR' in support.

Finally Rangers' slim advantage evaporated before the interval when Steve McMahon latched on to a diagonal through ball from Molby from the left before setting off on his own diagonal run from right to left inside Rangers left-back Ian Dawes, drawing goalkeeper Barron and coolly slotting home.

Liverpool pressured early in the second half but again with McDonald and Co. dominant created little and Rangers began to make an impression, with the lively Martin Allen proving a thorn in the Reds side, driving just wide and forcing a save out of Grobbelaar.

Then Rangers equalised on the night to put themselves ahead overall. Warren Neill's long right-to-left cross went into touch, but Gary Bannister closed down Mark Lawrenson from the throw, won possession and cut inside to find Mike Fillery who had a shot blocked by Craig Johnston.

The ball spun across goal where the left-footed Beglin, who should have cleared with his right, kicked the ball against Ronnie Whelan's legs and diverted it into the goal.

The game became end-to-end but with around 20 minutes left the Reds levelled the aggregate score again through Johnston.

Rush jumped in front of an unsighted McDonald as Grobbelaar booted the ball to the edge of the Rangers area. Johnston, with the ball drifting into the area, went in courageously to just beat Barron to it and lob it into the net.

v Liverpool 1986

Rangers substitute Wayne Fereday replaced Bannister with just less than ten minutes left and shortly afterwards helped make the goal which finally took Rangers to Wembley.

Warren Neill cut out a McMahon ball to send jet-heeled Fereday flying up the wing. The super-sub teased Hansen and elected to cross early to the near post rather than speed by him and Gary Gillespie diverted the ball into his own goal under pressure from Robinson with Grobbelaar out of position.

Cue celebrations behind the goal with Rangers supporters singing 'Que sera sera, whatever will be will be, we're going to Wembley, que sera sera'.

And as McDonald joined the supporters, Jim Smith, nicknamed the Bald Eagle, spoke of his 'pride and delight' and about how he was looking forward to leading a team out at Wembley for the first time, expressing the hope it was againsst his former club Oxford United.

But it was a case of being careful what you wish for as the final brought disappointment for favourites Rangers against the U's. A lacklustre display resulted in a 3-0 defeat in front of 90,000 at Wembley.

But none of the thousands 'bonding' with McDonald at Anfield will ever forget the moment when he and his Rangers team-mates proved too good for one of the world's greatest sides.

McDonald said in 2002, 'We had a phenomenal run through, we beat some cracking teams, I think it was Nottingham Forest, Chelsea and Liverpool in the semi-final and to be fair Oxford beat some great teams as well.

'I think to be honest we just froze on the day, we never played at all. It's probably the disappointment I look back on, because I can remember it like it was yesterday. The support was phenomenal, it was a beautiful day and the build-up had been tremendous.

'It was a crazy year for me, it was my first full season as a regular and in that season I got in a cup final for QPR and Northern Ireland qualified for the World Cup in Mexico. For me, in the space of six months I'd gone from being a reserve team player to playing in the World Cup and a major final at Wembley.'

Speaking to QPRnet.com, he added, 'That was my first full season. We had a lot of competition at centre-back, we had the likes of Steve Wicks who was a good player, and Terry Fenwick so for quite a bit of that season I was playing right-back. I enjoyed it, I mean I would have played left-wing to get a game!'

Rangers defender Warren Neill said to your author in July 2013, 'There were great celebrations afterwards with the champagne flowing in the away dressing room at Anfield. I saw a picture of me, Wayne and Dawesy in it for the first time hanging up at Loftus Road a few months ago.

'Unusual to get two oggies and probably had a bit of luck, which you needed at places like Anfield but you've got to say we deserved it. A great achievement as it was against the greatest team around. The manager had made us feel positive going in.

'I remember putting Wayne away for our first goal. Dawesy was about three yards outside the box for the handball for the penalty. They got every decision.'

37 v Chelsea **6-0**
Football League First Division. Loftus Road
31 March 1986. Attendance: 18,584

QUEENS PARK RANGERS:	CHELSEA:
Barron	Francis
McDonald	Lee
Dawes	Rougvie
Fereday	Pates
Wicks	McLaughlin
Fenwick (Rosenior)	Hazard
Allen	Nevin (Canoville)
James	Spackman
Bannister	Dixon
Byrne	Speedie
Robinson	McAllister

Referee: Martin Bodenham

QUEENS PARK Rangers striker John Byrne recalls with a quiet pride the first of his two goals which helped towards the greatest victory over the club's greatest rivals Chelsea at Loftus Road on a wet Easter Monday morning in 1986.

Byrne smiles as he describes it as a goal against a side with championship pretensions which could rival Diego Maradona's mesmerising, magical and momentous one against England in the 1986 World Cup finals in Mexico City a few months later.

Argentina talisman Maradona, infamous for his Hand of God goal earlier in that quarter-final, certainly showed the ying to his yang with the effort voted Goal of the Century by the website FIFA.com.

He picked the ball up just in his own half, turned and beat a succession of England players, including Byrne's club-mate Terry Fenwick, to seal victory and the global accolade.

Byrne's goal saw him take two Chelsea players out of the game, including Mickey Hazard, with a dropped shoulder and turn after controlling a chested ball back to him from a Wayne Fereday pass forward from the right flank.

The red sea of Chelsea shirts seemed to part as Byrne moved forward into space by gliding over the slick Omniturf.

Chelsea defender Colin Pates was deceived as the Rangers front-runner feinted to go right before switching feet and moving left.

Hazard tried to get back and snapped at his heels before Byrne skipped by a desperate sliding tackle on the edge of the penalty area and moved menacingly into the box.

Byrne, the latest QPR maverick to wear the number 10 shirt, maintained his composure and, as Chelsea stopper Steve Francis, in his last appearance for the club came out, glided the ball beyond the goalkeeper into the far corner.

He peeled away to the sidelines to acknowledge the home fans packed tight close to the pitch. Gregory and Robbie James came across and the player was enveloped in a group hug.

v Chelsea 1986

A pitchside advertising board by the celebrating Super Hoops displayed the legend 'pure genius' to advertise Rangers' shirt sponsors, Guinness.

But Byrne's effort certainly deserved such a description for his best contribution to the 6-0 crushing of Chelsea.

It might have had him sipping a Black Velvet afterwards by mixing the contents of the bottles of champagne and the black and white stuff brewed in Park Royal nearby given out to every QPR man of the match had not Gary Bannister hit a hat-trick.

Byrne said to your author in July 2013, 'It was sort of like Maradona's – but nowhere near as good! I remember picking the ball up just over the halfway line and going through about four or five players and ending up one-on-one with the goalkeeper and slotting it in on an angle.

'The QPR fans remember it. They always go on about it. It's up there with the best I've scored, especially as it was in the biggest win QPR have had against what the supporters will tell you are the club's biggest rivals.

'Funnily enough, though, I should have scored an even better one against Chelsea on another occasion when I actually went through the whole team and even went past the goalkeeper but missed from six yards. It was a bit like that famous one George Best scored when he played in America – but he actually hit the back of the net.

'But I'll take the one that actually went in on that Easter Monday. We gave them a lesson overall on that plastic pitch.

'Everything went right with the help of a decent atmosphere in a packed ground. It was a nice ground to play at when it was packed because the supporters were right on top of the pitch. And it was always like that when we played Chelsea.'

For many, extra endorphins were released on the magic Monday with the bitterest of rivals on the receiving end of a battering.

The two clubs first locked horns in 1968 with Rangers slumping to what proved to be their worst defeat against Chelsea until Byrne and Co. came on the scene. The 4-0 reverse was followed by two more losses.

Stan Bowles got the only goal of the game as Rangers completed their first victory over the Blues at the sixth attempt in an FA Cup tie in January 1974.

And Dave Sexton's side emphasised Rangers' growth into title challengers by overcoming their hosts 3-0 at Stamford Bridge for the first time at the end of that year.

Rangers brought the head-to-head in wins up to eight each by returning to SW16 to knock Chelsea out of the League Cup in the quarter-finals in January 1986.

Indeed the cup was still very much on QPR's minds when the Blues, in their all-red kit, arrived for the six-goal hammering, with Rangers having secured their place in the final against Oxford United with their last-four win against Liverpool at Anfield.

But Rangers' league form during the 1985/86 season lacked consistency and the hosts were in mid-table when former R's midfielder John Hollins brought his First Division high-fliers from SW6 to the Bush for the ambush which wrecked Chelsea hopes of ending a 31-year wait for a second top-tier championship crown, another reason for celebration by the one-eyed among the QPR followers.

The wind whistled around the stand and raindrops fell on the heads of those exposed to the stuff falling out of the sky in shower bursts before the morning kick-off.

The noise emitting from the collective throats of those vociferous folk in the Loft End was louder than normal as it was packed 100 per cent end to end and back to front with home supporters.

No away fans could gain entry to it on the day to reduce the volume as an advance-ticket only policy had been introduced.

The ears of Chelsea chairman Ken Bates must have been throbbing in the directors' box after they had been burned by the Super Hoops verbalising their anger at his criticism of their plastic pitch in the lead-up.

QPR, lifted by the Loft and the rest of their supporters singing 'Glory, glory Rangers', swept into an eighth-minute lead through Bannister.

Chelsea centre-back Joe McLaughlin climbed high to nod away a deep free kick from his opposite number Steve Wicks to his left to spark a triangle of one-touches from the quick-thinking, mobile Rangers to set the ball up for Byrne in a central position on the edge of the penalty area.

His left-footed effort was blocked but the ball spun loose to his left. Bannister latched on to it by controlling the ball with a back-spin flick before taking his time and rolling his shot across Francis and into the far corner from eight yards.

Home fans dipped into their American marching band song book to sing the surname of the goalscorer, emphasising the three syllables of his name.

A Loft End taunt, which is still familiar on grounds all over the country, followed to rub salt into the wounds for Hollins, his players and their 4,000 suffering supporters, 'You're not singing anymore.'

Bannister scored his and Rangers' second after 25 minutes. Sloppy play from Chelsea gifted QPR possession. The ball was quickly knocked back and long out to Byrne on the right. His dink to the near post was headed across goal by Terry Fenwick and Bannister headed home at the far from inside the six-yard box.

Again the home supporters maintained the high volume as they stole Chelsea's theme tune and sung, 'Well I never felt more like singing the blues.' It seems derby rivalry has no place for sympathy towards an opposition in dire straits.

Byrne made it 3-0 a minute before the interval with his Maradona-esque goal which evoked goals of Rangers' past number 10s.

The much-thumbed band book was opened up once more with 'John-ny Byrne, John-ny Byrne, Johnny Byrne' bellowed into the battered ears of the lads in red. Confidence had taken a vice-like grip with the Super Hoops faithful who chanted 'easy, easy'.

They had clearly forgotten what happened to Newcastle United at the same ground on the same artificial surface two years before, of course, when Rangers roared back from an even greater interval deficit to force a draw.

Chelsea, though, were unable to respond in the manner Rangers had in that extraordinary 5-5 deadlock.

With the visiting rearguard all over the place as the sunshine broke through, Bannister completed his treble in the 58th minute to make it 4-0.

A mis-directed header from Chelsea defender Doug Rougvie found Bannister who sprinted into the area and hit the ball low into the far corner from ten yards.

The electronic scoreboard flashed 'Gary Hat-Trick Bannister' in recognition of the front-runner who had proved Smith's predecessor Alan Mullery had found an able replacement for the prolific Clive Allen, now with Tottenham Hotspur, two years before.

Byrne made it 5-0 with his second goal six minutes later. He met a Bannister cross from the right to chip the ball deftly over Francis from close range with the Loft End taunting Bates by chanting 'blame the pitch' and 'easy, easy' once more.

v Chelsea 1986

And the New Year's Eve song book was produced by the Rangers supporters when Chelsea's volatile forward David Speedie was sent off for apparently catching Ian Dawes with his elbow as the left-back sprawled on the surface.

To the tune of Auld Lang Syne, they bastardised the lyrics to include 'bye, bye Speedie, bye bye Speedie'.

Substitute Leroy Rosenior completed the scoring eight minutes from time. A strong header out of defence by Fenwick was headed on to Rosenior who was in the clear as he ran from halfway down the left-hand channel before driving home off Francis from 15 yards.

Byrne said, 'QPR fans will never forget us beating Chelsea 6-0. That's one of the biggest wins they go on about.

'I remember when it was 6-0 Doug Rougvie wanted to "kill" someone. I said to Gary Bannister, I'm going to play on the left wing, I'm not getting injured for the League Cup final [against Oxford not long after].

'Banno said to me, "I'm going to play on the other wing." We were all just keeping away from Rougvie. He was spitting blood. Which is fair enough. If you are 6-0 down you've got to show a bit of pride. We just didn't want to get injured for the final.

'Chelsea were a decent side with the likes of Pat Nevin, David Speedie and Kerry Dixon, Colin Pates. That era. Good players. But we were decent too. QPR had a good side in the 1980s with good players like Fenwick, Gary Bannister, who was underrated, Wicks and Gregory. All good footballers.

'The manager Jim Smith was a great character. I liked him. He told it how it was, basically. He was a good character. He used to shout and swear a lot and throw cups across the dressing room. But we probably deserved it at the time.

'I had that number 10 shirt for a few years. They had a good tradition with it. You got to follow in the footsteps of Bowles and Marsh and be a flamboyant, skilful sort of player. I did alright. There was Simon Stainrod. And Roy Wegerle came after me. All skilful type players.'

Chelsea manager John Hollins said afterwards, 'It's been a very bad Easter for us, but I want to give QPR full credit for their performance.'

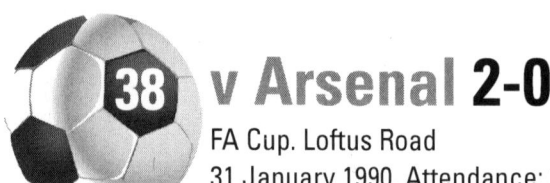

v Arsenal 2-0
FA Cup. Loftus Road
31 January 1990. Attendance: 21,547

QUEENS PARK RANGERS:	ARSENAL:
Seaman	Lukic
Bardsley	Dixon
Sansom	Bould
Parker	O'Leary
McDonald	Adams
Maddix	Winterburn
Wilkins	Richardson
Barker	Thomas
Clarke	Rocastle
Wegerle	Smith
Sinton	Groves (Merson)

Referee: Mr G. Peck (Kendal)

KENNY SANSOM and David Seaman helped Queens Park Rangers sing in the rain as they recorded an historic FA Cup victory against reigning First Division champions Arsenal on a glorious night for the Super Hoops under the Loftus Road lights on Wednesday 31 January 1990.

Left-back Sansom scored against his old club – with Andy Sinton adding the second – while stopper Seaman so impressed the Gunners they paid £1.3m for his services five months later to pave the way for him to become an Arsenal and England goalkeeping legend.

The two sides had only met twice in the competition. And that was SEVEN decades earlier.

Rangers overcame the Gunners 2-0 in the FA Cup at Loftus Road in 1921 in what was the first meeting between the clubs, and then lost 2-1 to the north London side at home the following season.

As far as knockout competitions were concerned there was a hiatus until Dave Sexton's Rangers side knocked the Gunners out of the League Cup in 1976 with a 2-1 win.

And when QPR boss Don Howe, the former Arsenal coach, and George Graham, the Gunners manager, took their places in the dug-out it was the first time the two clubs had met in a cup competition since.

And what they and those present witnessed was a blood and thunder cup tie in wild and woolly weather – and a shock result.

Rangers had revived under Howe but were still a mid-table outfit taking on the champions; 13th to the Gunners' third in the old First Division for the replay on a damp night in London W12.

QPR had proved their mettle at Arsenal to earn a goalless draw in front of the season's biggest FA Cup crowd of the season – 43,483 – at Highbury just four days before. New manager Howe, who had a respected and successful career as a coach with the Gunners

v Arsenal 1990

whom he helped to the 1971 Football League and FA Cup Double, used all the insider knowledge he possessed and Paul Parker was outstanding in protecting the Rangers goal.

The controversial Omniturf had been replaced by a natural surface by now and both sets of players had a good playing surface despite the rain earlier in the day with the help of sand under the turf and decent drainage.

The tie kicked off in mild dry conditions with Loftus Road heaving as the Super Hoops faced a Gunners side in their yellow change strip.

It was the days when Arsenal were known for their formidable back line. And that rearguard was well represented with Lee Dixon, Steve Bould, captain Tony Adams, David O'Leary and Nigel Winterburn all present and correct for the challenge of providing an impervious wall for Rangers to bounce off in front of goalkeeper John Lukic.

They also had a superb midfield three in David Rocastle, skilled, pacey and tricky, Michael Thomas, whose late goal against Liverpool at Anfield had sealed the title the previous season, and the dependable Kevin Richardson.

Up front was Alan Smith, an intelligent player with an unerring eye for goal, and the hard-working Perry Groves. But Rangers too were to be respected. There was Seaman, a big-money signing from Birmingham City four years earlier.

And, in front of him, the rock-like Alan McDonald alongside Danny Maddix, who had arrived at Rangers on a free transfer from Tottenham Hotspur, with the superb Paul Parker, in central defence.

There was the adventurous full-back/wing-back pair of David Bardsley, a converted winger, and Kenny Sansom, a class act with vast experience with England and, of course, Arsenal.

Class was the hallmark of their midfield with soon-to-be England winger Andy Sinton, talented Simon Barker and the legendary Ray Wilkins at its heart.

Colin Clarke, the big, strong, lion-hearted Northern Ireland international, and twinkled-toed number 10 Roy Wegerle provided a decent partnership up front.

Rangers had an early warning. Adams pushed forward and put Smith in but superb covering from McDonald blocked his view of goal and his low punt was saved by Seaman to his right.

Wegerle had Arsenal hearts in mouths soon after. Adams, pivotal in Arsenal's defence, miscued a long Bardsley ball into touch amid a cacophony of 'ee-aw' noises emanating from the Loft End which typified a trend among rival fans to nickname the Gunners' talisman and leader 'Donkey'.

Barker picked up the throw and put the ball down the right for a cross headed away by Steve Bould. But razor-sharp Wegerle pounced on the ball to rocket an angled volley which Lukic saved superbly.

The moment sent a frisson of excitement through the ground and the pace of the game stepped up with Arsenal, led by the foraging Dixon from right-back, looking to hit the front.

And the visitors carved a glorious opportunity for skipper Adams. Smith found him inside the area with a clear sight of goal but the defender blasted the ball over the bar.

Rocastle had a half-chance but Wilkins blocked his effort before the winger forced Seaman to save with Groves coming in late on the goalkeeper to provoke ire from the normally placid stopper.

The rain from before the kick-off had returned to create the sort of thrills and spills in the wet FA Cup tie atmosphere for which the competition is famous.

Adams, unperturbed by the taunts, surged forward from the back again on a superb solo run and shot which Seaman saved and safely held despite the conditions.

Rangers looked for holes in the Arsenal wall by building up patiently. And the approach came close to paying off when the ball was worked out to Sansom on the left.

He floated over a teasing cross which dipped, forcing Lukic to tip over the ball. Bardsley, storming forward, drove over as the rain became torrential.

Rangers made a quick break to create another opportunity as Wilkins hooked clear an Arsenal attack towards the halfway line.

The ball fell behind Kevin Richardson as the visiting midfielder waited underneath it but the alert Wegerle nipped in to gain possession as Richardson and team-mate Dixon were left floundering.

Wegerle beat Adams on a diagonal run to the left to supply Sinton but the winger delayed his return ball to the striker and the effort was blocked by centre-back David O'Leary.

It seemed as if a swift break, taking advantage of the vagaries of the weather, with the wind causing swirling conditions, would be the way to get on the scoresheet.

Rangers tested the theory by repeating a theme of the match with defenders from both sides getting forward. Marauding QPR duo Bardsley and Parker used pace, energy and bravado to get deep into the Arsenal half to create half-chances.

Clarke headed just wide from a cross from Parker, after he had stayed forward.

The breakthrough came for Rangers in the second half thanks to an error from Lukic, the brilliance and awareness of Wegerle and the dead-eye of former Highbury hero Kenny Sansom.

Lukic seemed sure-footed as he struck a goal kick, but he miscued to Wegerle just outside the penalty area.

The number 10 then did what Rangers' number 10s tended to do and mesmerised all opponents in his path.

He knocked the ball past a falling Adams and ran to the right to gather it. The covering O'Leary chased him. Wegerle slipped on the surface while he tried to control the ball and turn in one movement as O'Leary joined him on deck. The striker then sprinted for the ball as it went loose towards the right-hand touchline with O'Leary again in pursuit. Wegerle arrived first but appeared to be hemmed in by the Arsenal centre-back.

A deft feint to the left and Wegerle had beaten O'Leary. The South African cut back inside the Republic of Ireland international as he moved towards the area. He then touched the ball with the outside of his right boot and then pulled the ball back across to the left to beat O'Leary yet again.

And, with Arsenal defenders crowding around him, he spotted Sansom on the edge of the box. Sansom's right-footed pass was drilled first time beyond Lukic by the former Gunner.

It was Sansom's first goal in three years. And that last one, against West Ham United, was for Arsenal.

Rangers were pushed back as Arsenal searched for the equaliser. Alan McDonald and Danny Maddix combined to stop a jinking run inside the box from Michael Thomas following a Rocastle ball. And Seaman saved a thunderbolt from Dixon as the left side of the home defence failed to pick up his run onto a superb crossfield ball from substitute Paul Merson, who had replaced Groves.

A curled lob from Smith was only just wide of Seaman's left-hand post. And the keeper held on to a fierce Merson drive at the second attempt.

QPR held firm with Sansom in determined mood at the back despite being booed by a large contingent of Arsenal fans, perhaps for his defection from their club to Rangers via Newcastle United.

Sansom's side had been well drilled by Howe to maintain focus and stay organised to stave off George Graham's powerful and skilled side. All for one and one for all.

They stuck to the task, gave Arsenal limited space and generally left their opponents frustrated. But the tie remained in the balance with both sides knowing extra time could become a reality.

Rangers wrapped it up when Sinton scored his side's second goal from a late break with Arsenal caught with too many players forward.

Again Wegerle was the architect. He received a superb ball from the right inside the full-back from Clarke, who had turned Adams following a throw down the touchline by Bardsley.

Wegerle sashayed to the left and found Sinton who guided the ball low into the far corner from 15 yards.

The winger leapt in the air and celebrated with his team-mates and the crowd. Any danger that extra time could be forced had evaporated as Rangers completed a memorable victory.

The win secured a tie against Blackpool of the Third Division at Bloomfield Road in the fifth round of what proved a marathon run to the quarter-finals in which every tie went to at least a second match.

Rangers' opening round saw them dominate Cardiff City at Ninian Park. A host of chances came and went and Seaman was left largely idle throughout the 90 minutes of the goalless draw.

The Welsh side proved equally resistant for much of the replay at Loftus Road before late goals from Wilkins and Wegerle ensured a safe passage into their fourth round encounter with the Gunners.

And, you've guessed it, the tie with Blackpool was not settled after 90 minutes.

Clarke scored twice in the 2-2 draw on the Lancashire coast and Blackpool proved a hard rock to crack in the replay which ended 0-0 after extra time despite the hosts carving out a series of opportunities and having two goals disallowed.

Rangers won the toss to stage the third match and came through 3-0, although the goal floodgates only opened in the second half after a ball got wedged under the foot of Seasiders left-back Alan Wright to gift Sinton a chance he did not waste before Sansom scored for the second round in a row and Simon Barker added a third.

Rangers finally had a draw at home in the last eight against Liverpool, who had been pipped for the previous season's title by the Gunners.

The first game finished 2-2 in a thriller with Barker taking the tie to a replay with a late equaliser after John Barnes and Ian Rush had put the Reds in front after Wilkins had given R's a first-half advantage.

Peter Beardsley netted the only goal at Anfield to put the cap on an astonishing nine-match run across four rounds.

Ray Wilkins said to QPRnet.com, 'There were a few matches I remember and the one against Arsenal is one of them.'

39 v Liverpool 3-1

Football League First Division. Anfield
30 March 1991. Attendance: 37,251

QUEENS PARK RANGERS:	LIVERPOOL:
Stejskal	Hooper
Bardsley	Hysen
Brevett	Burrows
Tillson	Nicol
Peacock	Molby
Maddix	Ablett
Wilkins	Beardsley
Barker	Houghton
Ferdinand	Rush
Wegerle (Allen)	Staunton (Rosenthal)
Sinton (Wilson)	Gillespie

Referee: Mike Reed (Birmingham)

RAY WILKINS has become a perennial pick when fans vote for their all-time Queens Park Rangers XI. And he showed just why as he proved instrumental in helping relegation-threatened R's secure their first – and so far only – victory at Anfield against reigning champions Liverpool on Saturday 30 March 1991. The hosts were second, R's 16th. It was some shock.

Wilkins had enjoyed a stellar career at some of football's most glamorous clubs like Chelsea, Manchester United, AC Milan, Paris St Germain and Glasgow Rangers, earning 84 England caps along the way.

And it was thought the classy midfielder was winding it down when he arrived at Loftus Road in 1989 aged 33.

But those who believed that did not know Wilkins. He was an evergreen, as physically fit, mentally sharp, technically gifted and highly motivated as the day he began building his reputation as Chelsea's youngest captain.

The big bush of dark hair worn by the youngster nicknamed Butch had, to put it politely, thinned out.

It was a classic case of not judging a book by the cover as he proved a revelation to the ignorant as he cemented his place in Rangers' legend in two spells; the first lasted five years and the second saw him become the oldest player to wear the blue and white hoops aged 39 years 352 days in a 2-1 home defeat by Bolton Wanderers on 1 September 1996.

He epitomised his worth to the club by playing in every Rangers game during the 1990/91 season, leading from the front when taking the captain's armband. This was the season, of course, he took his Rangers to Anfield.

He was just the sort of player Rangers needed in the situation. Anfield personified intimidation. You walked through the main entrance and up the stairs carpeted in red and lined by silverware in glass cases not deemed worthy of the main trophy cabinet for the serial collectors for the then four-time European Cup winners, three-time UEFA Cup

v Liverpool 1991

winners who had been top-tier champions a record 18 times (11 since 1973), and winners of four FA Cups and four League Cups at the time.

The ghost of Bill Shankly, the presence of manager turned director Bob Paisley, the recent memories of managerial glories achieved by Kenny Dalglish, who had left with the reigning title holders top of the league the month before, hung in the air.

And the Reds, with Ronnie Moran in caretaker charge until Graeme Souness came in 16 days later, had destroyed Derby County 7-1 at the Baseball Ground in their previous game a week earlier.

They also included a team of superstars such as Ian Rush, Peter Beardsley, Steve Staunton, Jan Molby and Steve Nicol.

Then there were the fans. The passionate Scousers singing 'You'll Never Walk Alone' on the Kop, probably the most famous section of a ground in the game.

It was considered a home banker. BBC *Match of the Day* commentator Steve Wilson self-effacingly admits that was the reason he got switched to the match which launched his broadcasting career from his usual beat of 20-second update flashes from Third Division matches for Capital Radio at either Fulham or Brentford ('otherwise they'd have sent one of their more senior reporters').

The good news for Rangers was that they were in the middle of an unbeaten 11 match run reviving hopes of top-flight survival come the season's end. Also John Barnes, who had scored twice against the Rams, was missing from the home line-up.

Rangers manager Don Howe had pieced together a decent enough team which looked, on paper, one worthy of a position away from the struggle for their First Division lives.

And the bespectacled Howe, huddled and animated in his Anfield dug-out, clearly had a vision of how to topple the big red giant as the drama unfolded.

Howe had developed a reputation as a shrewd coach and tactician to help Bertie Mee's Arsenal win the Football League and FA Cup Double in 1971 and picked up managerial experience at West Bromwich Albion, Galatasaay in Turkey and the Gunners before succeeding Trevor Francis at Rangers the previous summer.

And it was evident in the opening minutes of the encounter. He had detailed Danny Maddix to stick like glue to Ian Rush, who had continued to be a goalscorer very much of legend in his own playing lifetime after returning from Juventus in Italy a couple of years before.

The defence as a whole looked well-drilled with Darren Peacock a rock at its centre alongside Maddix, David Bardsley and Rufus Brevett, with every player in a Rangers shirt buying into the team ethic. And Howe's heroes also had sharp Roy Wegerle, the latest number 10 maverick for QPR, and pacey Les Ferdinand, the powerhouse centre-forward, at the sharp end looking, well, sharp.

And Howe also had his on-the-field lieutenant Wilkins to help carry out his instructions, offer a voice of experience to the troops (like 'be careful – don't give them a chance' to team-mate Andy Tillson with Rush and Beardsley threatening at one point) to the troops, while spraying passes around and generally pulling the strings in the middle of the hallowed park.

Howe knew, as Wilkins did, that his captain was not going to rely on pace. After all if you have never had it you are not going to miss it. But Wilkins, though, was able to use the qualities already listed as he helped Rangers leave Liverpool red-faced.

Ferdinand led the early charge when he regained possession to let fly with a rocket 30-yarder which Reds goalkeeper Mike Hooper tipped over the bar.

Queens Park Rangers' Greatest Games

Liverpool came back and unmarked Rush squandered an opportunity when he headed wide from eight yards from a David Burrows cross after Rangers cleared an attack instigated by Peter Beardsley.

Wilkins then sparked a superb Rangers move. He cushioned a header from a panicky Liverpool clearance to Simon Barker and was immediately on the move. Barker laid the ball back for right-back David Bardsley to thread a pass through to Wilkins on the edge of the box.

Wilkins, with a back-heel flicks put in Andy Sinton behind the Liverpool rearguard and the winger rifled the ball just wide and over on the angle.

Liverpool hit back and Jan Stejskal, who had been applauded by the sporting Kop behind him as he took his place in goal before the kick-off, saved a Rush volley from a David Burrows ball. Rush and Ray Houghton had efforts from the loose ball blocked.

But Rangers remained threatening. Left-back Rufus Brevett put Barker away down the left and from the midfielder's cross Ferdinand slipped his marker to shoot.

His effort rebounded out and Barker again picked the ball up on the left. This time the skilled, hard-working number 8 crossed to the near post and Ferdinand dived for the ball under pressure from Gary Ablett to head into the net.

The Rangers fans packed behind the goal at the Anfield Road End were ecstatic and chanted 'we love you Rangers, we do'.

And their heroes doubled the lead through Roy Wegerle just before the interval. The goal was presented to the gifted South African forward. Burrows allowed a back-pass from Steve Staunton to go through to Hooper. The alert Wegerle popped up behind the pair, took one touch with his left foot to control the ball and another to pull it wide of Hooper and lifted the ball into the far corner with his right.

Rangers supporters sang and chanted throughout the interval while the rest of the spectators were left stunned as their side looked to be surrendering three points at home for the first time during the campaign – and the title to Arsenal.

Liverpool only managed to give themselves hope with a controversial penalty, converted by Jan Molby midway through the second half.

Rangers protested about the decision given after Ray Houghton was challenged by Rufus Brevett who lost his balance with the ball seeming to hit his hand accidently as he fell to the ground.

Houghton and Rush pleaded with referee Mike Reed who pointed to the spot. And Danish midfielder Molby put the ball past Stejskal as the goalkeeper went to the left.

But QPR made sure when substitute Clive Wilson scored with his first touch. Ferdinand latched on to a ball down the right and crossed.

The ball flicked across the head of an airborne Wilkins to Steve Nicol and then rebounded off the defender for Wilson to knock it in. Game over.

The Anfield faithful applauded Rangers from the field. There was general recognition they had deserved what they had dared not hope for – a victory and a place in the club's history books. It also provided a confidence boost which helped the R's ultimately successful bid to survive in the top division for another season.

Wilkins has revealed how he came to go to QPR, his attitude and why he thrived as a 'golden oldie'.

He said to QPRnet.com, 'There was no way I was just going there [QPR from Glasgow Rangers] to see out time, I looked around at the players they had at the club and I knew I was going to enjoy life at QPR.

v Liverpool 1991

'Thankfully I was able to play there for a good few years because I had some really good times and we had some fantastic results against some really good teams.'

What was the reason he produced some of his best football at Loftus Road? He said, 'I think it was the working environment: we had a great bunch of lads, a really exceptional bunch of fellas.

'We all got on well, enjoyed each other's company and worked hard for each other and it just went from strength to strength. I'd always looked after myself because I love playing football and enjoyed myself.'

Ferdinand told your author with a smile in July 2013, 'It was great to be part of the first time in the club's history they had beaten Liverpool up there.

'I remember having a particularly good game on the day. I remember Don Howe saying to me afterwards that he hoped I'd carry on playing like I had because I was unplayable in this league.'

The Daily Mail got players involved to reminisce about the day.

Maddix said, 'We had a great squad which could mix it with the best of them. We were confident. I remember when we saw the team sheet and John Barnes wasn't playing, that gave everyone a boost. Don Howe told me before the game to do a job on Rushy. It paid off.

'The thing which has always stayed with me was the reaction of the Liverpool fans after the game. To a man they stood up and clapped us off – that's what football meant at Anfield, they appreciated the way we'd played. It was the same with their players.

'When we finally got back to Loftus Road there was a whole group of fans waiting for us. I'd never seen that before, and it brought home to me what we'd achieved.'

Clive Wilson said, 'My goal must have been scripted. I was in shock. When the final whistle blew it really hit me, an overwhelming disbelief.'

Liverpool striker Ian Rush said, 'QPR had a decent side back then but, even still, losing to them in the manner that we did was a shock. That defeat was the sign that our title was slipping away from us.'

Gary Gillespie said, 'Perhaps complacency played a part. The main thing I remember about the game was Les Ferdinand's performance. He was always a handful and had all the attributes to be a top striker – he was strong, quick, skilful and good in the air. You could see he was destined for great things.'

v Manchester United 4-1
Football League First Division. Old Trafford
1 January 1992. Attendance: 38,554

QUEENS PARK RANGERS:	MANCHESTER UNITED:
Stejskal	Schmeichel
Bardsley	Parker
Wilson	Blackmore
Wilkins	Bruce
Peacock	Pallister
McDonald	Webb
Holloway	Phelan (Giggs)
Barker	Ince
Bailey	McClair
Wegerle	Hughes
Sinton	Sharpe

Referee: K. Barratt (Coventry)

SIR ALEX FERGUSON recalled in his autobiography how Queens Park Rangers striker Dennis Bailey thanked God for the hat-trick he scored against his Manchester United team at Old Trafford on New Year's Day (or rather evening) 1992.

The United boss added, 'I don't blame him, hat-tricks by opposing players are rare enough.' They are as rare as hen's teeth one suspects unless you are aware of an adult female fowl with full dentures.

Only nine other English league players have achieved such a feat before or since. The only other player to have the temerity to ruffle the feathers of Fergie in his own back yard as he established the most successful managerial reign in English football? Ronaldo.

And even then the great Brazilian was unable to avoid being on the losing Real Madrid side with United substitute David Beckham coming off the bench to inspire a 4-3 European Cup win. Bailey, known for his Christian faith and who has in recent years played for Renewal Christian Centre in Solihull in the West Midlands Christian League Division Two, said to *Backpass* magazine, 'That's the game I'm always going to be remembered for. The goal for the hat-trick? That was at the Stretford End, standing on the line, I couldn't believe it. I had to look at the linesman to make sure his flag was down before celebrating. It was a fantastic feeling.'

And his efforts helped provoke the song 'Dennis Bailey, hallelujah hallelujah' from the Rangers faithful.

Bailey, who wished his mum Lillian a 'happy New Year' during a post-match interview, said to QPRnet.com, 'I thought that was quite good. All the players started singing at me at the end. To be honest that's what I miss the most. The banter between the other players and with the supporters. To be part of that is something you never forget.'

It would have been hard to have imagined Scot Ferguson waking up the morning after celebrating Hogmanay along with his 50th birthday believing a striker who had played for six clubs in as many years before being signed by new QPR boss Gerry Francis from

v Manchester United 1992

Third Division Birmingham City before the start of the season, would provide a shock tripping-up of his league leaders.

After all a match against United was fast becoming the very definition of playing against the big boys.

Peter Schmeichel was rated among one of the best, if not the best, goalkeepers in the world. Steve Bruce and Gary Pallister, affectionately known as Dolly and Daisy, were sturdy pillars in the heart of the home defence with the assistance of former Ranger Paul Parker, who had left Loftus Road for Old Trafford for £2m at the start of the season.

Their midfield had the influential Paul Ince, the pace and trickery of Lee Sharpe, the industry of Mike Phelan, who was to become Ferguson's assistant, and the class of Neil Webb. And up front was the dynamic duo of tough-as-old-boots Mark Hughes, destined to manage Rangers in the new Millennium, and canny Brian McClair.

And on the United bench was 18-year-old Welsh wing whizz-kid Ryan Giggs, who has gone on to make over 900 appearances for the club at the last count as this tome was published.

Rangers had never won at Old Trafford before and went on to lose 12 and draw three of their 15 matches against United up until the end of the 2012/13 season.

Indeed their league position – just below midway – failed to give any indication they could turn it on in such irresistible style, although they were on an unbeaten run of six games and included classy international performers such as former United midfielder Ray Wilkins, striker Roy Wegerle and winger Andy Sinton.

In fact, most teams, no matter how well they had been playing, would not have been tipped to trounce the front-runners who had only lost once that season – at Sheffield Wednesday – and been impregnable at home. Not many could have seen United's worst defeat at Old Trafford since 1977, one later equalled by Liverpool and finally beaten by Manchester City, coming unless you had the self belief Gerry Francis managed to instil into his Rangers troops entering the Theatre of Dreams that day.

But it happened. It was the Theatre of Dreams Turned Reality as Bailey's treble and a goal from Andy Sinton revealed Francis's side had the potential to not only defeat a side of such stature, but destroy it in the last season the elite division was a member of the Football League.

This was the season before the Premier League, Sky and six-figure weekly player wages smothered those members and formed what is often referred to as the greatest league in the world. The result, the manner of the result and Bailey's astonishing achievement will forever have a place in the hearts and minds of all R's.

It might be hard to swallow for United fans spoiled for silverware in the 27 years Ferguson spent at the helm, but the 38,500 who were there and the millions watching it on ITV, including the injured Les Ferdinand, whose physical setback had enabled Bailey to take over the number 9 shirt, will verify they hadn't just experienced a fantasy. It really did happen. And how.

With the match being screened live by television, a traditional kick-off time at 3pm was eschewed so 5pm it was. It ensured those armchairs of the armchair viewers would be filled to capacity. The hangovers of party-goers were cleared. And it was not too late to interfere with any of them chasing the hair of the dog in the evening. Neither was it too late to send youngsters to bed.

It you are going to get embarrassed, this was getting embarrassed big style for Ryan Giggs and Co.

Queens Park Rangers' Greatest Games

Sinton got the ball rolling as he put Rangers 1-0 up after three minutes. It was a goal which left United embarrassed, with left-back Clayton Blackmore's complexion in danger of turning redder than the deep red of the shirt he was wearing.

He was caught in possession by Roy Wegerle after a throw down the line by David Bardsley. And as Wegerle wriggled passed him the defender was left on his backside with his legs akimbo. Steve Bruce rushed across to cover but Wegerle teased him too before laying the ball across to his left to Simon Barker as the move reached the right-hand side of the penalty area.

Barker, showing composure, intelligence and awareness despite being surrounded by red shirts, caught sight of Sinton to his left.

The midfielder touched the ball square to him and Sinton, unmarked despite SEVEN United players being in the box, was able to steady himself and guide his shot to the left of Schmeichel with his right foot and into the net from 12 yards.

Bailey netted his first to put Rangers 2-0 up two minutes later. Again hapless Blackmore was involved. A long throw from Clive Wilson was hooked high over the United rearguard. Bailey ran in behind Blackmore and held off the challenge of the home left-back close to the near post with his upper body strength to fire towards goal.

Schmeichel blocked it with his hands, but the ball looped up and bounced into the United goal at the far corner.

Bailey almost laid on a third. He took on Paul Parker down the left and laid it inside for Ian Holloway, a future manager, to fizz a 20-yarder just wide of Schmeichel's left-hand post.

The striker came within an ace of adding to his tally a few minutes later. David Bardsley knocked the ball back for centre-back Darren Peacock who hoisted a high curling delivery from deep out on the right-hand side and Bailey found himself in acres of space and one-on-one with Schmeichel. He tried to lift the ball over the giant Dane with his extended left foot as the stopper thundered out and the ball only just cleared the bar.

Bailey deserved the ruffle of his hair from Barker. Ferguson sat in the United dug-out stunned at what was happening before his eyes.

Statistics at the interval revealed Rangers had taken seven shots to United's two. And that both home efforts were wide of the target.

The so-far-unused Giggs was given a Young Eagle of the Month Award on the pitch at the interval, as, no doubt, Ferguson was giving his famed 'hairdryer' treatment to Blackmore and his team-mates back in the dressing room, probably at a temperature hot enough to peel the paint off the walls. On the resumption, Hughes worked an opening by twisting and turning by three QPR defenders to find Paul Ince who, despite a strong challenge by Barker, found Blackmore who rocketed a 20-yarder just over.

It was indicative that Ferguson might get the reaction he desired in the second half.

It seemed, though, that Giggs would have to be introduced to step up the bid to get something out of the game.

Phelan gave way to him. It was hoped he could get at Rangers' defence down the flanks to provide deliveries for the likes of Hughes and McClair, who had so far been largely starved of any service. But Rangers broke again. Barker found overlapping full-back David Bardsley down the right and he crossed to towards the D of the penalty area where an unencumbered Bailey chested the ball back to Sinton.

The winger, unhindered, switched feet to rifle a low left-footer which Schmeichel saved low to his left. Ferguson must have wondered whether his side could sew up the holes in its defence.

v Manchester United 1992

Apparently not because Bailey made it 3-0 moments later in the 58th minute, bursting through, outpacing Bruce and chipping the ball over Schmeichel as the goalkeeper came out. The stopper was left with his hands on his hips, his face a picture of disbelief as a smiling Bailey whirled his extended right arm above his head before accepting the hugs of grateful team-mates Wegerle, Barker and Wilkins.

But United kept going and from a free kick conceded by Wilkins, Giggs made a run down the right which brought another set piece for the home side on the edge of the box.

Giggs floated it into the area where Bardsley and then Peacock were forced to head away. Then Brian McClair reduced the United arrears six minutes from time. Parker put Giggs away for another bash at the left-hand side of Rangers' defence and crossed. Gary Pallister touched the ball first time into the box. Peacock tussled with Hughes and the ball broke for McClair who scored on the turn from eight yards.

But Rangers seemed determined to give the fans what they wanted after the Super Hoops' travelling army of supporters chanted 'we want four' and they did just that three minutes before the final whistle. And another Blackmore slip in midfield gifted possession to Sinton who sprinted through an unguarded channel.

Bailey was calling for it, but the winger carried on and with the Red rearguard in tatters he slid the ball across Schmeichel against the far post and Bailey was on the spot to knock the ball over the line and enter the record books. Cue whirling arm and the widest of smiles.

Bailey, who had run United ragged, did so once more as he turned Bruce on the left to lay the ball across for Wegerle but his strike partner drove high over the bar.

The striker told ITV's Gary Newbon pitchside, 'I've never played here. It was my first game at Old Trafford. I enjoyed every minute of it. We had gone six games undefeated and were playing good football. We came into the game confident we'd win.

'Birmingham City [his former club] was good but this is different class. It's the First Division. I did hear the announcement [that he had won the champagne as man of the match]. Thanks to all our great supporters and a happy New Year to my mum!'

Bailey, after collecting the ball, interrupted a Ferguson 'hairdryer' session by going into the United dressing room for their players to sign it.

He said to *Backpass*, 'My team-mates told me to get it signed by the United players. I guess I was quite naive because I went to their dressing room, opened the door, and looked ahead and they were all sitting down.

'Steve Bruce was directly in front of me and his head was bowed. I'm standing there with a big grin on my face saying "could you sign my ball, please?" I stood there for what seemed like ten minutes but it was probably ten seconds and then I said again "could you sign my ball, please?"

'But nobody moved or said anything so I had to walk back out again. I found out later that Alex Ferguson was giving them the hairdryer treatment and had been standing behind the door.'

Bailey admitted the attention in the media was 'like a circus'. He said to QPRnet.com, 'I tried to take it in my stride but how do you? It was something totally new to me and something I'd never expected. The manager was confident and instilled that confidence in us. Everybody was expecting them to turn us over.'

Ray Wilkins recalled the game on QPRnet.com, 'It's not often anyone gets a hat-trick at Old Trafford is it! We were in synch and battered them.'

41 v Everton 5-3

Premier League. Goodison Park
12 April 1993. Attendance: 19,057

QUEENS PARK RANGERS:
Roberts
Bardsley
Wilson
Peacock
McDonald
Impey
Wilkins
Holloway
Ferdinand
Allen
Sinton (Barker)

EVERTON:
Southall
Ablett
Hinchcliffe
Watson
Jackson (Barlow)
I. Snodin
Horne
Ebbrell
Ward (Radosavljevic)
Cottee
Beardsley

Referee: Steve Lodge (Barnsley, Yorkshire)

IT WAS an extraordinary season. Football as we knew it was no more. The Premier League was upon us, made up of clubs from the First Division who decided to split from the Football League.

Elitism ruled. The rich would get richer by providing a competition which would become rated the best of its kind on the planet.

It lifted the profile of the game against rival distractions to a level which ensured football would thrive, enabling players to cash in with a weekly wage comparable to the annual salary picked up by the British Prime Minister. And much of it was underpinned by Sky television money.

It would need something special, possibly unique, for an individual to make their own indelible mark in such a ground-breaking environment where the very nature of the ground-breaking was the lead story in itself.

Teddy Sheringham managed it when he scored the league's very first goal in a game screened live by Sky. It was for Nottingham Forest in a 1-0 win over Liverpool, an achievement which has remained a stock question for pub quizzes.

And Les Ferdinand scoring back-to-back hat-tricks over three days has also been picked up by compilers who host such occasions with a dodgy microphone and beered-up regulars.

The first treble was against Forest at Loftus Road. The second came against Everton at Goodison Park. Only four players have achieved the feat of consecutive trebles in the Premier League up to when the manuscript of this book winged its way to its publishers. Ian Wright, Didier Drogba and Wayne Rooney for Arsenal, Chelsea and Manchester United respectively, are the other men.

But it is Ferdinand's achievement which stands head and shoulders above the rest. It was the first and quickest – in the number of days it took to complete – as it all but sealed a 5-3 victory against Everton on Easter Monday 1993.

v Everton 1993

Ferdinand told your author in June 2013, 'It was a great feeling. It was extraordinary. Back-to-back hat-tricks are rare. Especially two in three days! It probably wouldn't happen today in such a short period. Saturday-Monday.

'I look at football now and most players who played on the Saturday wouldn't play the Monday. They'd rotate it.'

But he was far from surprised. He said, 'On the Saturday I'd scored my first hat-trick in professional football against Nottingham Forest. I can remember it being a topsy-turvy game. We scored, they scored. They went up. We scored.

'Then we travelled up the next day to Liverpool for the Everton game on Bank Holiday Monday for that other hat-trick.

'I was just in a rich vein of form. I just felt that every time I went out on the pitch I was going to score.

'Obviously I didn't realise I was going to score back-to-back hat-tricks, but there's a period in your career where you go out on a football pitch and you are thinking "I know I'm going to score". That was that purple patch I was going through at the time.

'I was having this discussion at work [coaching at Tottenham Hotspur]. That there was just a certain period of time where I just felt I was going to score. And nine times out of ten I did.'

Wright was next to achieve the feat but 14 days separated his away-day trebles against Ipswich Town and Southampton in March 1994. And during that time the former Gunners record goalscorer played in a European Cup Winners' Cup victory over Torino at Highbury.

There was a 16-year wait for Drogba to add his name and his efforts against Wigan Athletic and West Bromwich Albion and then there was the FA Cup Final, close-season and FA Charity Shield in between them in 2010.

Rooney's double treble was achieved when United played two league games in a row, against Arsenal and Bolton Wanderers at the start of the 2011/12 season and there was a gap of 13 days between the fixtures.

Ferdinand secured the first half of a remarkable achievement in a 4-3 victory against Nottingham Forest at Loftus Road on Easter Saturday, when Kevin Wilson slotted in the other Rangers goal from the penalty spot.

He remembers his first senior treble well, 'First one a clearance upfield from the goalkeeper Tony Roberts. It went almost the length of the field, bounced s couple of times and I hit it over their goalkeeper.

'Second? Someone played it in, I rounded the goalkeeper and put it in.

'For the third Andy Sinton crossed and I stooped in the six-yard box to head it in.'

But Ferdinand was clearly in no mood to rest on his laurels. It is often said that after a high comes an immediate low. It can be hard to either escape anti-climax or doubt whether such a high level can be sustained two matches in a row.

But there were no such thoughts clouding the mind of Ferdinand as he ran out with his team-mates on to the Goodison Park pitch, even though Rangers had only managed two wins at the home of Liverpool's blue half in their previous 20 visits.

And Everton fielded a strong side packed with internationals such as the great Neville Southall, Wales's world-class goalkeeper, striking duo Peter Beardsley and Tony Cottee, outstanding full-backs Gary Ablett, who tragically passed away in January 2012 from non-Hodgkin's lymphoma, and Andy Hinchcliffe, plus long-serving centre-back Dave Watson and tenacious Wales international midfielder Barry Horne.

Queens Park Rangers' Greatest Games

They were no walkover on paper, but Rangers manager Gerry Francis had pulled together an impressive line-up on his side.

Captain Alan McDonald and Darren Peacock made up a formidable partnership in central defence with full-backs David Bardsley and Clive Wilson equally adept at either defending or bombing forward.

And the midfield, led by the experienced Ray Wilkins, with strong support by England winger Andy Sinton and the hard-working Ian Holloway, were a match for most.

Above all, on this day of course, although they all combined for a superb performance on the day, they had Ferdinand to thank most for the victory. He was at the top of his game. The big, powerful, ruthless striker left the hosts licking their wounds back in the dressing room and reflecting on their biggest reverse in nine years.

Ferdinand's treble came in just 12 minutes. It might not have been as swift as the hat-trick which would be scored by Robbie Fowler of Liverpool in August of the following year, which took a record four minutes and 32 seconds against Arsenal who had former Ranger David Seaman developing backache.

But Sir Les bringing his season's total up to 21 with his first goals away from Loftus Road of the campaign in such a quick time left shattered Toffees boss Howard Kendall telling the *Daily Mirror* that Ferdinand did a 'one-man demolition job on us'.

And his own boss, Gerry Francis, was mightily impressed, insisting he was 'frightening with his strength and pace'.

Ferdinand needed time to take centre stage and sent on a warm-up act in Andrew Impey. The winger put the R's ahead by blasting home with his left peg after only five minutes.

QPR set about Kendall's men and Sinton and Ferdinand caused home hearts to flutter with efforts which went too close to hitting the back of Southall's net for comfort.

The diminutive Cottee relieved the tension being experienced by home fans and a squirming bench when leaping high to nod the ball down and beyond Rangers stopper Tony Roberts after 30 minutes.

Ferdinand then stepped into the limelight much to Everton's chagrin as he put Rangers back in front in the 38th minute. He rifled in his first goal from just inside the box after Andy Sinton and Bradley Allen, younger brother of former Ranger Clive and son of League Cup hero Les, had combined.

He reacted quickly to a mistake from Southall for his second from a few yards inside the box within seconds of the re-start. And he thumped home his third from 15 yards on 51 minutes. Right-back David Bardsley joined in the fun for rampant Rangers when he made it 5-1 with a 25-yard drive 11 minutes from time.

The west London outfit, though, were unable to shut up shop and conceded twice in the final three minutes, from substitutes Stuart Barlow in the 87th minute, and Preki Radosavljevic, in the 89th.

It might have salvaged some pride for Everton but Ferdinand-inspired Rangers had long since done enough damage to ensure victory.

It was clear to anyone who wanted to see goals that they should attend any match which QPR were involved judging by their showdowns with Forest and Everton. And they would then be able to see a striker in his pomp.

There were calls from Francis that Ferdinand was worthy of more than mere selection for Graham Taylor's England squad for the imminent World Cup game against Holland. Francis said he 'must have given himself a great chance of actually playing'.

v Everton 1993

Your author asked Ferdinand to recall the goals with which he made early Premier League history.

He said, 'My first one? I was played through and I hit the ball across the goalkeeper into the bottom corner on the run.

'The second goal was a great run from Andrew Impey down the line. It looked like he'd fallen over but he's crossed it. It wasn't a great cross to be honest. He might say it was a great cross!

'I remember Neville Southall fumbling it. I nicked it off him, went round him and just put it in the roof of the net. The third one was good build-up play. I did a one-two with Bradley Allen and I bundled it in. Wasn't the cleanest strike I've ever hit.'

How did he remember them in such detail? He said, 'When somebody mentions it to you, all of a sudden it comes back into your head. Not a bad thing to recall experiences like that.'

It was all part of a superb season for Rangers as they were London's top club when the final table of the first Premier League season was published. They ended in fifth place, four spots higher than Tottenham Hotspur with Arsenal, Chelsea, Wimbledon and Crystal Palace trailing in their wake.

Ferdinand said, 'The one thing with that team back then was that we weren't going to win the league but what we had was a good little team where everyone was comfortable on the football. When you look throughout our team, 99 per cent of the team were. It made for us playing some good attractive football.'

v Port Vale 4-4
Football League First Division. Vale Park
19 January 1997. Attendance: 5,736

QUEENS PARK RANGERS:	PORT VALE:
Roberts	Musselwhite
Graham (Maddix)	Hill
Brevett	Tankard
Murray	Jansson
McDonald	Griffiths (Holwyn)
Ready	Glover
Spencer	McCarthy
Peacock	Porter
Hateley (Dichio)	Mills
Brazier (Impey)	Naylor
Sinclair	Guppy

Referee: R. Poulain (Huddersfield)

ROBBIE WILLIAMS sang 'Let Me Entertain You'. Of course, there are plenty of ways in which a performer can achieve that albeit in the era of film, books, television and computers.

Williams's field is music and the Port Vale football fan just might have been inspired to write one of his biggest hits by the show his favourites and Queens Park Rangers put on at Vale Park in a second-tier league showdown on Sunday 19 January 1997.

Many thrill-seekers looking to be entertained seemed to have been looking at anywhere but Vale Park on this day judging by the paltry 5,000 crowd of spectators – with three-quarters of the ground empty – who bothered to come along for the game.

But it was their loss. There are comebacks. And then there are comebacks. The one which occurred when Rangers staged arguably the greatest of them all in the history of English professional football.

Queens Park Rangers were in a pickle. They had been relegated from the Premier League in 1996 and were trying to bounce back to the big-time.

And it was not going well on the afternoon they took on the Valiants at their hosts' headquarters.

They were 4-0 down at the interval and new manager Stewart Houston and his assistant Bruce Rioch were not enjoying, let alone being entertained by, this part of their settling-in process. But red-shirted, red-blooded Rangers roared back to force a 4-4 with Scotland international John Spencer smashing home the equaliser in injury time.

It is comparable to the achievement they pulled off 13 years earlier when they managed to secure a home point against Newcastle United despite trailing by four goals at the interval (as we have read in a previous chapter).

But the feat against John Rudge's stunned team – another in black and white – is all the more remarkable when one considers that the R's were 4-1 down with only five minutes left of normal time.

v Port Vale 1997

Houston compared the two halves graphically. He said to *The Independent*, 'It was like heaven and hell. I told the players that if Vale could score four goals in 45 minutes so could we. I didn't really think we would but it was one hell of a game.'

Rangers went one down after 24 minutes when the defence failed to pick up Lee Glover who ran to the near post to meet a low Jan Jansson cross and, unmarked, the former Nottingham Forest forward who served Brian Clough at the City Ground crashed the ball past Tony Roberts at the near post. QPR's Welsh international stopper kicked the ball out of the goal with a face like thunder.

Within 11 minutes Rangers had conceded a second goal. Steve Guppy, the future Leicester wing man, took on Mark Graham down the left and went outside his marker to sprint towards the goal line before crossing to the far post where Lee Mills dived to head the ball into the roof of Roberts's net.

Houston's side went 3-0 down after 41 minutes. A ball down the right from full-back Andy Hill was flicked on to put Tony Naylor clear. Naylor ran inside Rufus Brevett, checked and lofted a left-footer towards the far post where Guppy laid it back across the goalmouth first time for Swedish international Jansson, unmarked, central and eight yards out, to smack the ball beyond Roberts.

It became 4-0 to Vale in the last minute of the first half when Malcolm Brazier headed an in-swinging corner to the near post from Jansson into his own net. Stalwart R's centre-half Alan McDonald shook his head in frustration.

There was certainly no double decker bus parked in front of their goal. In fact if the hosts had owned one they would no doubt have had plenty of room to drive their way around it. There were certainly no road blocks on any route to the visitors' goal.

Rangers had a mountain which would have dwarfed Everest to climb in the second half. But it appeared that way when Alan Mullery's QPR trailed Newcastle United by the same score at the interval on the Omniturf at Loftus Road in 1984.

Mullery was unable to sound a rallying call to his troops against the Jack Charlton-managed Toon, which featured former Rangers players Glenn Roeder and David McCreery. He could see no hope and told them there was 'no way' they could pull the four goals back.

And yet, as we have read in a previous chapter, the miracle happened as Rangers salvaged a point; 4-0 became 4-3 became 5-3 became 5-5.

Now it was the same problem with a different team, different manager and different division in a different era.

This time, the boss was able to come up with some words of optimism to try and fire up his players in the privacy of their dressing room at Vale Park. He reckoned that, if the hosts could score four goals in 45 minutes, so could they.

Rangers increased the tempo at the start of the second half. There was a greater hunger. Mark Graham exemplified the new approach as he hustled and harried an opponent before coming away with the ball. He pulled it back for Trevor Sinclair to hit a cross to the far post towards the head of 6ft 3in Danny Dichio.

Vale defender Jermaine Holwyn, running back towards his own goal to intercept, got his head to the ball but instead of putting it over the bar he only succeeded in guiding it below it and into the net, falling on his back to stare at the sky in disappointment, hoping what had just happened was a nightmare rather than a reality.

The mountain was smaller for the R's but still looked insurmountable with a 4-1 deficit as the minutes ticked by until there were only five of them left.

Queens Park Rangers' Greatest Games

Yet Houston's men still kept battling and believing, refusing to give up on what looked like a hopeless cause before they got their reward.

Sinclair was full of skill and industry. He found Danny Maddix venturing forward and the defender crossed to the far post. Luckless Holwyn beat Dichio in the air but the ball fell to Andrew Impey 15 yards out. As Vale midfielder Jon McCarthy jumped and turned his back to block, substitute Impey caught the ball on the volley with his right foot to send it rocketing into the roof of the net.

Impey jogged over to the Rangers fans behind the goal and put four fingers up with his right hand and two with his left to indicate the scoreline. The subtext of the gesture was, 'We are going to do this.'

Hope springs eternal but the winger's goal gave him, his team-mates and the QPR supporters something substantial to hold on to. There was still a justifiable spring in the step of the fighters from London W12.

Houston and Rioch both stood on the sidelines, the epitome of synchronicity. Both had their right arms cocked and were looking down at their watches. How much time was there left? Would they be able, like Manchester United's fabled manager Sir Alex Ferguson, to squeeze a little 'Fergie' time from the referee?

Rangers' inner-belief was growing and, as the late legendary manager Brian Clough said, it only takes a second to score. And there were more than a few of those left – at least 120, for that now was how long it would be until normal time ended.

Defender Karl Ready pushed forward to try and put Dichio in but Vale held firm as the hosts cleared to Allen Tankard in midfield. The home player dwelt on the ball and was dispossessed by Alan McDonald as the heart-on-his sleeve-all-for-one-one-for-all defender charged forward before laying the ball off to Gavin Peacock.

The cultured Peacock threaded the ball to Dichio with his back to goal on the edge of the Port Vale area. The big striker found Trevor Sinclair who spread the ball into space on the right-hand side of the penalty area for Paul Murray to run on to.

Vale goalkeeper Paul Musselwhite quickly sensed the danger and flew out to narrow the angle. It left Murray little time but his speed of thought and execution was as near perfect as it needed to be.

The split-second before Musselwhite arrived at his feet Murray chipped a lob over him towards the far post and the ball nestled into the corner of the net for 3-4.

Was this really happening? Surely it was still too little too late must have been the reassuring thought running through the collective brains of the home side desperately trying to stay in the now rather than fast-forwarding their grey matter and imagining Rangers really could salvage a point.

Substitute Dichio rushed into the net to gather the ball so Vale restarted the game that much quicker. But Glover would not allow him to and the pair tussled in the netting at the back of the goal with Holwyn and the referee having to part them.

The visiting supporters were now convinced that somehow there would be enough time for an equaliser, something Houston had told his players they could achieve without, deep down, believing it a possibility.

But normal time had run out for them. They had to hope added time would produce what they so desperately wanted.

Suddenly Rangers had a free kick 20 yards out on the left-hand side of the penalty area. Dichio, the Notting Hill-born striker with Italian ancestry, had a shot from a short ball from the set piece charged down.

v Port Vale 1997

Rangers left-back Rufus Brevett picked up the loose ball as Vale stayed packed tight at the back defending what little they had left of the lead.

Their winners' flag was still implanted into what was once an unconquerable peak, except it was now blowing in the wind and being eased out of the ground.

Brevett played the ball forward and left to Sinclair, who in six days later would hit the headlines with a wonder goal (see the following chapter).

The winger moved inside Tankard and then slipped the ball down the left wing for Impey. The Vale supporters were frantically urging the referee to blow the whistle and their players were trying to avoid tightening up and just keep focused on the job in hand.

But the super-sub who had breathed life in his side's late, late bid to win a point was free. Red-shirted Rangers swarmed into the area as Impey thumped over the cross. Dichio was first to it and headed firmly and down. The ball headed with pace towards the back of the net, just inside Musselwhite's right-hand post.

But the stopper got down to claw it away with his left hand as he strained every sinew.

Time seemed to stop for a nano-second. Where was the ball headed? Straight to the feet of the lurking John Spencer, the Scotland international striker in the all red of Rangers, that's where.

And the £2.5m capture from Chelsea a couple of months previously lashed the ball with his left foot and it ripped between Musselwhite, trying to regain his feet, and the stopper's near post to nearly burst the net.

Spencer had done it. QPR had done it. The match-saver's celebration was low key and he walked off to the side, arms and hands at his side, a pugnacious look in his face, inner pride surging through his body as team-mates jumped on him in front of a deliriously happy Rangers faithful who had had their faith repaid.

The players also hugged their supporters hanging over the barrier before a policeman parted them. Mission Impossible, whatever you want to call it, had been achieved.

Houston's men had refused to abort. They had refused to panic. They kept plugging away and got what their approach and never-say-die attitude deserved. One observer doubted whether we would see that again. He probably had a point.

43 v Barnsley 3-2

FA Cup. Loftus Road
25 January 1997. Attendance: 14,317

QUEENS PARK RANGERS:	BARNSLEY:
Roberts	Watson
Maddix	Eaden
Brevett	Appleby (Liddell)
Murray	Bosancic (Jones)
McDonald	Moses
Ready	De Zeeuw
Spencer (Hateley)	Hendrie
Peacock	Redfearn
Dichio	Wilkinson
Impey	Marcelle (Bullock)
Sinclair	Sheridan

Referee: Not known

THERE ARE moments in football which stay with its ardent followers forever; moments they are convinced will never be surpassed. One such incident came in the 74th minute of Queens Park Rangers' FA Cup fourth-round tie against Barnsley on Saturday 25 January 1997.

Trevor Sinclair launched a bicycle kick which hurled him into a Hall of Fame as the scorer of the club's greatest goal in its 130-year history. Or so those ardent folk would have you believe. Now one such ardent fan was Nick Saloman, one of many musicians who love the R's. He might not have the cache of QPR fans like Mick Jones out of seminal punk band The Clash, or Pete Docherty of The Libertines and Babyshambles, who helped produce an R's fanzine. Or even Bruce Welch of the influential Shadows.

But the season ticket holder and QPR supporter of 50 years is rated a 'cult guitar hero' by the estimable *MOJO* magazine, judged from the recording and performing of his own songs for his band The Bevis Frond. And he knows and works with the one-time girlfriend of the tragic Kurt Cobain, the last global rock legend.

Saloman invited American singer-songwriter Mary Lou Lord, who immediately preceded Courtney Love in the Nirvana frontman's affections, to attend her first football match when Sinclair made his bid for QPR immortality.

It was 2-1 to Rangers. John Spencer and Gavin Peacock had replied to an early effort from Neil Redfearn for the Tykes, who were being cheered on by Barnsley-born fan Sir Michael Parkinson, the television presenter and journalist, although the hosts had been left hanging on due to Andrew Impey being sent off.

Sinclair took centre stage to emulate the 1976/77 feat of QPR's Gerry Francis and become the winner of the *Match of the Day* Goal of the Season despite the competition of an effort from the halfway line by David Beckham for Manchester United against Wimbledon.

Sinclair had picked up a position inside the D on the edge of the penalty area with his back to goal. A red-shirted Barnsley defender was breathing down his neck.

v Barnsley 1997

John Spencer spotted the dreadlocked figure in the blue and white hoops and slung over a first-time high cross from the right from a Danny Maddix pass.

Sinclair kept his eye on the ball as it winged its flight over from the right-hand touchline and as it arrived at head height just in front of him he sprung in the air. And as the airborne Sinclair leaned back he brought up his right leg in an arc and connected his right foot with the ball. Detonation!

The spherical object was propelled seemingly at the speed of sound, if not light, towards the top-left corner of Barnsley's goal. Tykes stopper David Watson was only a mere mortal trying to cope with the attempt destined to elevate its practitioner above such confines.

Sinclair fell to the green sward on his back and half lifted himself enough to turn and witness the net bulge. There was a collective silence as Sinclair's wonder strike hit its target, as if no one in the ground could believe what they had just witnessed.

But then the penny dropped and both sets of supporters showed their appreciation, the Tykes with respectful claps and the home support with exhortations so loud those noise abatement people just might have paid a quiet visit to the Shepherd's Bush area shortly afterwards to discover there had been a run on deaf aids in the aftermath among its population.

Sinclair climbed to his feet he turned and ran off to the left-hand touchline with his arms up in the shape of the V, his dreadlocks springing around and with almost certainly the biggest smile on a Rangers player since Dennis Bailey scored his hat-trick at Old Trafford five years before.

Saloman, along with most in the 14,000 crowd, went ape. Mary Lou turned to him and said amid the din, 'Hmmm, not bad.' To which Saloman responded, 'Not f****** bad?! That's the best goal I've ever f****** seen.'

He told your author in July 2013, 'It wasn't very gentlemanly of me but for her one and only ever football match, Mary Lou saw a super-tense 3-2 victory, with five goals, a controversial sending off, and the best goal ever scored in the FA Cup. We even witnessed a full-on knife fight in the White City Estate on our way back to the car!

'She was still a bit lukewarm in her analysis later. "Yeah, I guess I can see why people dig soccer so much," she said with not much conviction.

'I tried to impress upon her that it wasn't like that every week, and just how exceptional Trevor's goal was, but she didn't really grasp the enormity of the situation.

'Later that night I heard her talking to her husband, back in Boston, Mass., on the phone, "Yeah, so this dude kinda did a backflip and made a goal … everyone went crazy, I guess it musta been somethin' kinda special". She wasn't wrong.' It certainly lifted the spirits of the bemused R's faithful following relegation and general upheaval.

Their precious club had gone down after 13 seasons in the top flight the previous term, following the £6m move of top scorer Les Ferdinand to Newcastle United before the start of the campaign, despite the best efforts of Sinclair, who came from Blackpool in 1993, and loyal Simon Barker, who had featured in the historic Old Trafford victory five years earlier.

Long-term Rangers supporter Chris Wright, the chairman of Chrysalis Communications – developed from a respected record label – bought the club from chairman Richard Thompson before the start of the season

A month into the campaign player-manager Ray Wilkins, two years after replacing Gerry Francis, departed with the official line stating he wished to concentrate on playing.

He was, after Frank Sibley had taken caretaker charge, replaced by Stewart Houston with assistance from Bruce Rioch, who had been the new manager's boss at Arsenal.

Queens Park Rangers' Greatest Games

After a poor start to the Houston-Rioch reign Rangers moved up to sixth by the turn of the year and completed a league double over Barnsley three days before beating Huddersfield Town to secure their fourth-round FA Cup date against the Yorkshiremen, who would be promoted to the Premier League by the end of the season.

The unforgettable meeting in the fabled knockout competition came on a chilly Saturday afternoon.

Redfearn put the visitors ahead on 13 minutes. The midfielder had been in good goalscoring form and was rated 9-1 by bookmakers to score the first goal of the game. He guided an under-hit 20-yard free kick through the wall which squirmed into the net with goalkeeper Tony Roberts caught out.

Gavin Peacock equalised for Rangers. But for Sinclair's spectacular effort later, Peacock's goal would have got more plaudits. Roberts, making amends for his part in Barnsley's goal, lofted a long kick upfield which was headed on to Spencer who flicked the ball first time into the path of Peacock.

The striker surged past one challenge, altered the angle of his run to avoid a second and lashed the ball into the top corner from 18 yards.

A little and large striking partnership combined to put QPR 2-1 ahead after 27 minutes. A Sinclair ball was half-cleared to Peacock who combined with Paul Murray for Alan McDonald to loft an angled cross deep into the Barnsley area to the giant unmarked Danny Dichio who touched the ball across to his right for the diminutive Spencer to tap in.

It seemed Spencer, a £2.5m signing from Chelsea in November 1997, had the sign on Barnsley, having hit a hat-trick against the Tykes in the 3-1 home win two weeks earlier.

Impey was ordered off shortly after the re-start for violent conduct with Barnsley full-back Nicky Eaden prostrate on the pitch before Sinclair's moment of magic eased nerves.

But deep-lying striker John Hendrie pulled one back for Barnsley four minutes from time. He managed to sidestep two Rangers defenders as he moved to the left on the edge of the home box and rifled low to Roberts's left and into the corner.

But the match was about the one moment above one-eyed bias from Trevor Sinclair.

When Rangers visited the Selhurst Park scene of Beckham's wonder chip which rivalled Sinclair's effort in the eyes of *MOTD* in the next round to take on Wimbledon there was no further glory on offer.

Mark Hateley scored Rangers' consolation goal in a 2-1 defeat, leaving the hopes of 8,000 travelling supporters deflated after being pumped up by the dreadlocked winger in the previous round.

Sinclair told the media of his quintessential moment in an impressive career which also featured spells at West Ham United, Manchester City and the 2002 World Cup finals with England. He said, 'I try them all the time in training but they've never come off like that.'

During a spell with Cardiff ten years later, he said to *The Independent*, 'A few of the lads have been giving me grief about it. They say, "I can't believe you're still on about that goal after ten years."

'I try to recreate it in training and they have a chuckle. But as your back gets stiffer and you get older it's not so easy. I know it's a popular clip on YouTube, and people still ask me about it. It's nice to be remembered.'

v Crystal Palace 6-0
Football League First Division. Loftus Road
9 May 1999. Attendance: 18,498

QUEENS PARK RANGERS:	CRYSTAL PALACE:
Miklosko	Miller
Breacker	Frampton
Baraclough	Woozley
Kulscar	Austin
Linighan	Petric (Tuttle)
Maddix	Thompson
Scully	Foster (Burton)
Peacock	Zhiyi
Rowland (Murray)	Martin (Carlisle)
Slade	Morrison
Kiwomya (Gallen)	Mullins

Referee: Peter Rejer

CHRIS KIWOMYA remembers the day he became a Queens Park Rangers hero, when he was applauded and cheered loudly by the majority of the all-seater record 18,498 crowd at Loftus Road on a tension-racked Sunday afternoon in May 1999 as he was substituted five minutes before the whistle for club legend Kevin Gallen after a match-winning hat-trick. It was as if the European Cup Final had been won by his efforts. It was Alfredo di Stefano for Real Madrid in Glasgow in 1960. Trevor Francis (the future QPR manager) for Nottingham Forest in Malmo in 1979. Alan Kennedy for Liverpool in Paris in 1981. Didier Drogba for Chelsea in Munich in 2012.

It was as if he would return to either the centre circle or a balcony in the posh seats to collected a winners' medal and to lift the most prized club trophy in European football.

Who would have believed the treble were goals which had just helped save Rangers from relegation to the third tier of English football even though the atmosphere created by the outpouring from the Super Hoops appeared one for the biggest stage in club football?

Praise on such a scale, though, is an aphrodisiac to the ego. It could go to the head for whomsoever received it. Not so Kiwomya, who arrived at Loftus Road via Ipswich Town, where he made his name, Le Havre, Selangor and Arsenal.

Kiwomya, of Ugandan descent and Yorkshire birth, is as down to earth as the image his home county perpetuates. When you hail from Huddersfield it is unseemly to act the big-time Charlie.

Nonetheless there is no doubting the significance his eye for goal (and those of George Kulscar, Tony Scully and Tim Breacker that day) meant to the Rangers faithful.

But for it Rangers would have returned to the level they had sought to escape from since their arrival in the Football League until that magical year of 1967 which also brought the club the League Cup.

Kiwomya appreciates players play a largely fleeting role in the history of a football club, but supporters are there through thick and thin, no matter how thin the gruel.

Queens Park Rangers' Greatest Games

He said in July 2013, 'It was a day I am happy to remember.'

The cause was helped by Palace, who were reduced to nine players by the final whistle with Fan Zheng Zhiyi and David Woozley sent off for the south Londoners.

It was an out-of-the-blue result in a season which lacked consistency in performances and results which made the Great Escape the hardest job returning manager Gerry Francis had ever experienced.

Francis came to Rangers for his second spell as manager in October 1998. The former Rangers midfielder and captain had performed wonders in his first spell in charge, guiding them to fifth spot in the first season of the Premier League with the help of hot-shot Les Ferdinand. It was the highest position of any London club, an admirable achievement given the glamorous assortment of clubs from the capital including Arsenal, Tottenham Hotspur and Chelsea.

Francis had shown his potential to match an outstanding playing career while cutting his teeth in management at lower league West Country clubs Exeter City and Bristol Rovers. Indeed, he used a few of the players he helped cultivate at Rovers, along with showing faith in Les Ferdinand. But the reign ended in November 1994 with suggestions he felt undermined with owner Richard Thompson's plans to make Rodney Marsh, the club's 1960s idol, chief executive. Francis accepted the opportunity to manage Tottenham Hotspur. He took over from Ossie Ardiles, whose adoption of what was perceived as gung-ho tactics, involving the Famous Five forward line, was deemed too gung-ho.

He brought a more pragmatic approach and signed Ferdinand in a £6m deal from Newcastle United at White Hart Lane.

High-profile clubs like Spurs, though, can wear many bosses down. He went close to glory in 1994/95 by taking the club to the FA Cup semi-finals and two spots from a UEFA Cup place.

There was a slow tailing off and pressure was building for the team to achieve glory. Francis decided to resign in November 1997 and take his first break from the game in 32 years.

He told *The Guardian*, 'When I left Tottenham, I had not been out of football since 1967 but I didn't miss the job at all. I have three young children and I needed to spend some time with them.

'I took them off to America and spent a full Christmas with them, something I hadn't been able to do before and I enjoyed doing normal things. I turned down a dozen jobs including Sporting Lisbon because I needed some time off.'

But when Rangers came calling there was a difference. The heart over-ruled the head. He had played for several clubs, but he considered his football home was Loftus Road and Queens Park Rangers.

R's faced a drop into the third tier of English football. Ray Wilkins, Stewart Houston (who unpopularly showed loyal defender Alan McDonald the door) and Ray Harford, the trio who had held the reins since his first spell, had been unable to lead the club back to the Premier League following relegation in 1996.

Chairman and owner Chris Wright thought a tug at Francis's heart strings might be what was needed after a disastrous start to the 1998/99 season, without the departed John Hollins, David Bardsley and Simon Barker, which put them in the relegation mire. Wright lived up to his name as he was right, of course.

Francis took over as director of football with Iain Dowie player-coach, caretaker following Harford's resignation, and Bobby Ross, who had spotted Les Ferdinand in

v Crystal Palace 1999

non-league, and Des Bulpin back after serving the comeback boss first time round as members of his backroom staff.

Francis knew the money situation – Rangers were in the red. The club reported in February 1998 they were £3.5m in debt in the half-year up to the previous November with record signing Mike Sheron sold for £1.5m to Barnsley, a new shares issue announced and Wright digging into his own pocket to help balance the books.

Even new goalkeeper Ludek Miklosko was understood to have paid some of the £50,000 fee R's had to give West Ham United for him in December.

But Francis had set about the task in typically pragmatic style by introducing talented youngsters like Richard Langley and playing then loanees Miklosko and Tim Breacker from West Ham and later Rob Steiner from Bradford City.

After a couple of losses, results improved and, even though the situation remained far from perfect they scrimped and scrapped their way up to 17th by the turn of the year.

But they slipped two spots with the gap increasing between QPR and those immediately above and Francis's brow became furrowed because of how a job he considered the toughest of his life was turning out.

Kiwomya, a free transfer from Arsenal at the beginning of the season, bagged his first goals for Rangers in a 4-0 thumping of Swindon Town, with Steiner and Keith Rowland also chipping in.

On the March transfer deadline day, Francis sealed permanent deals for Jermaine Darlington and Ross Weare from non-league and Andy Linighan and Luke Cornwall, from Crystal Palace and Fulham on loan.

Unfortunately, it failed to spark a winning run. Rangers drew 1-1 at home to Huddersfield Town and crashed 3-1 against Ipswich Town at Portman Road with Kiwomya scoring the consolation goal against the club where he made his name.

Rangers managed to scrape a 2-1 home win with defender Karl Ready and forward Gavin Peacock on target.

Any crumb of comfort was blown to the four winds with what followed. The not-so Super Hoops totted up FIVE defeats on the bounce – against Grimsby Town, Sheffield United, Birmingham City, Bradford City and Port Vale (no big comeback this time). They only managed a single goal, from Kevin Gallen, throughout the sequence.

It left Rangers facing Palace on equal points with Bury in a battle to avoid the last relegation spot with Oxford United and doomed Bristol City occupying the final two places. It was a Save Ourselves Sunday for R's. They needed to either win or improve on whatever result Bury, who faced Port Vale at Gigg Lane, could manage if they were to ensure survival.

Oxford played Stockport County knowing they would only stay up if Rangers and the Shakers both lost and that they netted four more goals than QPR.

Rangers fans welcomed their team with banners and balloons flying on a blazing hot day. And the balloons played a part in Rangers taking the lead through Kulscar after eight minutes.

Keith Rowland found Kiwomya whose cross made it through the balloons which had drifted on to the pitch and it was half-cleared to Hungarian striker Kulscar to volley home from the edge of the penalty area. The ground erupted with ear-battering noise, to break a huge dam of tension.

Rangers doubled their lead through Kiwomya two minutes before the interval. Ludek Miklosko launched a long punt which caught Palace's back line out and Kevin Miller on his line and lightning-quick Kiwomya pounced to head home a rebound after his first effort had hit a post.

Palace shot themselves in the foot shortly after the re-start. Zhiyi, over-eager to get possession of the ball after Palace were awarded a throw-in, shoved referee Peter Rejer in an attempt to claim the ball as the official kicked it towards the touchline, and was sent off.

Kiwomya scored his second on 56 minutes. Scully put a free kick in the box and Steve Slade headed it across for ice-cool Kiwomya, surrounded by Steve Coppell's red-shirted visitors, to turn and net.

Scully volleyed home a corker for Rangers' fourth goal from an Andy Linighan ball after 76 minutes.

Breacker made it 5-0 six minutes later. Woozley received his marching orders after fouling Scully in the penalty area. Miller saved Kiwomya's spot-kick and the defender followed up for his first Rangers goal.

Kiwomya took a second chance to complete his treble and the 6-0 scoreline five minutes from time. His first two efforts from a Scully cross were saved by Miller but it was third time lucky as he touched the ball over the line from close range.

And Gallen, who had come on for Kiwomya, came close to putting Rangers in seventh heaven with a shot on the turn from a Paul Murray ball which drifted just wide of the far post.

Any details of what was going on up at Gigg Lane were being relayed around the crowd for those who could pick up radio signals.

But there was no edge-of-the-seat concern as the whistle blew. Those in the know knew Bury had won by just 1-0. Those in the know and the rest of those in white and blue roaring and applauding the slight figure of Chris Kiwomya had something to celebrate even if it wasn't winning the European Cup.

It was, however, something that would enable QPR to build a team capable of competing at the top of the table rather than in its lower reaches.

The lowering of confidence and the reduction in attractiveness to players needed to develop such a team which would have come with demotion would have all but destroyed such ambitions.

'One Chris Kiwomya, there's only one Chris Kiwomya.' Almost certainly an undeniable fact, true (unless those in Huddersfield and Uganda know different). But if 90 minutes can define a player at one club then that 90 minutes had just taken place

The following season Rangers were flying in the early part of the season as they prepared for their next meeting with Palace. It was at Selhurst Park in November 1999.

Francis, ever the realist, said to *The Guardian* at the time, 'I feel we're already over-achieving at the moment as we're very thin on the ground in terms of numbers. My target is still to go up but it's going to be difficult.

'In my opinion, being in the top half of the table is a job and a half very well done. It's been very difficult turning things around, particularly off the field. I love the club and I want to see it set up for the future.'

Rangers fell away eventually that season – but at least they achieved the aim of competing for those leading spots once more thanks to Francis and Kiwomya.

One fan posted on the internet, 'The 6-0 was certainly among the best atmospheres I have seen at Loftus Road, so much tension and then an explosion of joy and relief as the game unfolded. The reaction to the first goal especially was incredible.'

v Oldham Athletic 1-0

Football League Second Division play-off semi-final
Loftus Road. 14 May 2003. Attendance: 17,201

QUEENS PARK RANGERS:
Day
Kelly
Carlisle
Shittu
Padula (Williams)
Gallen
Bircham
Palmer
McLeod
Thomson (Pacquette)
Furlong

OLDHAM ATHLETIC:
Pogliacomi
Low
Armstrong
Haining
F. Hall
C. Hill
Murray (Duxbury)
Sheridan (Carss)
Eyre (Corazzin)
Andrews
Eyres

Referee: Mark Clattenburg (County Durham)

MIX A 34-year-old who cost Glenn Hoddle £2m when he signed him for Chelsea, a winner of the Britain's Brainiest Footballer title a year before and a striker with blue and white running through his veins.

What have you got? Three players – Paul Furlong, Clarke Carlisle and Kevin Gallen – central in helping to ensure Queens Park Rangers made it to a play-off final.

They helped Rangers beat Oldham Athletic 1-0 at a rocking Loftus Road to complete a 2-1 aggregate victory in the semi-final of the 2003 Second Division end-of-season gut-wrencher, money-spinner and dream-maker/wrecker.

Furlong scored the goal which sealed a Millennium Stadium date with Cardiff City. Carlisle made the goal. And Gallen showed why he had received the club's Player of the Year and the Players' Player of the Year awards at the recent supporters' club presentations night with an outstanding display.

And the efforts of QPR's Three Musketeers had helped give the club's long-suffering support something to cheer.

R's and their manager Ian Holloway had been through the mill. A Premier League outfit seven years earlier, they had, during the 27 months of Holloway's reign, been relegated to the third level of English football, gone into administration and endured a transfer embargo. And only seven months before Oldham they had suffered a humiliating FA Cup defeat against non-league Vauxhall Motors in a replay shoot-out at Loftus Road, one in which Carl Nesbitt, who worked in the motor company's Ellesmere Port plant, notched one of the penalties.

Furlong and Carlisle were in a result rated one of the most embarrassing since Rangers first became a Football League club of substance.

Now the pair, along with Gallen and the rest, were 90 minutes away from promotion.

Furlong had arrived at Rangers on a second spell on loan from Birmingham City in pre-season. The striker – who started out at non-league Enfield – had had a series of

Queens Park Rangers' Greatest Games

big-money moves via Coventry City, Watford and Chelsea, of course, to Brum but was considered long in the tooth.

But Holloway appreciated what he was getting and the temporary arrangement soon became permanent – and it paid off in goals from the very start when he netted in the opening-day home victory over Chesterfield, netting 13 as Rangers finished their 2002/03 league fixtures in fourth.

Carlisle returned to first-team duty after a 20-month absence in a 4-0 victory over Mansfield Town to kick off a five-match winning run to underline an already impressive start to the season and largely kept his place with a series of solid displays for the rest of the regular campaign.

Local hero Gallen, born in Chiswick and raised a Rangers supporter, had shown the reliability, effort and goals which made him such a favourite with the crowd.

His striking instincts saw him banging in his eighth league strike of the season, against Wycombe, to help end a nine-match winless mid-season run which included five games on the spin in which R's were unable to even find the net as they tried to hang on to a play-off spot.

Rangers, though, struggled for victories and slipped to tenth by Christmas – and just ten points from the drop zone. A series of sendings off was a contributory fact.

Their New Year wish came true as they scored four wins and clean sheets on the bounce with Carlisle scoring at Peterborough United and Gallen at home to Stockport County.

After a defeat at Tranmere, Holloway won the Manager of the Month award for February with Rangers winning two and drawing two, while Gallen pledged his loyalty to the R's by signing a new two-year deal.

QPR occupied the last play-off spot but it was tight. Goalkeeper Chris Day returned after a long-term injury, winger Kevin McLeod signed from Everton and Tottenham Hotspur right-back Stephen Kelly was brought in on loan to plug gaps caused by returning loanees and injuries as Holloway attempted to keep the show on the road.

Rangers were defeated just twice in 12 to put themselves seven points clear of seventh with five matches left. And they cemented their play-off place in fourth in their last home game which produced a goalless draw against Crewe Alexandra even though Carlisle and Kelly saw red.

The 1-1 draw in the first leg at Boundary Park put Rangers in the driving seat for a trip along the M4 to Cardiff to face the city's team at the 'neutral' stadium opened three years earlier which was being used with old Wembley transforming into new Wembley.

It had been a curate's egg of an experience for R's in the Greater Manchester town internationally famous for its leading role in the Industrial Revolution through cotton and textile manufacture in the 19th century.

Iain Dowie's team wanted to weave its way into the town's history books in a more prosaic manner. And all seemed to be going well for the hosts when they took the lead through 39-year-old winger David Eyres.

But Richard Langley, the talented midfielder introduced to the Super Hoops' first team by Gerry Francis, equalised two minutes after the re-start.

But Langley was banned from the second leg when he was sent off. He picked up two bookings in 30 seconds from referee Steve Bennett ten minutes from time. The first was for simulation and the second for catching Eyres with the back of his head.

Holloway remarked in *The Guardian* the following day, 'That [the sending off] marred it for me. When are we going to learn?

v Oldham Athletic 2003

'You've got to be professional on occasions like these but we have shown signs today that we cannot handle it and I won't have it. We have got to deal with ourselves in a more professional manner, a less emotional manner, otherwise we will shoot our foot off.

'We can't keep blaming referees, we have to take responsibility for our own actions. Yes, I've spoken to Richard about it and that's why I'm out of the dressing room. Right now, I'm not a very happy man.'

But then came the Wednesday night in London W12 when the smile returned to his face.

The atmosphere of the momentous second leg is recalled as one of the most electric of nights under the Loftus Road floodlights by club historian Gordon Macey.

And that includes the European evenings in the 1970s when Stan Bowles and Co. provided the thrills, spills and glory.

The visit of Oldham had extra spice with former QPR player and manager Iain Dowie in charge of the Latics.

But, most crucially, it was the craving for some crumb of comfort from an era bereft of it which gave the crucial edge.

Craving is defined as an intense, urgent or abnormal desire or longing. And most of the 17,000 packed in were suffering from the condition as County Durham referee Mark Clattenburg blew the whistle to start the second leg of a stirring play-off semi-final.

Holloway knew nothing could be taken for granted, especially as Oldham had ended their 21-match unbeaten home run in November 2002.

He shuffled the pack for the second leg with full-backs Stephen Kelly and Gino Padula, centre-back Carlisle, and striker Andy Thomson replacing Terrell Forbes, Tommy Williams, Matthew Rose and, of course, Langley.

It meant Gallen would support Thomson and Furlong up front with Carlisle slotting in centrally at the back alongside Danny Shittu.

There had been ill feeling left over from the first leg which manifested itself in a series of late tackles and backchat which spoiled the occasion to a certain degree.

And it was more than self-evident in the final seconds when Oldham's Wayne Andrews got his marching orders from Clattenburg for violent conduct.

But overall it was a victory for Rangers to savour. It involved enough incident, characterisation and storylines to turn it into a compelling film manuscript; the 'dodgy' referee, spot-kick appeals which got the brush-off from the official, the red card, and, of course, the match-saving stop from a goalkeeper only recently recovered from a long-term injury, never-say-die visitors and the late winner by a home hero way beyond the flush of youth. Maybe one day we could see Samuel L. Jackson as Paul Furlong, Daniel Radcliffe as Mark Clattenburg and Ian Holloway as Ian Holloway.

Furlong put McLeod through early on but the flanker shot straight at Oldham goalkeeper Les Pogliacomi.

Rangers centre-back Shittu, built like a giant outhouse, powered forward as Argentinian full-back Gino Padula floated in a free kick but his effort went into the side netting.

Dowie's resilient outfit almost stunned the hosts from the breaks but the unmarked Andrews squandered a golden opportunity.

Shortly afterwards the Super Hoops were adamant that they deserved to be awarded a penalty. Gallen, a thorn in the visitors' side, crossed and it seemed as if Latics' Darren Sheridan had handled it inside the 18-yard box. But Radcliffe, sorry Clattenburg, waved away home appeals.

Queens Park Rangers' Greatest Games

Furlong, belying his years, was looking hot and he frightened the wits out of Oldham by heading the resultant corner from Sheridan's 'offence' against the woodwork.

Sheridan went close to putting Latics ahead close to the half-hour. He struck a fierce volley which was deflected just beyond the far post of Chris Day.

Would-be super-sub Richard Pacquette, the supporters' Young Player of the Year, thought he had put Rangers ahead when he took a cross from McLeod on the volley from close range but the superb Pogliacomi somehow blocked it.

QPR, roared on by the vociferous crowd willing them to score, maintained the pressure. And they got their reward just eight minutes from time.

A kick out of the penalty area from Pogliacomi went straight to Carlisle. The defender, who went on to become PFA chairman, spotted a run from Furlong and guided a high ball from just inside his own half through the middle and behind the visitors' rearguard.

The striker controlled the ball by heading it down. Oldham defender Fitz Hall came across to tackle him on his left. But Furlong, using his upper body strength, kept Hall at bay before firing into the corner of Pogliacomi's goal from eight yards as the stopper came out to try and save his shot.

Furlong pulled off his shirt and ran to the fans to celebrate as team-mates rushed across to offer their congratulations.

Andrews was ordered off after kicking out at Kelly late on before Chris Day, so long on the sidelines through injury, got down to his right to pull off a wonder save from Hall after Lee Duxbury headed the ball across to him 15 yards out.

So a happy ending for Rangers. Supporters and other staff joined the players on the pitch in celebration as 'Hi Ho Silver Lining' was sung around the ground. Holloway joined in, jumping into the arms of his players. And back in the dressing room champagne flowed as the players chorused, 'We're all going to Cardiff'.

The journey into Wales and the final saw their hopes ended by a single goal in extra time by substitute Andy Campbell.

But no one will ever forget the Loftus Road thriller under lights against Oldham on the evening of 14 May 2003 when one Furlong added up to far more than a mile for a club hoping to drive their way back to the next stop on a return to the big-time.

Holloway said to *The Guardian* the following morning, 'We've got the ingredients to go there and give ourselves a chance. It's another test for us but we've passed them all so far.'

Furlong said to QPRnet.com, 'Goal? I remember Clarke around the halfway line pushing the ball through the middle and I thought I'd race on to it. To be fair I thought Fitz Hall was going to get a little touch on it and knock it wide but I managed to keep him off and slot it.

'Afterwards it was pure shock really, the time we scored was perfect and what it meant was just fantastic. The whole night there was one I'll never, ever forget. It will stay with me for as long as I live. Amazing, amazing happenings.

'That night is one of the highlights of my career. I've played in Europe with Chelsea but to score that goal and see what it meant to the whole place was fantastic.'

46 v Sheffield Wednesday 3-1

Football League Second Division. Hillsborough
8 May 2004. Attendance: 29,313

QUEENS PARK RANGERS:	SHEFFIELD WEDNESDAY:
Camp	Pressman
Edghill	Geary
Padula	Barry-Murphy
Rose	Dean Smith (Carr)
Carlisle (Gnohere)	Wood
Ainsworth	Mclaren
Bircham	Mcmahon
Johnson	Cooke
Rowlands (Cureton)	Brunt
Gallen	Robins
Furlong	Shaw

Referee: Mark Clattenburg (County Durham)

'EVERY DOG has its day and today is Woof Day and I just want to go off and bark somewhere.' So said Ian Holloway with a typically off-beat turn of phrase to sum up the occasion.

Moments earlier Holloway had stood in the centre of the Hillsborough pitch in his black top with the legend 'IH' emblazoned in white on his swelling chest and smiling broadly. His arms were up in a V for victory shape in front of an estimated eight to ten thousand deliriously happy Queens Park Rangers fans.

The eyes of the Super Hoops' super manager were alive. His right hand might have been squeezing tight an empty plastic water bottle, but he was oblivious to the distortion he was causing to its shape. He was, it seemed, oblivious to anything other than the undiluted emotions of pride and joy which was rushing throughout his mind and body.

The fact his contract and eight of his players' deals had just expired with the blow of referee Mark Clattenburg's whistle seconds earlier seemed forgotten.

The suffering endured by relegation, administration and the rest of the upheaval which almost sucked the life out of the club which first played on a field owned by a dairy behind a pub in the 1880s seemed forgotten. Ollie was lost in the moment. The side he built almost from scratch had just sealed the club's first promotion in 21 years on the last day of the 2003/04 regular season with a 3-1 win over hosts Sheffield Wednesday.

The club was rising out of the ashes as well as the third tier just three years after demotion and being on the verge of extinction due to its money troubles.

Rangers had suffered the agony of missing out on elevation from the third tier the previous season when defeated by an extra-time goal in the play-off final against Cardiff City at the Millennium Stadium.

But goals from Kevin Gallen and Paul Furlong and an own goal from home substitute Chris Carr got Rangers over the line against Wednesday without recourse to the roller-coaster ride which the bit tagged on to the regular season always provides.

Queens Park Rangers' Greatest Games

Former Rangers player Holloway had been thrown in the deep end when he returned as manager on the recommendation of predecessor Gerry Francis, who had signed him as a midfielder for Bristol Rovers with his own money – £10,000 of it – in February 2001.

He discovered 51 professionals on total wages adding up to £5.3m, with half of them injured, no youth players to promote to the first team and owner/chairman Chris Wright losing £100,000 a week of his personal fortune before the administrators came in to try and sort the financial mess the club were in. And, of course, the team were likely relegation candidates with a run of one win in 13 sealing their fate.

The administrators left Holloway with just seven fit players for the following season, 2001/02, after slashing the wage bill to keep the club operating.

But he managed to piece together a squad by picking up bargains and bringing back crowd favourite Kevin Gallen, to achieve a top-half finish with the club out of administration and Nick Blackburn replacing Chris Wright as chairman. And he got Rangers rolling forward to their ultimately unsuccessful play-off bid in 2002/03 by signing others who cared about the club, such as Mark Bircham and Paul Furlong.

And he breathed even more life into the side as he wheeled and dealed in the transfer market before and during the 2003/04 season, with players such as Gareth Ainsworth, who became a Loftus Road icon and manager, Martin Rowlands, Tony Thorpe, Richard Edghill, Arthur Gnohere, Richard Johnson, Lee Camp and Jamie Cureton coming in.

The signs were good as Rangers began the 2003/04 campaign with a 5-0 home win over Blackpool (a club Holloway was to manage) after a minute's silence for the tragic passing of former manager Ray Harford through cancer the same morning.

Gareth Ainsworth scored twice on his debut and Gallen once, while skipper Steve Palmer and Richard Langley completed the nap hand. Optimism had replaced pessimism among the faithful.

There were reality checks with defeat at Brighton & Hove Albion and the squandering of a 3-1 lead – which included an Ainsworth double – in the following away game at Rushden & Diamonds.

But home victories against Bournemouth and Chesterfield, with Furlong on the mark in both, kept the mood buoyant.

And the reverse against the Seagulls was the only one in the opening 13 fixtures.

In fact there was only one more defeat – at Port Vale – and Holloway's army was on the march again and another unbeaten run lasted seven games and included five wins.

The only downer on high-flying Rangers' season seemed to be the alcohol problems of a depressed Clarke Carlisle, the defender who had set up the play-off semi-final winner against Oldham the previous season. In fact, another Ollie-ism eased the pressure on his troubled centre-back when the media bombarded him with questions about why he had been absent from the early season victory over the Spireites.

Holloway deflected his questioners into being more interested in the performance rather than his defender. Trying to explain he was happy with the result and not the display, he said, 'It's like when you meet a bird who's not the best looking. You talk, things go well and she gets in a taxi with you, get her back home and lovely jubbly, let's have a coffee.'

Holloway felt his sense of humour was misinterpreted as 'madcap' and that it was – and remains – a useful tool to develop an empathy with his players which he insists is essential as a manager.

He also helped himself in the 2003/04 season by curbing regular outbursts of anger after taking part in a BBC documentary called *Stress Test*. He took on board the advice

v Sheffield Wednesday 2004

given him by an assigned psychologist who believed his displays of bad temper were caused by his belief that nothing he ever did was good enough. And he feels his decision to control it was fundamental to him guiding Rangers to promotion.

He said in his autobiography, 'I believe the things that happened in the next few months wouldn't have happened if I hadn't changed.'

Holloway continued to plot a path which, although it involved too many draws for his liking, kept his side in the hunt for going up. Rangers wobbled coming into the home straight, including a 1-0 defeat against promotion rivals Bristol City at Ashton Gate.

Then came a pivotal game at Tranmere Rovers. The boss was upset his side did not get awarded a free kick and Rovers won a penalty from the break with the visitors reduced to ten men for the offence. But stopper Lee Camp saved the re-taken spot-kick as it bounced off the post and R's came away from Prenton Park with a 0-0 draw. Was fortune now favouring the braves of London W12 who edged one point ahead of Bristol City?

Unfortunately R's lost 2-0 at Plymouth Argyle who sealed the title with the victory.

The defeat had reduced their chances of an automatic promotion spot with two games left, but at least Bristol City had also suffered a reverse that day.

Holloway knew that victories in both remaining games would be enough. The benefits of his anger management therapy paid off when he resisted knee-jerk changes to keep the side beaten at Home Park for the visit of Swindon Town to Loftus Road. A Rowlands goal gave the hosts three more precious points.

But City maintained the pressure by also scoring a win – 1-0 at Barnsley – which left the race going down to the final game. Rangers took on Sheffield Wednesday on 8 May 2004 as Danny Wilson's Bristol City entertained Blackpool.

Bristolian Holloway used a league championship medal he won while playing for the city's Rovers, and incorporated Rangers fans in the reception of the Sheffield hotel where the squad had stayed overnight for his pre-match motivational speech.

He said in his autobiography, 'I sat down with our lads and invited the fans to come over and sit with and among us as I did what I hoped would be my pep talk. We'd been over our tactics in training, so this was purely aimed at getting something in their hearts and minds that might just edge things our way.

'I began, "I've had some special times in my life and it was the people I was with at Bristol Rovers that helped me win this medal – my team-mates, but I just want you to hear what these supporters think of you regardless of what happens." I asked a young kid to step up and say something to the lads and he smiled, took a deep breath and said, "You've been brilliant! Absolutely brilliant."'

Rangers were tense and tentative after referee Mark Clattenburg got the game going in front of close to 30,000 at Hillsborough.

Their nerves tightened further when the electronic scoreboard at the ground revealed Bristol City had taken a 1-0 lead at home to Blackpool. It left Holloway incensed by the operator's lack of sensitivity given the situation.

City's name was up in lights once more a few minutes later revealing Rangers' rivals had increased their advantage to 2-0 to put Wilson's men in the automatic promotion spot as things stood.

Another negative distraction was the last thing R's needed and Wednesday fans underlined QPR's plight by singing about how the west Londoners weren't going up.

Holloway kept a lid on his emotions as he bubbled up with fury inside and told his skipper Palmer to calm Rangers down.

But the visitors only settled on 35 minutes when Kevin Gallen, proving why he was still such a hero among the supporters, gave them the lead.

He turned in the area surrounded by three Wednesday players as he controlled a Richard Edghill ball to put Gareth Ainsworth away down the right. Ainsworth got to the byline and crossed to the near post. Paul Furlong tried to get a touch as Dean Smith attempted to clear.

The ball went loose and the unmarked Gallen slammed it into the net of stopper Kevin Pressman, making his final appearance after a 20-year career with the Owls, from six yards.

Furlong doubled Rangers' advantage two minutes after the re-start. Bircham charged down an attempted clearance and took a return ball from Gallen to put over a cross which hit the head of a defender and looped into the goalmouth.

Furlong controlled the ball with his chest as he turned and held off a challenge to thunder his shot on the volley from eight yards to the left of a diving Pressman.

But Jon Shaw pulled one back from a Terry Cooke back-flick from 18 yards for Wednesday with half an hour left to destroy any presumptions Rangers might have had that they were home and hosed.

Wednesday followed it up with a bombardment of Rangers' goal. A close-range effort from Carr from a Chris Brunt ball was blocked

Time slowed to a crawl for Holloway. And his nerves led him to visit the toilet three times. But as he returned from his final visit he witnessed Martin Rowlands helping to make it 3-1 with 20 minutes left.

A minute earlier a crucial tackle from Rangers' long-haired Argentinian full-back Gino Padula on Shaw denied the Wednesday scorer a second.

But then Rowlands, Rangers' man of the match, broke up the left wing and his cross was mis-kicked over his own head and into his own net by Owls substitute Chris Carr.

The clock slowed even more for the Rangers bench for the remaining minutes. Then QPR goalkeeping coach Tony Roberts hugged Holloway and the rest of the bench joined in. Clattenburg had ended their agony to turn the Rangers mood at Hillsborough – and at Loftus Road where thousands had been watching on the big screen – into one of ecstasy.

Rangers had beaten Bristol City by a point. City boss Danny Wilson rung up Holloway to congratulate him and was sacked after his side lost the play-off final to Brighton & Hove Albion. Holloway got his new deal.

Holloway said in his autobiography, 'We all took memories of that season which will stay with us forever.'

He said to *The Observer* post-match, 'I am so proud, for the first time in my life I can't really put it into words. I've experienced promotion as a player, but this feels better. When I came to this club, I had seven fit players.

'There's been such hardship at this club, but everyone has worked so hard. I'd like to change the name to Queens Park Rangers United, such has been the feeling of unity here.

'Life's about passion – you have to have it – and if you get knocked down you have to get up and carry on.

'Half the players on that pitch, along with myself, are out of contract at the end of this season, but we have all put the club before any selfish motives.'

Mark Bircham, his hair dyed Rangers blue, summed up the Holloway effect when he said to *The Guardian* in the immediate aftermath, 'He is essential to this club's hopes of moving forward. Everyone, in or out of the team, wants to play for him.'

v Watford 2-0

Football League Championship. Vicarage Road
30 April 2011. Attendance: 15,538

QUEENS PARK RANGERS:
Cerny
Orr
Hall (Shittu)
Gorkss
Connolly
Derry
Taarabt (Ramage)
Faurlin
Routledge (Buzsaky)
Helguson
Smith

WATFORD:
Loach
Hodson
Taylor (Bennett)
Mariappa
Doyley
Eustace
Cowie
Buckley (Murray)
Deeney
Graham
Sordell (Whichelow)

Referee: Neil Swarbrick (Lancashire)

NEIL WARNOCK had been a manager for 31 years. He had served 11 previous clubs and had achieved six promotions with five of them, two (Notts County and Sheffield United) into the top flight.

But his seventh with a sixth, Queens Park Rangers, in 2010/11, was special. He rated it his best. He had found a club in danger of relegation back to the third tier when he took over just 13 months before and seeking stability after an unsettling four years since the departure of Ian Holloway as manager.

Gary Waddock, John Gregory, Mick Harford, Luigi De Canio, Iain Dowie, Gareth Ainsworth, Paolo Sousa, Ainsworth again, Jim Magilton, Paul Hart and Harford, again, had been tried at the helm.

And the revolving door of bosses had quickened when Flavio Briatore took over from Gianni Paladini as chairman in 2007 before stepping down for Ishan Saksena a month before Warnock's arrival. It will no doubt stand as Warnock's crowning achievement in a managerial career built on innate Yorkshire grit and wit.

Made in Sheffield is the title of his autobiography and it reflects Warnock's steel-like determination and passion to succeed.

A lengthy subtitle could have reflected his many more colourful characteristics, such as his charisma, controversial actions, outspokenness, humour, a teller of tales of the unexpected and love for his role as a family man.

It was all there when goals from skipper Adel Taarabt, who had lit up the division with his skills and goals all season, and Tommy Smith defeated Watford 2-0 at a sun-drenched Vicarage Road on 30 April 2011 in the penultimate match of the regular season to seal the Championship title and a return to the Premier League after a 15-year absence, confirmed seven days later when the FA announced the club would not be deducted points over a breach of transfer rules.

Charisma? The cameras zoomed in immediately on the white polo-shirted 62-year-old receiving and offering congratulations to and from his playing heroes in blue and white, coaches and backroom staff as he moved from the touchline on to the pitch as referee Neil Swarbrick sounded the final whistle.

Controversial actions? Refusing to leave the pitch despite the pleadings of stewards until he had saluted the 2,171 Rangers fans as they chanted 'there's only one Neil Warnock', and defiantly staying amid a group of them who had encroached onto the playing area and were singing 'we shall not be moved'.

Plus he told the public address announcer ordering the supporters to desist from their encroachment and leave forthwith to keep his orders to himself.

Outspokenness? Revealing (with a twinkle in the eye) how shocked he was to settle in London after parting ways with his beloved Sheffield United because he thought anything south of Watford was 'the pits'.

He told Taarabt, the Championship Player of the Year who had drawn comparisons with Rangers mavericks such as Rodney Marsh and Stan Bowles in his style of play, that he had to be more dedicated and be a better listener to succeed in the Premier League.

Warnock had already blasted the media for turning the training ground 'into a morgue' in the build-up to Watford for talking about how the FA could deny Rangers the crown, even automatic promotion, by docking them points over a deal involving Argentinian Alejandro Faurlin, who played against Watford.

They were just fined £875,000 with the verdict coming through hours before their final league game, a 2-1 home defeat by Leeds United, after which they were presented with the trophy and their medals.

The humour? Telling *The Sun* newspaper how he celebrated the greatest moment of his career with a cheese and pickle sandwich in his pyjamas.

Tales of the unexpected? Revealing to the same publication how he destressed from the pressures of management by following deer around Richmond Park.

His love for his role as a family man? Saying the support of his wife Sharon and children Amy, William, James and Natalie was vital to survive in management.

I knew Warnock when he was a winger with Aldershot and I was assistant sports editor on the town's bi-weekly newspaper in the 1970s and he was already 'good copy', telling me how he lived in a caravan and was a qualified chiropodist.

He was a chiropodist not afraid to tread on a lot of toes, not afraid to be approachable, not afraid full stop.

Warnock is the sort of character who helps make football what it is – the number one sport on the planet. Without his like the sport would be dull. Perhaps the fact Warnock has provided so much entertainment will be his greatest legacy.

Certainly most Super Hoops remain forever grateful to the manager who led them from a low ebb back to the Promised Land in such quick time.

He said to *The Guardian*, 'To get this team out of relegation to winning the league in such a short space of time is incredible, it's the best job I've done. You have to roll your sleeves up in the Championship, and the players have done that, they've been magnificent. I can't fault anyone.

'I'm pleased for the fans, too. Some of them probably had raised eyebrows when they heard Neil Warnock was the QPR manager but they have helped bring pride back to this club. The whole experience has been interesting for me, you don't plan too far ahead at QPR but I told the owners when I came that I wanted to be in the Premier League within a season and that's what we've done.'

v Watford 2011

Rangers were firing on all cylinders from the start of the season as they battered Barnsley 4-0 on day one of the season and they were top at the end of August.

Warnock said to the club website, 'The attitude of the players has been superb. Adel Taarabt's doing well. We play a system that suits him. It's all about teamwork and getting the best out of everyone.'

With QPR under the ownership of billionaire steel magnate Lakshmi Mital, son-in-law Amit Bhatia and motor racing's Briatore and Bernie Ecclestone, Warnock signed Taarabt, who had been on loan, on a permanent deal from Tottenham Hotspur, and added Paddy Kenny, Clint Hill and Shaun Derry as he pledged promotion by the end of the 2010/11 season. He also brought in Tommy Smith and Rob Hulse before the transfer window closed and Rangers stormed on, extending an unbeaten run to nine – including seven wins, two draws, 22 goals scored just two conceded and eight clean sheets – to go six points clear of their rivals.

QPR conceded their first goal in six games but made it eight wins in ten against Warnock's previous club, Crystal Palace. They maintained their unbeaten run but four deadlocks saw them drop to second behind Cardiff City.

But they re-gained the lead and Taarabt scored the match-winner when the Bluebirds arrived at Loftus Road in late November.

Rangers' unbeaten run came to an end in the 20th game, at home to Watford, but the Super Hoops bounced back and destroyed Swansea City 4-0 with a magical display from Taarabt. Rangers were dealt a major blow when outstanding forward Jamie Mackie suffered a double leg break in an FA Cup defeat at Blackburn Rovers in January but they held on to top spot with Warnock signing returnees Danny Shittu, Wayne Routledge and West Bromwich Albion's Ishmael Miller in the transfer window.

QPR only dropped four points out of 18 in February and saw off Crystal Palace and Leicester City in front of a packed Loftus Road crowd to end the following month nine points clear.

Rangers began the final push with a 3-0 win over another of Warnock's former clubs, Sheffield United. A surprise 4-1 reverse at struggling Scunthorpe United was swiftly brushed aside as QPR pipped Barnsley by a single goal at Oakwell. A 2-2 draw at Cardiff City then set up the promotion and championship-clincher at Watford.

Goalkeeper Paddy Kenny suffered a shoulder injury in the warm-up with former Tottenham Hotspur stopper Radek Cerny, 37, stepping in.

Rangers faced a Hornets side which had only managed one league win in seven and twice went close to taking the lead through Heidar Helguson. The striker hit the side netting from a Taarabt cross and saw Watford goalkeeper Scott Loach keep out his header.

Watford refused to be overawed, buoyed by their 3-1 win in the reverse fixture at Loftus Road as they tested the resilience of a defence which had lost its first-choice goalkeeper.

Unmarked home striker Danny Graham wasted a chance by heading wide following a marauding run from full-back Lloyd Doyley.

But tricky Taarabt was a jack in the box who kept popping up to cause the hosts consternation. Loach was unable to hold a wicked free kick from the Moroccan magician and had defender Adrian Mariappa to thank for a timely clearance.

Taarabt then found Faurlin just inside the penalty area but the Argentine cleared the bar with his rising effort.

After the re-start, Taarabt combined with the midfielder again to supply him the ball direct from his lowly-struck corner and Loach pulled off a superb stop.

Queens Park Rangers' Greatest Games

But, generally, Rangers were unable to hold on to the ball and the momentum swung towards the Hornets.

Faurlin got in the way of a Troy Deeney drive after the Watford front-runner had been put in by his winger Will Buckley.

QPR were in panic stations following a back-heel from Marvin Sordell towards Deeney, but managed to clear their lines.

A goalless draw would be enough for promotion, subject to the FA decision, of course, but not the title.

Then Taarabt put Rangers ahead 14 minutes from time. Tommy Smith ran with the ball to the left-hand byline and looked up. He saw the raised right hand of Taarabt as his skipper moved into the goal area and crossed to the near post.

The Moroccan let the ball bounce, waited for Loach to come out and guided his shot into the far corner from close range for his 19th goal of the season. And he soon went close to a second goal as he bent a shot just wide.

Helguson squandered a golden opportunity before Smith made it 2-0 from the edge of the penalty area in injury time to put the seal on their 25th victory of the season, promotion and the championship.

The former Hornet declined to celebrate scoring against his old employers but he was the only one in blue and white – on the pitch, sidelines and stands – who didn't.

It was also QPR's 25th clean sheet of the season – having conceded only 30 goals in 45 games with just five defeats – which combined the stonewalling of a rock solid defence, a hard-working and goalscoring midfield and strike force, plus the sprinkling of Moroccan magic, in a side largely put together by Warnock in double-quick time, to put Rangers back in the big-time.

The players pogoed in their Vicarage Road dressing room afterwards singing in unison, 'We are Premier League, say we are Premier League'. The champagne flowed. The architect stood off in the corner of the room, with beads of sweat across his brow from the energy spent on the on-field celebrations, applauding his players. It was a feelgood moment to be savoured. Contemplation on how Rangers would cope in the top-flight was for another time.

48 v Liverpool 3-2
Premier League. Loftus Road
21 March 2012. Attendance: 18,033

QUEENS PARK RANGERS:
Kenny
Traore (Taiwo)
Young
Ferdinand
Onuoha
Diakite
Derry
Taarabt
Barton (Mackie)
Cisse (Buzsaky)
Zamora

LIVERPOOL:
Reina
Jose Enrique
Carragher
Kelly (Coates)
Skrtel
Gerrard
Downing
Spearing
Adam (Henderson)
Suarez (Carroll)
Kuyt

Referee: Howard Webb

MARK HUGHES sensed it. His players sensed it. And so did the fans, with new chairman Tony Fernandes in their midst, when Shaun Derry scored in the 77th minute.

They sensed that Queens Park Rangers could pull off one of the most dramatic comebacks in the history of the Premier League – and they did to lift themselves out of the relegation drop zone.

Rangers were 2-0 down at home to high-flying Liverpool with 13 minutes left and won 3-2 with Derry's goal added to by former Reds striker Djibril Cisse and, in injury time, Jamie Mackie after Sebastian Coates and Dirk Kuyt had put the visitors in the driving seat.

Their opponents had just won the League Cup and reached the semi-finals of the FA Cup and were chasing a Champions League place that was thought to be their birthright during the playing days of their manager Kenny Dalglish. Superstars Steven Gerrard and Luis Suarez were stoking the Reds' fire.

Rangers had been on a nightmare run of results with just two points collected from the previous 18 available with their remaining fixtures including meetings with every member of the top five.

Their hopes of survival in their first season since returning to the Premier League had been written off by many BEFORE their visitors had set off from Anfield for the Wednesday night encounter under the Loftus Road lights.

Monty Python comic actor Eric Idle sang 'Always Look On The Bright Side Of Life' in the film *Life of Brian* but even the most fervent preacher of positivism might have struggled to find any good news for Rangers before Adel Taarabt took a 77th-minute corner on the right.

But seconds later Derry, with more grey than dark hair, found spring in his 33-year-old legs to out-jump two Liverpool defenders and head Taarabt's looping, dipping kick to the far post beyond Pepe Reina.

Queens Park Rangers' Greatest Games

Manager Hughes said, 'Our first goal created a momentum and the fans – who were fantastic – sensed it, and we rode the wave.'

But belief on its own is not enough for a great escape. You also need drive, determination, a never-say-die, unquenchable spirit. And a hero. Enter substitute Jamie Mackie who ticked all the boxes on an unforgettable night.

Cisse making it 2-2 four minutes from time produced a scoreline Hughes was ready to accept as the thriller entered the first minute of injury time. Not Mackie.

The forward, who had returned from a double fractured leg after seven months out earlier in the season, latched on to a Luke Young headed ball. As Liverpool defender Jose Enrique slipped and missed the ball, Mackie found himself eight yards from Pepe Reina's goal and one on one with Reina who came out to narrow the angle.

The player known for his lung-bursting runs, boundless enthusiasm and willingness to put himself on the line for his team-mates displayed yet another attribute as he weighed up his options with the Spanish goalkeeper becoming larger and larger in his line of vision – composure. And the Scotland international calmly guided the ball into the far corner to Reina's right.

The match-winner calmly walked away and outstretched his arms as if to say, 'How about that?' Those wearing blue and white shirts, tracksuits and favours, and the manager in his smart two-piece suit, shirt and tie, went ballistic. Kapow. An explosion of noise. Football never ceases to surprise but this was one of major proportions.

Rangers should know, having experienced remarkable comebacks before. They had trailed Newcastle United and Port Vale 4-0 at half-time, the first at home and the second away, and got a point (as you have read).

But with due respect to the Toon and Vale, the Reds represented a higher mountain to climb given their status, achievements and all-star cast. And it seemed like Mackie had put R's in Fantasy Land with his goal.

A click of the fingers, a knock to the side of the head by the palm of the hand and a shake of the cranium and a double take at the electronic scoreboard brought anyone who had staggered into the world of make believe back to reality. Fairytales can come true. As long as you have a Jamie Mackie.

In front of James Bond himself, actor Daniel Craig (a Liverpool fan), Rangers were in 0-0-Heaven. Craig's Liverpool favourites had had the living daylights punched out of them and there was no solace for him, quantum or otherwise.

Hughes said afterwards, 'We'd have taken 2-2 but thankfully Jamie Mackie didn't feel that way. It made for a great night for him and everybody.

'When Jamie comes on he gives you huge energy and we needed that to pick us up. Maybe it was dropping. He will always give you that – and more.

'Hopefully people [urging Hughes to bring him on in place of Joey Barton after 62 minutes] will think it was the right decision. I know it was.

'The comeback is right up there with any I've experienced. We looked dead and buried. We had nothing to lose and thought "let's go for it" and we did. We took the game back to Liverpool. We were not to be denied.

'Everybody sensed the emotion and significance of the result. As the season progresses we may well look back on this result as the one that changed it all for us.'

The manager was swift to heap praise on the supporters who turned Loftus Road into a cauldron of positivity. He said, 'I thought the crowd were fantastic as they never lost faith in us. Once we got a little bit of momentum they drove us over the line.'

v Liverpool 2012

The win convinced Hughes, head of the escape committee, that his POWs were building a strong enough tunnel underneath the barbed wire and armed sentry posts of what seemed an impregnable camp to enable Rangers to get out and taste freedom from the mind-fracturing torment of an immediate return to the second tier of English football.

Hughes knew he could talk to his players until he was blue – and white – in the face about his belief that they would keep their place in the top flight.

The defeat of Liverpool gave him, his team, the club board and the supporters something more tangible. Something that was of as much of a boost to him as it was to them. He said, 'You need results to back up what you say.'

It had not, of course, always been thus that season. The club had stuck by manager Neil Warnock as it entered a top-flight season for the first time since 1996. It was the least the 62-year-old veteran deserved after guiding them, up as champions, to his seventh promotion success with six different clubs.

Malaysian business tycoon Tony Fernandes, through his company Tune Group, became a majority shareholder in August 2011 after buying out Flavio Briatore and Bernie Ecclestone's 66 per cent interest, with the Mittal family retaining 33 per cent.

And he became chairman with Amit Bhatia restored as vice-chairman. The Warnock-Fernandes axis seemed harmonious.

Warnock's side bounced back from a 4-0 opening-day defeat against Bolton Wanderers at Loftus Road to score victories over Everton, their first away in the Premier League in 15 years thanks to a Tommy Smith winner, Wolverhampton Wanderers and Stoke City.

The highlight came when, as Warnock said at the time, his side entered 'dreamland' by overcoming arch west London rivals Chelsea, Didier Drogba et al, who eventually won the Champions League for the first time that season, to record their first home win in the top flight since 1996 thanks to a Heidar Helguson penalty.

But the wheels came off the Rangers wagon from the end of November, through Christmas and into the New Year with six defeats, two draws and no wins and Warnock was sacked on 8 January 2012 and replaced two days later by Mark Hughes, the former Manchester City and Fulham boss and ex-Manchester United and Barcelona striker.

Hughes secured a victory over Wigan Athletic in his first home game in charge and signed Cisse and Zamora but his new charges only managed to glean two points of the next 18 available going into the Wednesday evening meeting with Dalglish's side. The atmosphere was tense among the Hoops contingent as they gathered in the stands, the boardroom and dressing room prior to the kick-off against the Reds, but they also dared to dream that a deed of derring-do was about to take place.

They felt that somehow out-of-touch Rangers would find their touch and take a crucial three points to give them enough impetus to go into a run-in which could reasonably be described as daunting with hopes high they would bowl over a few big names and stay up.

Clint Hill, a veteran defender who had proved an astute purchase from Crystal Palace by his former Selhurst Park boss Neil Warnock the previous season, was injured and Luke Young came in for him with Anton Ferdinand, the cousin of Rangers legend Les and brother of Rio, and Nedum Onuoha in the centre of the back line with Armand Traore at left-back.

Talisman Adel Taarabt, the Championship Player of the Year the previous season, came in for Shaun Wright-Phillips with Shaun Derry, Samba Diakite and captain Joey Barton making up the four across the middle. Cisse and Bobby Zamora, signed from Fulham, were at the sharp end.

Queens Park Rangers' Greatest Games

Rangers, who had lost the reverse fixture, were given encouragement with the knowledge that the Reds had lost three of their previous four league games – and, coincidentally, three of their last four away.

Nonetheless Liverpool took control at the heart with red wave after red wave crashing against a sturdy Rangers back line forced on to the back foot but the interval arrived with the game goalless.

A Paddy Kenny save denied Suarez after an Onuoha slip and Martin Skrtel and Kuyt had efforts blocked by a stonewall R's rearguard.

Rangers came back and Cisse shot into the sidenetting but Suarez and Gerrard maintained the Liverpool charge to find a chink in Rangers' defence.

Liverpool went in front thanks to a wonder goal from Coates nine minutes into the second half. The Uruguayan centre-back, who had come on as a substitute for Martin Kelly, was lurking just inside the QPR penalty area as a Gerrard corner was half-cleared.

Stewart Downing powered in a shot which was cleared off the line by Rangers striker Bobby Zamora. Coates waited as Zamora's kick floated towards him and he jumped to bicycle-kick the ball past Kenny.

Kuyt made it 2-0 in the 72nd minute. A piece of Suarez brilliance saw the Uruguayan twist and turn and swivel his way past two defenders before shooting against the far post.

Downing picked up the rebound and beat three players in blue and white hoops as he cut across from the right to get a low left-footed shot away. Kenny got a strong right arm on it but the ball sat up for Kuyt to bundle home from close range in his 200th Premier League appearance.

More doom and gloom seemed to have descended on Hughes and his club in a season mostly made up of the combination.

But then Derry scored his first goal for the club and first in five years to spark the comeback.

Cisse drew them level when he got behind his marker Martin Skrtel to head a cross from Taye Taiwo, who had been set up by Zamora, firmly past Reina from six yards. And Mackie then wrote his name into Rangers' history books.

Hughes, known for his battling qualities as a player, displayed them in words as he issued a warning to others and a rallying cry to his troops with Rangers taking on the Premier League top five among their final games.

Bordering on the evangelical preacher, the Welsh dragon emerged from within as he said, 'People might be writing us off because of the tough games we have left but they do that at their peril. I know what I've got in the dressing room. We can stay up without a shadow of a doubt.

'The fact we beat a big name like Liverpool and the manner of it given the circumstances gives us huge belief. But this is just the beginning as we have a huge job in front of us.'

Rangers were up to it, winning their remaining home games against Arsenal (2-1), Swansea City (3-0), Tottenham Hotspur (1-0) and Stoke City (1-0) to complete a great escape which would have made Steve McQueen proud.

And they came close to finishing off the season in style against Manchester City at the Etihad Stadium in a sensational game. They led 2-1 in injury time before Roberto Mancini's hosts came back to win 3-2 to seal the title and deny holders and neighbours United the title with two goals in stoppage time.

49 v Fulham 2-1

Premier League. Loftus Road
15 December 2012. Attendance: 18,233

QUEENS PARK RANGERS:	FULHAM:
Green	Schwarzer
Traore	Riether (Kelly)
Hill	Hangeland
Nelsen	Hughes
Onuoha	Riise
Faurlin	Duff
Mbia	Sidwell
Wright-Phillips (Da Silva)	Baird
Taarabt	Richardson (Petric)
Cisse (Ferdinand)	Berbatov
Mackie	Rodallega (Dejagah)

Referee: Martin Atkinson (West Yorkshire)

THE JURY remained out on Adel Taarabt until 15 December 2012. That was the day he guided Queens Park Rangers to their first Premier League victory of the season at the 17th attempt and off the bottom of the table, preventing the club from setting the record for the worst start in the English top flight for 109 years.

The 2-1 success over Fulham in the west London derby at Loftus Road also marked the first win under Harry Redknapp following three draws at the start of his reign with the club looking for indications of a recovery process.

Taarabt scored both goals and dazzled Rangers' near neighbours who were like rabbits caught in the headlights of his brilliance. He scored twice and put on a virtuoso performance which left those either present or watching on their iPads, laptops, mobiles and even television gasping at the jaw-dropping nature of the football he produced. He had the wow factor in spades; flash with a finish.

'One of the all-time great performances, the boy's a genius, he could play with anybody,' was how his manager Harry Redknapp, who had bossed the likes of Gareth Bale and Luka Modric, and played alongside Bobby Moore and Geoff Hurst, described it.

He added, 'Adel's got ability like not many people you've ever seen in your life. He can do things that nobody else can do. He's my type of player, I love people with that ability. I had Paolo Di Canio at West Ham and he's like that.'

Fulham manager Martin Jol, who knew Taarabt from their time together at Spurs and got him to Craven Cottage on loan for 2013/14, said, 'He's a wizard.'

Various descriptions had had Taarabt down as a magician, an outrageous talent. Usually, though, the hyperbole used in trying to pin down what positive characteristics the playmaker and goalscorer offered football was often followed by the word 'but'.

There followed a list of negatives – that he was lazy, inconsistent, temperamental and a luxury. The Moroccan sprinkled his stardust all over the Championship to be named its most outstanding player in the 2010/11 season. He captained Neil Warnock's Rangers to the title with performances and displays of skill which drew the breath away and earned plaudit after plaudit. There was a superlative performance against Swansea City on Boxing Day which ended a mini blip of two successive defeats.

He made the first for Jamie Mackie after beating Joe Allen and Garry Monk, won the second (a penalty converted by Heidar Helguson) and scored the remaining two – the second a brilliant solo effort from 20 yards after nutmegging Allen – in a 4-0 dismantling of Brendan Rodgers's side. And he added the goal in the title clincher against Watford at Vicarage Road (see earlier chapter).

Yet the 'buts' persisted. Different 'buts'. That it was all very well mesmerising opponents and being the glory boy in the second tier of English football, even if the division has been rated among the top five in Europe in terms of average attendance and sixth richest, but could he hack it in the Premier League, rated in many quarters as the finest league in the world although those in Spain and Germany may beg to differ?

His first season back in the top flight – he had made the occasional appearance with his previous club Tottenham Hotspur – left cynics unconvinced the mercurial talents of the Moroccan could sustain him at that level.

There was speculation linking him to a move to France – where he had grown up near Marseille and idolising Zinedine Zidane – and Paris St Germain and Italy with Napoli.

New signing Joey Barton replaced him as captain. These two factors appeared to affect Taarabt and it was reckoned his form had dropped off from the high standards he had set the previous term.

He said, 'It was difficult because perhaps I thought it was going to be the same in the Premier League as it was in the Championship. Teams knew how I played.'

It was understood he was unable to keep a lid on his temperament and it was reported that he had a disagreement with Neil Warnock after the then Rangers manager had substituted him at the interval during a 6-0 defeat against Fulham at Craven Cottage. He was hauled off at half-time as QPR lost 3-1 at Spurs and left out altogether against Manchester City and Stoke City. He was also absent through international duties and injury.

Warnock, it was said, was willing to accept an offer and critical of the player's agents with speculation linking him to other clubs. But Taarabt returned to the side and his performances picked up again, scoring goals in vital wins over Arsenal and Spurs as Rangers successfully fought for their Premier League lives.

He signed a three-year contract in July 2012 and showed decent form in a struggling side as the 2012/13 season kicked off, scoring his first goal of the campaign with a superb solo effort against West Ham United and a volley at West Bromwich Albion.

Taarabt was rediscovering his mojo when Redknapp replaced Mark Hughes in November. Rangers chairman Tony Fernandes said, 'Harry was our number one target, the unanimous choice of the board and we're delighted.'

Taarabt was delighted because he had a manager who brought the best out of him, even though Redknapp had been the Spurs manager who unloaded Taarabt to QPR and once labelled him a 'complete fruitcake'.

Taarabt said in the *Daily Telegraph*, 'What's a fruitcake?'

When told he added, 'Ah, I've got a strong character and if I'm not happy, I say things. Maybe some other players will keep it to themselves. I'd rather have it out there face to face.' In harness with Redknapp, who dealt with a few 'face-to-face' situations with the maverick he had willingly inherited, Rangers began to see a more mature approach.

v Fulham 2012

His tendency to showboat was reined in a little. The simple was tried more often. The decision about when to either pick out a comfortable pass or to dribble, drag-back and/or nutmeg was more often than not the correct one.

He said to various media outlets, 'I've improved a lot. I mix my game. Keep it simple and when my opponents believe I'm going to do that surprise them with a dribble and shot. I anticipate what the defender thinks I'm going to do.

'I know before I get the ball what I'm going to do. I feel very calm. It's important your first touch is good because nothing bad can happen to you. I know I'm an important player for the team. I am the player who can score and win the game for my team. I can make things happen.'

Taarabt's wondrous performance which ripped apart Fulham – a reality not underlined by a flattering scoreline in favour of the Cottagers – reflected the extra confidence Redknapp had instilled in him along with his maturity.

Neil Warnock ('was like a father to me') and Mark Hughes ('a great manager') had both helped him. But Redknapp's man-management style made Taarabt feel so good about himself he desperately wanted to show his boss how much.

Taarabt said, 'He has something that not a lot of managers have. A lot of managers can organise the team and so on but Harry wants a player to feel he is the best.'

Fulham fielded another great talent, Dimitar Berbatov, the languid former Manchester United striker whom he had known during their time together at White Hart Lane.

Yet Redknapp told Taarabt he reckoned he was better than the Bulgarian who had cost the Reds £30m when their manager Sir Alex Ferguson signed him for the Old Trafford giants from Spurs.

Taarabt, again in the *Telegraph*, said, 'He [Redknapp] came to see me and said, "I think you've nothing to learn from Berbatov because I think you can be better than him."

'So I'm thinking, "If he thinks that then I'm going to show him he's right and that I am better." And this is Harry. He will tell you, "I won't change you for anyone."

'And not just me. He's said the same to the other players and when a manager says this to you and you go on the pitch you want to show him he was right.

'I saw it at Tottenham also. Modric was there and Juande Ramos didn't play him. We played at Stoke and Luka was put on the floor. He wanted a free kick and Ramos turned and said, "He's not a player for English football." Harry arrived and just said "fantastic player". And after that Luka, game after game, wow.'

Taarabt went out and kept Berbatov in the shadows to deservedly claim the headlines with the display which mixed his undoubted skills with a more considered, developed approach throughout the 90 minutes.

The fact the Moroccan's brilliant display came shortly before Christmas provoked colourful recollections from expert observers such as Paul Jiggins of *The Sun*. Jiggins said it was a time for a miracle and that it 'came to pass' with Rangers 'being led by a bright star from across the desert'.

It was pure delight for the QPR faithful to see the player who put his talent down to being 'gifts from God' become a more complete player against Fulham.

It made him a worthy successor in the number 10 shirt (having switched from wearing number 7) to the likes of Rodney Marsh, Stan Bowles, Tony Currie, Simon Stainrod, John Byrne, and Roy Wegerle. He was a maverick with a work and team ethic.

Redknapp put Taarabt in a central position behind the front man Djibril Cisse, so he could weave his spells between Fulham's defence and midfield, playing deep enough to bemuse the visiting rearguard, unsure whether to keep its position or go and seek him out. And he thrived.

Taarabt might have had a reputation for being a lightweight and of being likely to go AWOL if the going got tough. But he proved, along with his other attributes, that he was just the individual needed. He was the epitome of when the going gets tough the tough get going against Jol's team. He made an almost instant impact by putting the recalled Cisse through, but the French striker, seemingly fouled by Aaron Hughes, had his effort saved comfortably by Mark Schwarzer.

Jamie Mackie missed a golden opportunity when he nipped in behind as John Arne Riise played a pass back to Schwarzer without looking but Mackie slid the ball wide from six yards one-on-one with the stopper.

Taarabt put Rangers ahead seven minutes into the second half. He picked up a ball from Alejandro Faurlin in midfield and was allowed to run and run before beating Schwarzer from 20 yards with the help of a deflection off the boot of Fulham defender Brede Hangeland. Cisse curled an effort just wide before Taarabt made in 2-0 on 68 minutes. It was sensational; pure ability, intelligence and confidence; entertainment mixed with end product and something for the heart and mind.

Taarabt picked up a short ball down the right at halfway. Hangeland came across to challenge. Taarabt feinted left and moved to the right as he swayed his hips.

For a split second the ball was tangled between him and his opponent, but a quick reaction and touch saw the Moroccan magician emerge with possession to hone in on the Fulham penalty area, his black-gloved hands flapping and his black-stripped opponents unsure what to do.

Taarabt went by the right of Riise and rolled his right foot over the ball to bemuse the Fulham rearguard still further and gain a few inches of space before striking his shot early with the outside of his right boot to send it curling into the right-hand corner of Schwarzer's goal in the blink of an eye. Soon after, the error-strewn Baird was caught in possession just outside his own penalty box, but his mistake went unpunished as Cisse curled his shot just past Schwarzer's left post.

Dimitar Berbatov had been outstanding for Fulham in a victory over Newcastle United five days earlier but his light remained dim in comparison to Taarabt's full beam ahead.

Visiting substitute Mladen Petric pulled one back for Fulham with a shot deflected off Faurlin and beyond Robert Green, Rangers' England World Cup goalkeeper, two minutes from time to give an otherwise dominant, Taarabt-inspired side a few anxious moments to play out before tasting the long-awaited victory.

A late flying header from Cisse, saved by Schwarzer, would have given the scoreline a fairer reflection. Still Redknapp and his bench, the players and the long-suffering fans were able to feel relief and triumph simultaneously largely due to a 23-year-old with magic in his feet. It was all in stark contrast to the previous season when Taarabt left Craven Cottage at the interval to get home via public transport after being substituted during that 6-0 defeat against Fulham.

Redknapp, Fernandes, his team-mates and the fans might well have clubbed together to hire him a Rolls-Royce as his mode of transport on this occasion.

Redknapp said after the game, 'We deserved it. We are on a good run and if we can get six points every four games we'll stay up. I met Tony (Fernandes) for the first time. I met him for the first time after the match. He was just so pleased. The people here deserve it. They're nice people.'

v Chelsea **1-0**
Premier League. Stamford Bridge
2 January 2013. Attendance: 41,634

QUEENS PARK RANGERS:
Julio Cesar
Hill
Onuoha
Nelsen
Da Silva
Derry
Taarabt (Dyer)
Granero (Park)
Mbia
Mackie
Hoilett (Wright-Phillips)

CHELSEA:
Turnbull
Ivanovic
Luiz
Cahill
Azpilicueta
Bertrand
Lampard (Ramires)
Oscar
Moses (Mata)
Marin (Hazard)
Torres

Referee: Lee Mason (Bolton)

THE DEFINITION of 'great' according to the *Merriam-Webster Dictionary* is: Of an extent, amount, or intensity considerably above the normal or average. And the victory rock bottom Queens Park Rangers secured against European Cup holders Chelsea in their arch rivals' own back yard deserves the adjective to describe the achievement.

The win over the team Rangers fans enjoy beating most was against all odds. Big time.

After all it was their first top-flight success against the Blues at Stamford Bridge in 34 years and first away Premier League capital derby win since a Les Ferdinand double helped overcome Wimbledon in March 1995. It was secured late on by super-sub Shaun Wright-Phillips against one of his former employers, who once thought him worth £21m when buying him from Manchester City. There is nothing like putting one over your old team so they say, though woe betide you if the feat sees you overtly celebrate it.

And the three points were not earned adopting a brand of breathtaking attacking football, a style associated with teams which have Harry Redknapp at their helm, although Wright-Phillips's clincher provided an excellent icing on the winning cake.

The style was pragmatic and defensive with no one critical of Redknapp's abandonment of his more adventurous footballing philosophies. There appeared a resolve to park the bus in front of your goal. This is a phrase which describes the adoption of an extreme defensive policy to defend what you have with a collective human vehicle.

It became familiar to Blues fans when Portuguese Jose Mourinho had made them aware of the expression from his native land in the Iberian Peninsula during his first spell in charge at Stamford Bridge. There are, you see, many ways to overcome seemingly insurmountable obstacles to achieve greatness. And Redknapp had found one.

Even though the stats – on top of the ones already revealed – alone presented enough of a barrier, albeit a psychological one, no side bottom of the Premier League at the turn of the year had ever clawed clear of the drop by the campaign's finale.

Queens Park Rangers' Greatest Games

But that mattered not to Redknapp's determined team whom he had imbued with the Three Musketeers' spirit of togetherness.

Nor did the fact Rangers had been unable to win an away game in the previous 24 attempts and they had been unable to keep a clean sheet on their travels since November 2011. Nor QPR not having been able to defeat Chelsea at Stamford Bridge since goals from John Gregory and Tony Sealy overcame their hosts 2-0 en route to the second-tier title in 1983. And even that was when the Blues were trying to avoid dropping down to the third level of English football.

The Chelsea side was an altogether different proposition in 2013. They were holders of the European Cup for starters and were going along very nicely in the league under interim manager Rafa Benitez. Chelsea had won their last four on the bounce and had stuck EIGHT into Aston Villa's net in their previous home game, and were en route to a Champions League spot and victory in the Europa League. Harry Houdini impersonations are all very well but Rangers had to develop a skill beyond escapology to reach such levels. Being stuck in a locked box in chains and working your way into the public gaze free of them to take a bow – or however you describe wriggling free of relegation – is impressive.

A celebration of success at the top end of the table, though, elicits more kudos. It is positive proof you have the mental, physical and technical strength to compete with the best and, if you fall short, it is not half as stressful as finding a way out of tight situations and the trap door of demotion.

The dullest scenario is mid-table mediocrity, something that, although not pleasant, can be lived with.

In order to try and get a squad capable of mixing it with the biggest of the big boys, Rangers, or rather chairman Tony Fernandes and his fellow owners, had ploughed in millions to bring in no less that 12 new permanent signings in the summer transfer window, including goalkeepers Rob Green and Julio Cesar, England and Brazil internationals respectively, midfielder Esteban Granero, full-back Jose Bosingwa, midfielder Samba Diakite, after his loan the previous season, winger Junior Hoilett and striker Andy Johnson.

But Rangers made a disastrous start to their second season back in the top flight which put them rock bottom. They kicked off with a 5-0 home defeat against Swansea City and lost a total of eight and drew four of 12 when Mark Hughes was dismissed following a 3-1 reverse against Southampton, a former club, on 17 November 2012.

It was time for a re-appraisal of the approach. A Harry Houdini impersonation was required and a man who had earned the moniker for leading successful relegation fights for Bournemouth, Portsmouth and Tottenham Hotspur was the chosen man.

Harry Redknapp also had a good pedigree at the top end, winning the FA Cup with Portsmouth in 2008 before taking over with Spurs anchored to the bottom of the Premier League later in the year and leading them into the Champions League within two years.

So Tony Fernandes and Co. could plan both short and long term with someone of Redknapp's experience in the managerial hot-seat it seemed. The theory was to keep QPR from a return to the second tier in the first season before starting to aim for the stars the next. It sounds good on paper, but the reality is often different. A manager is only as good as his players and their abilities and attitudes. It needed a backs-to-the-wall, all-for-one-one-for-all group to fight to the very last drop of blood in the cause to go with the physical and technical qualities. Redknapp had inherited a massive squad of players which he had to get to know. He certainly made s solid start. After watching Rangers lose 3-1 against

v Chelsea 2013

Manchester United at Old Trafford on the afternoon of his appointment, he got to work. Three draws followed at Sunderland and Wigan Athletic and home to Aston Villa. Then, as we have read, two Adel Taarabt goals earned QPR their first league victory of the season, against Fulham.

Low-level optimism, though, was forced to take a back seat with three reverses on the bounce, including a 3-0 home defeat against Liverpool who were clearly determined to not give a bone to Rangers' dogfight like they did in the previous season.

But Redknapp reiterated to anyone who asked him that Rangers would survive in the top flight after the last ball had been kicked in anger in the 2012/13 season.

And QPR proved it was not empty rhetoric when they faced their bitterest west London rivals at Stamford Bridge on 2 January 2013.

Redknapp shuffled his pack after the disappointing home defeat against Liverpool on the Sunday, with Taarabt a deep-lying lone 'striker'; a central role comparable to that played by Barcelona and brand new to the Moroccan. It was a move which Redknapp hoped would enable his talisman to bewitch and bedazzle between the two Chelsea lines at the back and in midfield when the visitors broke forward. Taarabt played it to perfection and sweated blood for the cause with tireless running to block off the hosts whenever the opportunity presented itself in contrast of the perception of him as a lazy performer.

Redknapp was forced into an early change when winger Junior Hoilett pulled a hamstring and was replaced by Wright-Phillips after 15 minutes.

Benitez opted to give star midfielders Juan Mata and Eden Hazard a breather on the bench, along with Ashley Cole, arguably the best left-back in the world.

The interim Stamford Bridge chief, who eventually brought on Mata and Hazard after an hour with Rangers proving a tough nut to crack, reasoned his players, no matter how influential, could not perform at their optimum if they were expected to play 90 minutes of every game in a heavy schedule of matches.

Rangers' 'bus' proved a road block Chelsea struggled to get around. The visitors offered blood, sweat and tears and constant support for each other.

Their only early break of significance before the winner came when eventual hero Wright-Phillips drove wide of Chelsea stopper Ross Turnbull's goal.

Rangers' gargantuan task might have been eased as early as the fourth minute when midfielder Stephane Mbia was flattened by a seemingly reckless challenge by Marko Marin, who was making his first league start. But Bolton referee Lee Mason elected to show yellow rather than red to the German international.

And the hosts seemed at a loss as to how to break down Rangers' steel-like back line without the creative attacking input of Mata and Hazard.

Fernando Torres, the £50m striker from Spain, was largely bereft of service from the midfield and surrounded by opponents defending deeply and in numbers. Blues defender Branislav Ivanovic tried a couple of shots but both were way off target.

Blues' Brazilian defender David Luiz, whose fuzzy hairstyle launched the production of wigs for Chelsea fans to sport, tried a volley, but the downward trajectory of the effort saw it hit the surface and loop over the bar of his compatriot Julio Cesar's goal.

Oscar, another Chelsea Brazilian, was lively. He had a shot which was deflected wide by QPR defender Clint Hill before Cesar stopped another effort from him, one which had hit Blues midfielder Frank Lampard on route, with his legs and Victor Moses put the rebound over the bar. And Rangers continued to deny the hosts any clear-cut openings for the rest of the half. They remained content to soak up each Chelsea wave of attack with Taarabt furthest forward in a 4-5-1 formation, but his roving role enveloped him in midfield activity rather than providing a cutting edge up front.

Chelsea's quality of play improved after the interval but it was a similar pattern as more half-chances for the hosts came and went. Moses just missed a Marin cross and Lampard had a shot deflected wide. Chelsea did get a clear sight of Cesar's goal when the goalkeeper had to save from Luiz but it only came from a loose ball from a block.

But Ivanovic faintly touched the top of the bar with a header and Cesar pulled off a stunning stop from Torres from eight yards after the ball fell to him after a Luiz blaster had rebounded off Wright-Phillips.

Lampard had the ball in the net for an effort which would have put him level alongside Kerry Dixon as the club's second all-time goalscorer but what would have been his 193rd goal for the Blues was ruled offside. Yet Rangers were also creating opportunities. Granero, following a break led by Wright-Phillips and Taarabt, flighted a delightful curling drive which Turnbull kept out. Then Jamie Mackie, put through by Taarabt, was only denied by a last-ditch Gary Cahill tackle. Wright-Phillips, with his first goal since May 2010, scored the winner 12 minutes from time.

Taarabt provided the killer ball with a delicate, classy first touch square to the right after Oscar had headed away a Granero left-wing corner to him just outside the penalty area.

England international winger Wright-Phillips's aim was true as his low drive sped by Turnbull into the bottom corner.

Ivanovic missed the chance of an equaliser and Mason blew his whistle to spark frenzied celebration among the Super Hoops who had opted for a change strip of all red on a red letter day – or rather night – for a club with red-for-danger lights flashing concerning their stay in the top flight extending beyond the end of the season.

Redknapp said to the BBC afterwards, 'It was good for the fans. We had a great support. They haven't had a lot to cheer travelling away from home watching QPR. Two years without a win. And we couldn't have come to a more difficult place to get it.

'That was for them. They are the people that matter. That's all I'm interested in. I'm here this year to try and keep them in this league and if I can achieve that I'll be happy. That's the most important thing. This is one of my greatest ever victories. Everyone knew their job, worked their socks off and got their rewards. We deserved it. It was a fantastic performance. They have set the standard and to get out of this mess they have to do it every week.'

Benitez said, 'We were tired and weren't precise. We made a mistake and gave them their chance. I don't regret the changes because we can't carry on with the same players in every game. If you're playing a team at the bottom of the table at home, you have to trust your players and I trust them.'

QPR remained bottom, five points adrift of safety, but after three straight defeats, the win gave them renewed hope that survival was not beyond them.

And Rangers tried to turbo-boost those hopes with six signings, including £7m striker Loic Remy and £12m defender Christopher Samba in the January transfer window.

The fact that Rangers ended up planning an opening fixture against Sheffield Wednesday at Loftus Road in the Championship for the 2013/14 season meant, of course, the club were ultimately unable to prevent demotion, but at least they were able to look back on the famous night they brought down the holders of the greatest club trophy in Europe deep inside enemy territory while they themselves were looking up at the rest of the Premier League.